AN EXECUTIVE'S COACHING HANDBOOK

An Executive's Coaching Handbook

Mary Jean Parson

Facts On File Publications
New York, New York • Oxford, England

AN EXECUTIVE'S COACHING HANDBOOK

An Executive's Coaching Handbook

**Library of Congress Cataloging in
Publication Data**

Parson, Mary Jean.
    An executive's coaching handbook.
    Bibliography: p.
    Includes index.
    1. Personnel management. I. Title.
HF5549.P284   1986   658.3   85-20524
ISBN 0-8160-1164-8

Printed in the United States of America
10 9 8 7 6 5 4 3 2 1

For
Ursula Clark Parson

ACKNOWLEDGMENTS

I never thought I would combine my work at the Yale School of Drama with personnel counseling. And when I was asked by Marie McWilliams (vice-president of personnel) in 1972 to serve as ABC's associate director of employee relations, I said, "But I am not a professional personnel person." And she said, "Didn't your work as a director prepare you to coach people and listen to people and aid them in role playing?"

Since my answer had to be yes I accepted the opportunity to help recruit and counsel women and minorities as part of effecting that company's affirmative action program.

That led to a number of years of work in the personnel field, including the opportunity to formulate and write personnel policies and procedures for a division at ABC and at Blair TV/Radio.

Personnel is really people…and the most complex job a manager will do in business. I'm not sure what a "professional personnel person" knows that the rest of us managers don't, except they spend their whole business lives dealing with the "people issue" in a company, while the rest of us do it part-time.

I've known managers who do it well and managers who do it badly. We've all had successes and failures. This book is based on observing those successes and failures and dedicated to those people who keep *trying* to understand the human equation. And it's dedicated to John Gassner, the Sterling Professor of Playwriting at Yale, who tried to teach me that out of human relationships and interaction can come dramatic moments which—at their best—can enlighten and educate.

Finally, the conversation with Kate Kelly, my editor, one night at an Irish restaurant, brought about the possibility of helping managers manage people without resorting to yet another book of rules and regulations but, rather, through a book of dialogues.

Maybe, through this device, we can combine the techniques of theater with the needs of management counseling.

Mary Jean Parson
Teaneck, N.J.
May, 1985

Contents

INTRODUCTION

In recent years the words "personnel department" have been replaced by "human resources." This is more than a semantic change. It is a recognition of the basic part that all employees play in the success or failure of a company.

It is a further recognition that the management of those human resources involves more than job descriptions, salaries, and benefits. It involves the personal needs of employees, their private agendas, their need for self-respect, and their vision of the future.

Many fine volumes have been written on this subject as guidelines for contemporary managers. And they continually stress the two words "human" and "resources."

The element which is stressed in this book is *Relationships*.

All the theory, all the hints, all the guidelines, all the practical advice is useless without the understanding that the relationship, one person with another, is the overriding determinant of success or failure in the management of people.

This book is not necessarily written for the professional personnel or human resources practitioner. It is written for the *manager*—that person who must direct people, events, or financial activity—and who has probably arrived at that position without professional training in psychology, philosophy, or personnel practices.

Most such managers learn their craft through on-the-job training and observation. Consciously or subconsciously, they absorb habits and techniques, good and bad, from those above them and around them. They learn by *example*.

This book is filled with examples—all of them gleaned from years of observation and practice. They are not absolutes, because there is undoubtedly no right or wrong in a universal situation. There are too many variables—the situation in the company, the cast of characters, and the intent (or private agenda) of each participant.

However, these examples are constructed as dramatic vignettes to allow you, the manager, to test your skills and imagination in resolving a typical manager/employee situation. There are Action Asterisks (*) along the way, to allow you to stop and ponder how *you* would handle the encounter in the next phase. And because the examples are written as dialogue, you can also use them as training sessions with your employees. They can be read as scenes, and when you reach the Action Asterisks, you can stop the dialogue and open a discussion on "what should the manager do next?"

Remember, these are examples, *not* absolutes. Every situation is different from every other in significant ways. But *all* situations between managers and employees revolve around one pivotal issue—human relationships.

The roles we play in business society can be enhanced and strengthened and made more enjoyable if we observe, practice, and remember. The Action Asterisk is a useful tool to employ in every such encounter.

1. Pause. (What's your hurry?)
2. Reflect. (What path have we gone down so far?)
3. Remember. (What is my *real* agenda? What do I hope to get out of this encounter? Where do I have to lead this conversation to accomplish that goal?)

Managing other people is the most challenging and rewarding task of any manager. Some do it very well. Some do it badly. Most of us muddle through with a few wins and a few losses. It is my hope that these examples will show some of the roads some good managers have taken over the years. The characters and situations are, of course, fictional, created to *illustrate* a point; they are not recreations and should not be construed to represent actual people or events.

The chapters that follow cover a number of personal situations which can confront a manager. In order to weave a fabric of people, responsibilities, and interactions that will more logically reflect the realities of the workplace, we have created a company—Salvo.

Salvo is a medium-sized computer software company located in a large city. Salvo was founded six years ago by three partners with a variety of experiences in the software field. It has been very successful with games and business programs, and this year has begun an acquisitions program of buying several small companies specializing in personal business software programs.

Although you can dip in to chapters that deal with subjects which interest you, you may also read the book in total. By creating a whole company with many departments and many personalities involved, we hope to make you feel at home in the book, recognizing the behavior and attitudes which can make departments and companies stand above others in human relations and employee motivation.

1 CREATIVE HIRING

Introduction

One of your responsibilities as a manager is the hiring of personnel. Many books, articles, and courses are available on the subject, from the points of view of both the interviewee and the interviewer. Several elements affect our choice of people to fill employment positions:

- The skills and experience detailed in the job description
- The makeup of the department currently, and what each candidate will add to the mix
- The chemistry between you and the interviewee, those indefinable feelings which make one interviewee seem more "right" than another

Only the first element is based on specific information which can establish guidelines for our selection. And in many instances, the specific requirements of a position are the fundamental elements we will require in hiring a person, whether the other elements are absolutely compatible or not. If the position requires a CPA, we don't often consider people who are not CPAs. If the position requires specific technical or scientific education, we choose from a pool of people with those credentials. If the job

1

requires fluency in certain languages, tests for that fluency will weed out the deficient.

But when specific education, skills, and certifications have been met, managers rely on the other elements to make their final selections. And more often than not, they seek someone who has done the job.

While there is a feeling of security in hiring someone who has performed the same job at another company, there is also a lack of imagination and even some risk in doing so. The person has learned the procedures and techniques of one company and will have to unlearn them or develop new ones to adapt to your company. The person may also be rather set in his or her ways and unreceptive to your company or your management style.

Of course, if you promote from within your own department or company, you are rarely promoting someone who has already done the job. You are promoting someone whom you think *can do* the job, because of a combination of skills, work habits, and achievements in other positions. With few exceptions, it is better to promote from within if a qualified person is available because you help build employee confidence and loyalty, you save time in recruiting and hiring, and you cut the lead time in training for the new position because the person is already familiar with the company. All good managers know this and do it instinctively. But we may not be aware that when we do so we are engaged in *creative hiring*. We have put people in a job which they have not *done* but which they *can do*.

Once we understand that, it becomes obvious that we can practice the same creative hiring with people we recruit from the outside. We can broaden our pool of potential employees by considering those who can do the job as well as those who have done it. We can then add a fourth element to our list describing how we hire people:

• Consider skills, education, and accomplishments acquired in other fields which are applicable to the position's requirements

We all know that America is a mobile society with people moving from job to job and place to place in record numbers for career advancement. But with our burgeoning technology and exploding new fields and ventures, our population is moving from *industry to industry* as well. We are becoming, more and more, a population—at least in the white collar sector—of transferable skills.

The sharp manager will take advantage of this growing pool of skilled, mobile people and practice *creative hiring*: matching skills, education, and accomplishments to the job requirements, rather than trying to match title for title, job for job, industry for industry. By making that leap of imagination, by not playing it quite so safe, a manager may draw on a larger pool of skilled, accomplished, ambitious potential employees.

The Situation

Once the designers in Salvo's product development department design new software programs, they turn them over to MIS development teams who create the systems and packages for production.

They have been very innovative and very successful. But over the years, the types and ranges of systems have proliferated and there is some concern that they have become too many, too varied, and too complicated.

Herman, the manager of MIS, has decided to bring in a systems designer to review the current inventory and, where possible, consolidate and alter them for more uniformity, but more importantly, to transfer them to the solid, ongoing systems and hardware successes in the marketplace. He further wishes this "heavy hitter" to analyze all future developments and keep Salvo's product in the mainstream of computer and systems technology and not on the esoteric fringes.

To that end, he has run a series of ads for the position and the personnel department has screened many applicants, narrowing the field to eight. He has interviewed five and is not quite satisfied. In each case, he has given the applicant a project to analyze so that his judgment will be based on more than instinct. He has reviewed the analysis before each interview.

The Characters

Today Herman is interviewing Eric, who teaches in the computer department at the local state university. He holds two degrees, was involved in the massive system implementation at the New York Stock Exchange, did some industry consulting for several years, and has been teaching for four years.

Herman was one of the first employees at Salvo and is proud of the part his department has played in its success. He knows that his people are good and that their work is creative and successful. But the company has grown so quickly that he knows he needs another pair of eyes, with the leisure to analyze and reflect, to assure that the decisions made for the future are viable.

Eric is about Herman's age, with a different background. As a consultant and teacher, he has operated less in the pressure cooker of industry and has had the leisure to develop his considerable skills as an analyst and innovator. While he enjoys teaching, he would welcome the opportunity to test his skills in a more challenging environment and to be part of a company's growth and success.

Manager's Objective

To hire the best person possible to analyze current and future systems for coordination with industry trends and Salvo's strengths.

The Dialogue—Example 1

Eric is brought to the door by Herman's secretary.

HERMAN	Come in. Come in. Have a seat.
ERIC	Thanks.
HERMAN	Thanks for coming in.
ERIC	Thank you for inviting me. I enjoyed talking with your personnel manager and hoped I'd have the chance to meet you.
HERMAN	Jane does a very good job. She was very complimentary of your background and experience.
ERIC	I'm glad.

* ACTION ASTERISK

This may all seem like meaningless small salk, but at the start of any job interview, common courtesy requires some polite exchange and compliments, as well as some common references—in this case, the personnel department, which brought them together.

HERMAN	I especially liked your analysis of the program I sent you. It was well-written and your ideas were interesting.
ERIC	It's an interesting program. Is it still on your list?
HERMAN	Yes. It's one of our old standbys. Every new generation of kids seems to love it.
ERIC	I can see why. It has some interesting tricks. It may become dated, however.
HERMAN	So you said.
ERIC	The system it's based on is becoming dated. And the hardware is pulling way ahead in capability for the price.

* ACTION ASTERISK

Eric is being critical of a very successful product and this is risky. Will Herman interpret it as interested and helpful or as critical and arrogant?

HERMAN	Our marketing department stays pretty up-to-date on those trends. We think we're pretty safe with it.
ERIC	Probably for a while. It depends on how long you projected the life cycle for a product like that, designed for kids and attractive to a new generation every three or four years.
HERMAN	We've made plenty of money on it.
ERIC	I'm sure you have.

* ACTION ASTERISK

Herman has effectively turned off this discussion of changing a program to extend its marketing life. He has chosen to see Eric's comments as criticism and to dismiss them, although analysis of old programs is a part of the job description.

HERMAN	Your resume shows very little work in industry. How could you handle a pressure cooker like this?
ERIC	I don't know what that means.
HERMAN	That's what I mean. How could you take the pressure?
ERIC	Every development job has its pressures and its demands. The New York Stock Exchange job wasn't exactly a picnic. And as a consultant I'm used to working under deadlines I have nothing to do with.
HERMAN	Do you like deadlines?
ERIC	I'd rather set them myself. Or at least, have a hand in setting them. Deadlines are necessary when they make sense.
HERMAN	They're pretty tight around here.
ERIC	Most places I've seen set them pretty unrealistically. But if everyone knows the facts, you can generally get agreement.
HERMAN	There's a lot of midnight oil around here because we try to roll out three or four products each quarter.

ERIC	Night work doesn't bother me as long as it makes sense. But I think in systems work it's important to do good work, not fast work.

* ACTION ASTERISK

Herman is trying to scare him with threats of deadlines and night work, but he won't be scared. He is obviously a mature professional with his own work ethic and achievement code. Herman must realize that he can't dominate him. This is a peer in age and intellect and experience—albeit different experience.

HERMAN	How do you work with other people?

ERIC	Which people? I've worked with hundreds over the years.

* ACTION ASTERISK

Eric has a careful mind. He simply won't be taken in by the usual trick interview questions.

HERMAN	Well, basically you're a teacher now, working with young people who know little about programs and systems. Do you work on projects with other people who have your knowledge?
ERIC	Occasionally. The college has a staff of five. But that's one reason I'm interested in leaving. I miss that give-and-take in problem-solving.
HERMAN	Can you give up being a teacher and be just another toiler in the vineyards?
ERIC	I like to think that in systems work we're all students as well as teachers. It's solving the problem that is the real teacher. We learn from that experience.
HERMAN	This job is a problem-solver, sometimes alone, sometimes in teams.
ERIC	I'd like that.
HERMAN	But we don't have the luxury of pure science. Here, it's solution upon demand. I've got to find someone who can analyze the past and plot the future.

ERIC	I've brought a list of my references. (*He hands a paper to Herman.*) You might wish to check with them to see if I meet those criteria.
HERMAN	Thanks. I'll be honest with you. I have concerns about your making the transition from class to crunch. I like your background and I like your work. But I want to think about it.
ERIC	I understand. And I'll be happy to supply you with any information you may want.
HERMAN	Good. I'm scheduled to interview some other people and then I'll narrow down my choices. You'll hear from me. (*He rises.*)
ERIC	(*Rises*) I look forward to it. (*They shake hands.*)

Comments

Was the manager's objective achieved? Not yet. Herman has to go through the rest of the process.

What we have dealt with in this example is *attitude*. What is Herman's attitude toward the new, untried position? Is he looking for someone who has *done* the work or someone who *can do* the work?

Eric appears to be his intellectual and professional equal who happens to have had consulting and academic experience instead of industry and commercial experience. Is the job so specific that Eric should have done it, or is the challenge so new that the successful candidate should be able to do it?

We're back to attitude. Should Herman be bound by predisposition or should he be open to people and ideas which can enhance the department rather than simply follow a predetermined job description?

The Dialogue—Example 2 (continued)

ERIC	The system it's based on is becoming dated. And the hardware is pulling way ahead in capability.
HERMAN	We have some concerns about that. You seem to think that we can adapt it.
ERIC	Oh, you can. The issue is, is it worth it? If the game is

popular, you may want to invest the time and money. But it wouldn't be cheap.

ACTION ASTERISK
Eric has shown he can think creatively to extend product life and also is aware of cost/price ratio.

HERMAN	Do you deal in budgets at the university?
ERIC	Only in the most cursory way. I have to plan and run my departmental budget, of course. But I have no control over the whole thing. Although in a strange way, I do.
HERMAN	How's that?
ERIC	Part of the reason for bringing me there was to overhaul and consolidate the whole planning and budgeting system. That took about three years, in order to consolidate it with the state system.
HERMAN	What took so long?
ERIC	Bureaucracies move slowly. Nothing is decided instantly.
HERMAN	Do you work well with deadlines?
ERIC	I can. They're not terribly firm in academia.
HERMAN	You don't have much of an industry background. How do you feel about the pressure we work under?

* ACTION ASTERISK
Herman is continuing his interview with an old interviewing method—how will the candidate cope in an environment which he tries to paint as different.

ERIC	What kind of pressure do you work under?
HERMAN	Marketing wants it done yesterday.
ERIC	And you?

8

HERMAN	I try to get it done today. Or tomorrow morning, at the latest.
ERIC	Is that why you take shortcuts?
HERMAN	Who said we did?
ERIC	The program I saw has shortcuts. They don't hurt it. But for a more sophisticated environment, shortcuts won't do.
HERMAN	I repeat the question. How are you at deadlines?

* ACTION ASTERISK

Herman is beginning to go with the flow. This conversation is going easier, with clipped sentences and both men on the same wavelength.

ERIC	If I set them, I'm fine. If other people set them, there can be problems. There is no magic in systems and programming. It's just hard work.
HERMAN	What's your greatest skill?
ERIC	Analyzing a problem until I can see a solution.
HERMAN	What's your greatest weakness?
ERIC	Analyzing a problem until I can see a solution. (*They both laugh.*)

* ACTION ASTERISK

Herman has used the old interviewing ploy of asking Eric to analyze himself and Eric has fielded the question with humor and finesse. Also with honesty.

HERMAN	Would you rather create or re-create?
ERIC	I'm not sure they're different. Especially in programming.
HERMAN	Why would you want to work for us?
ERIC	Because there is more variety in the challenges than my current job. When you teach, you're required to do a

9

few things over and over until other people learn them. I love to teach and I'm good at it. But I'd rather have a broader palette.

HERMAN   Do you want to teach here?

ERIC   In the best environments, everybody teaches and everybody learns.

HERMAN   (*Pauses.*) This could be interesting.

ERIC   Thank you.

HERMAN   I have some procedures to go through. There are other people to interview. We have to check references. I'll probably ask a couple of you to solve a problem for me within a time frame. Does that bother you?

ERIC   No.

* ACTION ASTERISK
Herman has sensed the strong inner core in Eric and is not frightened of it. He has enjoyed the interchange and wants to see more of this man's ability.

HERMAN   I'll be back in touch.

ERIC   Good. I look forward to hearing from you.

Summary
Was the manager's objective achieved? He's closer than most managers get.

Herman has taken an attitude which has allowed him to see some of Eric's capabilities without being upset about his lack of commercial experience.

He has also not been threatened by Eric's maturity and intellect. By letting the conversation flow in an easy give-and-take, he has seen the stability of the man, his intellect, his humor, and his professionalism. He has been offered a list of references to check and plans to have Eric "audition" with some problem-solving.

Eric could bring a new dimension to the department if he is hired and, although there may be some initial adjustment problems all around, this kind of creative hiring can add depth and new challenges to a department.

2 OVERWORK OR DELEGATE?

Introduction

Webster defines the verb "delegate" as "to entrust authority to another." Experience shows that managers don't always understand it that way.

To some, delegate means to give a subordinate *their* work to do. When this is the case, the words "entrust" and "authority" are lost in the definition. The subordinate is usually *instructed* to do the work and is given the *responsibility* to complete it, but no *authority* to make changes or to rethink it.

"Trust" is the fundamental root word in the definition of "entrust." A manager must trust the subordinate to do the job and allow that subordinate the authority to do the job in his or her own way.

This is not to be construed as giving someone a job to do and then walking away from it and allowing it to fail or succeed depending on the subordinate's ability. Delegating is not "out of sight, out of mind." Neither is it, "This is what to do and how to do it." Delegating requires constant communication, agreeing on the work to be done and the time needed to do it, agreeing on procedures and resources, counseling, and monitoring. If this sounds like Management by Objectives, you're right. Delegating succeeds in MBO because all parties are in agreement, all are aware of

11

progress and problems, and all work in an atmosphere of mutual trust. The subordinate has both trust and authority and, therefore, success in the activity is more likely.

The good manager, the good delegator does not simply give an order and expect a subordinate to perform like a robot, no questions asked, with no imagination or personal contribution involved.

This all sounds very simplistic and self-evident. However, in your experience, have you ever encountered a manager who delegated by giving orders and expecting compliance? The answer is undoubtedly yes. In fairness, *all* managers have probably behaved in that way at some time, but the best managers don't behave that way consistently. It's a military way of doing business, and while it may serve a purpose in the military, it has little use in ongoing, productive relationships in the business world.

Conversely, there is the other kind of manager who holds everything close to the vest. This may work well in a poker game but, again, it can be disastrous in the business world.

We've all encountered those kinds of managers too—those people who turn out volumes of work, who come in early, stay late, do a lot of their work themselves, turn their staffs into well-paid clerks, and exude a slight air of distrust always.

Inevitably, these managers then complain of overwork and about staffs who can't take responsibility. Does that sound familiar too? Sometimes it's a personality trait. More often than not it's the result of the Peter Principle—people have been promoted a step above their abilities and are expected to manage (which requires delegation) without learning how to manage.

Managers manage something—people, time, resources. And by implication (and with rare exceptions), they cannot perform their functions alone. Learning to trust others, to be able to give up the day-to-day responsibility and authority, to see the whole picture and not be driven to know every detail are the special challenges to a manager who wishes to succeed. If these attributes are not part of a person's nature, they must be learned, because the alternative is to be bogged down in minutiae and wake up to find a staff both unwilling and unskilled to perform without constant supervision.

Close to the vest management is as perilous as "do it my way" management. At the very least, "Let's do it our way" should be the slogan on the wall.

The Situation

Jim has been with Salvo since its beginnings and is now vice-president of finance. Recently he had "direction of acquisitions" added to his job description and has hired an analyst, Judy, to do the acquisitions studies of the prospective companies.

Also reporting to Jim are Joe, the controller, who directs all the accounting sections, and Herman, the director of MIS, which handles all the company books in addition to all the sales and customer records, and software analysis and development.

The rapid growth of the company, coupled with the acquisitions policy, has put a burden on all departments. Reports from each department have begun to miss deadlines, and when Jim investigated, he discovered the classic domino theory. When one report is late, it impacts on the schedule of the next department needing the information, making the next report later. The reason offered, in most cases, has been that the needs for the acquisitions studies have delayed the normal work schedule and caused the delays and foul-ups. While no one has blamed Judy, the analyst, her name has come up in all discussions because she has been the requestor of data in order to do the research and analysis necessary for a good business decision.

Jim is sympathetic to the problem because he needs the material from Judy in order to write up the acquisitions recommendations for the president and the board.

Overtime has increased in some departments, but the report schedules are still erratic. Jim has insisted on greater effort and longer hours from all the departments during this "temporary phase," but the end result has been continued lateness and hard feelings among the hardworking staff who are beginning to see their loyalty and efficiency questioned.

Jim has already talked to Judy about working longer and faster on the projects so that his final recommendations can be delivered on time. He is tired of long hours into the night himself.

Another report was late yesterday and he has called Judy to come to his office.

The Characters

Jim is forty and a workaholic. He is proud of the company and the part he has played in its growth, beginning as the bookkeeper with the three founding partners that have taken a software game idea into a hundred-million-dollar business and a respected place on the stock exchange. He has assembled a good staff in an orderly way, and takes pride in the fact that they are up-to-date in their analysis and reporting, helping the company to stay ahead of the competition.

The staff is lean, well-paid, own stock in the company, and don't expand unless there is a real need for new personnel. Jim likes to say that he doesn't expect anyone to work harder than he does. (Of course, they understand that he likes it if they work *as hard* as he does.) He is likely to work late at least twice a week, but lately it has been nearly every night. He is also disturbed that he has not been able to meet the deadlines the president expects in the acquisitions studies. His degree is in accounting and he is a CPA, with a healthy respect for sound business practices and accurate, timely financial records.

Judy is thirty-two and an MBA with eight years' experience in three other, larger companies. Her work has been in the analysis and planning departments, and she made this move to a smaller, growing company in anticipation of a planning slot when the company grows larger and the department is created.

She is meticulous, orderly in her thinking, a good analyst, and a good writer. She too is frustrated by the delays, because she is accustomed to larger companies with larger staffs, able to accommodate multiple requests. She has never lost her temper, but has been quietly and persistently insistent about getting the material. (Some call her a nudge.) She has good work habits but Jim is concerned that she may be getting weary of the many late nights, especially when she sees other people in other departments leaving at five P.M.

Manager's Objective

To get the work done in a timely way, without immediately increasing staff. There is a possibility of redelegating.

The Dialogue—Example 1

JIM   Good morning, Judy.

JUDY   Good morning.

JIM   Come in and close the door. (She sits.) How are you coming on the QTC analysis?

JUDY   We're behind. Herman hasn't finished the compatibility report yet.

JIM   What's the problem?

JUDY   When I talked to him last night it was about half done. He's running their programs against our matrix to see what is compatible with our current base, and what we would have to add to our programming to accommodate it.

JIM   Do you really need that?

JUDY   Yes, it could make an impact on our transfer and
                  startup costs and you'll need that information to make a
                  good judgment. If it's substantial, it could mean that we
                  need to increase the price of the product.

JIM   Why not just make two assumptions: one, that it is
                  compatible, and two, that it isn't? I'm due with the in-
                  itial recommendation day after tomorrow.

JUDY   I know. But in the other reports, you've needed this
                  data.

JIM   But we're running out of time. When can you finish?

JUDY   Will the president accept partial data?

JIM   It depends on how *I* analyze it.

* ACTION ASTERISK

They have reached a point of confrontation. Judy is trying to understand
why he has changed the ground rules on this report. Jim has not ex-
plained his change of mind. He has taken her questions as an im-
pertinence, so he has reprimanded her.

JUDY   Oh, I know that. But so far, he's had *all* the material
                  I've analyzed to make the decision.

JIM   Our decisions have been made on a lot more knowledge
                  than your reports.

* ACTION ASTERISK

He has slammed the door on her questions and wants to get on with
solving the problem.

JUDY   Of course.

JIM   Are you sure that Herman is the real problem with this?

JUDY   I didn't say Herman was the problem. I just said that the
                  work isn't completed yet.

JIM   (*Picks up the phone and dials.*) Herman? Jim. When

15

will you finish the QTC report? (*Pause.*) No sooner than that? (*Pause.*) No, I don't want any overtime. What else are you running? (*Pause.*) Who's handling it? (*Pause.*) Doesn't he handle the monthly statements too? So that's the holdup! Why don't you take over the QTC material and put him back to work? If you start now and work through lunch we can get it out of the way. What? (*Pause.*) You don't need to go to that luncheon. All you computer guys do is drink martinis and kill two hours. A sandwich won't hurt you. Listen. Get onto it and I'll send Judy up to get it this afternoon. (*He hangs up.*) He'll have it by five o'clock.

* ACTION ASTERISK

Jim has taken over the direction of the MIS department and reduced its manager's status by ordering him to work through lunch, do an operator's job, and miss an industry luncheon. He has also forced another late night on Judy without including her in the decision.

JUDY   Oh. Not any sooner? Can I get partial material by noon?

JIM   What's the problem? Do you have a hot date?

* ACTION ASTERISK

Whether this is said lightly or not, it is automatically insulting. Her plans, and his opinion of them, are irrelevant.

JUDY   No.

JIM   Listen, Judy, we all work hard around here. We don't watch the clock, we spend the time it takes to get the work done.

JUDY   I don't watch the clock! I've worked many late nights on these projects.

JIM   Good. And the work's been pretty good. Now get on back to work and Herman will have the material for you to analyze tonight.

JUDY   There is one other problem.

16

JIM	What's that?

JUDY	I'm still finding some delays in getting consolidations from accounting.

JIM	They're pretty busy down there, you know.

JUDY	I know. But the more companies we acquire, the more need we have for a unified consolidation method. I wonder if we could start talking to Joe about it.

* ACTION ASTERISK

Although Judy has had a very bad meeting with Jim so far, she is concerned about another incipient problem, and is probably also concerned about being blamed for it. So she ventures bringing it up to elicit Jim's help.

JIM	Joe hasn't complained about it.

JUDY	He's been very helpful. But there *is* a backup.

JIM	Listen, Judy, you may have stayed in those bigger companies too long. We don't have a big staff sitting around here. We're like a family. We're lean and mean and we plan to keep it that way. You can't come here and start complaining about every department you work with.

JUDY	I'm not complaining. I'm concerned that we may have more delays in the future if...

JIM	Don't you worry about the future. You get that analysis done tonight so that you can write up the report for me tomorrow. Your future depends on what you do *now*, not on what other people are doing.

* ACTION ASTERISK

This is the ultimate putdown, and with her experience in other companies, Judy would know better than to argue any further. She can only nod and rise to leave.

JIM	Call me in the morning and let me know when the narrative has been completed.

JUDY   Sure. (*She exits.*)

Comments

Were the objectives of the meeting fulfilled—to get the work done in a timely way, without immediately increasing staff?
Yes and no. Jim has exerted his decisiveness and instructed his employees to work harder and get the work out on time.

However, in the process, he has alienated Judy and Herman and increased their sense of resentment. He has also ignored warning signals that things may be piling up in accounting and that Joe may need some relief too.

Making people work harder is not delegating. Working harder is not necessarily working smarter.

In a high-pressure position such as Jim holds, is there another way to handle overwork, delegation, and getting extra work out in a timely way?

Let's take the same situation and see if he could have handled it differently.

The Dialogue—Example 2 (continued)

JIM   Do you really need that?

JUDY   I don't want to say, off the top of my head, but I could have that done by noon.

JIM   And you can finish the rest of the narrative by tonight?

JUDY   Yes. I'll structure it a little differently. I'll do all the history and marketing and personnel section. Then I'll chart the compatibility and pricing on the three standards of "best," "worst," and "probable." If that's good enough for a preliminary look, it will give Herman some breathing space to finish the matrix run.

* ACTION ASTERISK

Judy has just implied that the MIS department needs more time, but she has done it without criticism or blame. How can Jim pick up on this, to assure more, not less, cooperation between departments?

JIM   We've done three of these so far. Does Herman use the same matrix for all of them?

JUDY   I'm not sure. All of the reports have the same general information at the top. But each has a section on special problems.

JIM   (*Picks up the phone and dials.*) Herman? This is Jim. Where do we stand on the QTC report? (Pause.) No sooner than that? (*Pause.*) No, I'd prefer not to have overtime. Let me ask you something. When you run those compatibility analyses, are they all run on the same matrix? (*Pause.*) I know they're all different, but we're trying to find the similarities to *our* programs. (*Pause.*) O.K., don't let this stand in the way. Get that report to Judy as soon as you can. Tomorrow afternoon will be fine. (*He nods at Judy. She nods back.*) Yes, she'll work around it. Meantime, when that's done, I want to talk with you about a universal matrix to test these things. (*Pause.*) I know, I know. But if you build a matrix to test all that's compatible, then we can spend the extra programmer time on the exceptions. Think about it and let's talk the first of next week. Call Joyce and get on my calendar. Also, think about whether we should have the other companies run the tests, at least on the nonproprietary stuff. That would free us up for the hard parts. Yes. Yes. There are going to be more of these down the road and we'll have to free up your shop from the extra work. You can do the new programs in downtime. (*Pause. He laughs.*) Yes, Herman, I know that's a new word. But we'll find some. Thanks. And let's talk next week. (*He hangs up.*)

* ACTION ASTERISK

Jim has just taken charge of the jam-up in MIS. He has sympathized with the overwork, taken the immediate pressure off the pending report, placed no blame, and started a new modus operandi—but delegated to the manager to think it through.

JIM   Let's go with the options we talked about. And Herman should have the detail in time for us to digest it for the board next week. Will that do it?

JUDY   Yes. But I'm still worried about the future.

JIM   Oh?

19

* ACTION ASTERISK

The problem isn't over in Judy's mind. This temporary solution is fine for now, but what about the future? Even with the speed-up of the material she needs from MIS, she knows that the demands on her analytical and writing time will increase with every new acquisition. And what about the planning department she hopes to start? When will she have time to launch that? Jim is glad to have this crisis over and wants to move on to his next appointment. He wonders if there's something else lurking in the wings to occupy his time.

JUDY   Well, this solves the problem right now, but if we keep on with these acquisitions—and I hope we will—we're liable to end up in the same boat again.

JIM   If Herman can work out a universal matrix it should speed up everything in the future.

JUDY   I know. And that would be terrific. But with every company we add, the pressures will mount in accounting to incorporate their books into ours. And I'm finding more delay in getting consolidations.

* ACTION ASTERISK

Judy is treading on more toes. Although she has couched the problem as overwork, there is an implied criticism that Joe's people can't handle the workload. Although it may hold up her own work, it is not her territory.

JIM   He hasn't complained about it. They've had a little overtime, but that's to be expected at crunch time.

JUDY   I'm just anticipating when we get to a consolidated planning period. Those delays could be crucial.

* ACTION ASTERISK

Jim knows Judy is ambitious and wants to launch a formal planning function. He also knows she is good and is a hard worker. He doesn't want to kill that enthusiasm. But he doesn't want her to invade Joe's authority in accounting.

JIM   Who do you work with in accounting?

JUDY   Oh, Joe gives me all the material. He has Ralph or Gloria work on it whenever they can.

20

JIM   Do you work with them directly?

JUDY   Sometimes, when I need some explanation of the detail.

JIM   I'll get with Joe next week and see if we can rearrange some workloads. One of them might handle all the acquisitions and consolidations, and work more directly with you.

JUDY   That would be great!

* ACTION ASTERISK

Jim should beware of this; it could be construed as the classic "Don't do today what can be put off until tomorrow." However, if he truly has an open mind about the growth of the company, he will work with Joe as he worked with Herman—he will pose the problem of reallocating workloads within the department and challenge him to come up with some creative solutions. However, in his heart of hearts, he must know that a growing company will ultimately require more people. He is opening the door to adding more people in accounting or transferring someone to a new planning department or both. But he is involving his managers in the process.

JIM   Good! Thanks for coming in. I'll see you at noon for that first report, and we'll get the rest done tomorrow. (*Judy exits.*)

Summary

Were the objectives of the meeting—to get the work done in a timely way without immediately increasing staff—fulfilled? Yes.

How was it done?

It must seem obvious that although Jim is a workaholic and very demanding of himself and everyone else, he is not bound to habitual ways of doing things. At the very outset of the meeting, he challenged the necessity of the content of the report, even though he had set the original criteria himself. He was able to look at the problem from a different vantage point: not how can we get this work *done on time*? but what *content is necessary* to make a preliminary decision? This is the secret to flexible, dynamic management—to be able to hold up the problem independently of other impediments and analyze it from a different point of view.

However, he almost misjudged his employee. Judy is a meticulous, conscientious analyst and took his question as a sudden change of requirement. They almost reached a confrontation at the very beginning of the meeting. However, both of them have as a personal agenda—the doing of good work. The both also have the ability to *pause, reflect, and remember*. When she joined him in the search for a new answer (after she realized that such a compromise was possible), the meeting went very well.

Throughout the meeting, Jim involved all his managers in the solution process—Judy, Herman, and Joe. By involving them in reaching solutions, he has given them a greater stake in making the solutions work. Also, with more people involved, more ideas will be presented, considered, discarded, improved, and eventually selected. It is not a recipe for Management by Committee but it *is* a good example of Management by Objectives.

Jim did not add to staff today, and he will be able to discuss the potential of the QTC company with the president, with a high degree of accuracy. By the time the material is due for the board next week, it will be ready. Further, he will have three strong managers working on the possibility of building a better mousetrap for the future.

When he *does* have to add staff (and it is probably inevitable), the techniques and formula will be greatly improved, and again, they will be able to operate at a high efficiency level.

People many times are overworked. However, delegation does not mean giving them more work, or *your* work. Delegation means involving them in the process of deciding *what* work needs to be done and creating new methods of getting it done.

3 THE NO-SHOW (Always Late)

Introduction

No department or company is free of the unexpected no-show—the person who calls in sick, arrives late to work, gives no warning for his or her unexpected absence.

None of us is guiltless of being a no-show. Upset stomachs, the flu, a sudden illness in the family have kept each of us from work unexpectedly. Each of us has been late to work, intentionally or unintentionally. The train or bus breaks down, the car won't start, the dog runs away, a child has an emergency, the plumbing breaks—the list is endless and familiar.

Any manager who gets annoyed at an employee whose tardiness and absences become an inconvenience should reflect on his or her own work experiences and remember that everybody has been a no-show sometime.

Yet no-shows are not to be ignored simply because everybody has done it. Occasional incidents in an employee's work record are to be expected and, indeed, can be accommodated in departments which can function with staggered hours and in companies which have floating holidays and a flexible personal day policy. The manager's concern is the habitual no-show, the person who exceeds the company policy, who is away from work in a discernible pattern, who seems to take advantage of the manager's understanding attitude. These are the people who are difficult to deal with. Are they taking advantage of the company or not?

The problem is doubly difficult if they are generally good employees, if they do their work well, if they are cooperative and well-liked, if they abide by all other company rules.

That can become, as the King of Siam said, a puzzlement. Why do otherwise good employees seem, occasionally, to goof off and betray both their managers and their co-workers by simply not showing up when expected?

It's easy to go by the book. Well-run companies have personnel policies and procedures which define the actions a manager should take in most situations. Typically, the manager would meet with the employee to identify the problem and warn that it should not happen again. The meeting would be written up for the record. The employee would be warned once or twice (for serious infractions) and given a final warning (for the third or fourth infraction). If it happens again, the manager is expected to go by the book. The rules are there to help managers be consistent and apply the rules equally to all.

However, applying the rule., going by the book without sensitivity to individual character and needs accomplishes little in the long career of a successful manager.

There is no black or white in managing people, only many shades of gray. In the matter of the no-shows, a manager would do well to consider more than the rules. Is the person who is tardy or absent really abusing the company and the manager's authority? Or is there a personal problem which is causing the erratic behavior?

A manager needs to know the difference and must be very careful about the method of discovery. How do you pry into someone's private life to discover those things which may be affecting work performance? What rights does the employee have to retain his or her privacy? How far can you go in searching for reasons? The answer, of course, is not very far.

The no-show could behave that way for a variety of reasons.

First of all, is the employee a day person or a night person? Does he or she do the best work in the middle of the day, in the morning, or in the evening? While many scoff at the idea, data indicate that individual metabolism and energy levels do differ at different times of day in different people. The people on your staff may not function best at the hours your department traditionally schedules work. Not everyone is a nine-to-fiver. Sometimes the conflict gets too stressful and people drop out or arrive late. It's hard to determine such a factor, but it is important to remember and suggest that hours of work should be at the employee's peak period, if at all possible.

Second, the employee may simply be taking advantage of your good nature. There *are* people who will abuse the privileges of sick days and personal days, and the compassion and sensitivity of a company. It is a manager's job to know that and to discipline it. Don't be fooled; it's a difficult, sensitive issue and you *can* misunderstand. But people who take advantage risk being disciplined, and it is important to do so because the trust and cooperation of other employees is involved.

Third, people *may* have problems which complicate their working life. Those problems can range from marital problems to problems of being comfortable in a new ethnic environment to financial problems to...well, you fill in the blanks. Though we would like to think otherwise, our personal life *does* intrude into our business life on occasion and affect our behavior.

That is when a manager earns his or her money. The trust, the persistence, the dedication necessary to penetrate to the source of the problem without alienating the employee is the mark of a creative and caring manager.

It's worth the extra effort, but the risks are high. We are treading on private ground and must use care that the employee always knows that our concern is for his or her well-being, not for corporate gain or private knowledge. A manager wants an employee to feel good and work well in the company environment. That can only begin with communication and an attempt at understanding.

The Situation

Salvo has many of the personnel problems and opportunities all companies confront. Even in a company as successful as Salvo, with vigorous, aggressive personnel, the problem of tardy or chronically late employees occurs.

The Characters

Herman runs the systems department, and is very proud of its staff and their productivity. Computer systems and programs are at the very heart of Salvo's success, and Herman has been with the company from its beginnings. He came in as a systems analyst, working for one of the partner-founders of the company. Slowly, he has built an aggressive, cooperative staff since becoming the manager. He is in his forties and takes his job as manager very seriously. His staff is mixed in sex, age, and race, but all of them are "his kind of people." They accept a challenge, delight in it, and love to solve it. They don't watch the clock and are more interested in results than in being nine-to-fivers. They work well as a team because Herman is a good team leader. He understands the requirements of the company and expects his staff to be available during company hours to respond to all requests. He is also understanding about personal needs and problems. He knows that systems is a demanding profession and wants his staff to enjoy it as well as take it seriously. They play well together as well as work well together; there is generally a birthday celebration at least once a week in the department, attended and enjoyed by all. Herman is ambitious, and knows that his progress in the company will be measured by the productivity and responsiveness of his staff.

After high school graduation, Sam went to computer training school to create a career for himself and is now attending college at night to get a degree in computer science. He is twenty-three, very personable, very cooperative, and very good at his job as a systems analyst on one of the program development teams. He is well-liked by his co-workers and his good nature is a valued asset on the team. He has a very active social life with his girlfriend, family, and friends. He makes a good salary and enjoys the pleasures that it affords him.

But this summer he is either late on Monday morning or calls in sick. He also seems to be sick on occasional Fridays. Salvo has a liberal sick day policy, so Herman has deducted Sam's absences from the pool of days he has available. On two occasions, Herman has called Sam to his office to tell him that days away are deducted from his total available. Sam has simply nodded and said, "O.K." On the two Mondays when Sam has arrived late (over two hours on one occasion), he always had a reason. His car broke down, his mother had to go to the doctor. Herman warned him in each instance that the department depended on his being in on time so that the team's development work could proceed on schedule. In each case Sam was amiable, contrite, and totally in agreement that his lateness wasn't a good thing. Yesterday, it happened again. Sam arrived at eleven-thirty on Monday morning with a sunburn and the excuse that his dog had an attack of something and had to go to the vet. Herman has summoned him to his office.

Manager's Objective

To try to discover the facts of Sam's behavior and to get him to come to work on time.

The Dialogue—Example 1

Sam comes to the open door and taps on the facing. Herman looks up.

HERMAN   Come in, Sam, and close the door. (Sam does so.) You probably know why I asked you to come in.

SAM   Yes.

HERMAN	I've been pretty upset that you keep coming in late this summer.
SAM	I know.
HERMAN	This is the third time in five weeks, you know.
SAM	Yes.
HERMAN	And you've had three sick days on Fridays.
SAM	Um-hmmm.
HERMAN	It's caused some problems in the shop, you know, with people having to double up on the work.
SAM	I'm sorry about that.
HERMAN	Sam, what do you do on Mondays and Fridays?
SAM	What do you mean?
HERMAN	You know what I mean. You're late on Mondays. You stay out on Fridays. You come in here with a sunburn. It looks to us like you're taking long weekends without anybody's permission.
SAM	I've told you what happened each time.
HERMAN	I know you've told us.
SAM	Are you saying you don't believe me?

* ACTION ASTERISK

Herman is getting very close to calling Sam a liar. And that's a dangerous accusation, particularly with no proof.

HERMAN	I'm saying it's *hard* to believe you. You don't get sick during the week. You don't come in late during the week. You even kept good hours in the winter! But it looks like you take off in the summer with no concern about the job.

SAM	I'm concerned about it. But I can't help those things.
HERMAN	You've run out of personal days. Last time we talked, I told you it couldn't go on. You know our policy about warnings.
SAM	I know.
HERMAN	And it's happened again.

* ACTION ASTERISK

Herman must give Sam formal warnings. If he really thinks Sam is a good worker, he must find a way to keep him by making him more prompt. Without formality the warnings are meaningless.

HERMAN	Sam, what do you think I ought to do?
SAM	I don't know. Fire me. I guess.
HERMAN	Do you want to be fired?
SAM	No.
HERMAN	Do you like it here? Do you like the work?
SAM	Yes.
HERMAN	Then why the hell are you pulling this stuff?
SAM	What stuff?
HERMAN	Showing up late on Mondays and taking Fridays off! We see your sunburn. We can count days. Who do you think you're fooling?
SAM	I'm not trying to fool anybody. I told you what happened.
HERMAN	Yeah. I know what you told me.
SAM	You keep saying that. Are you calling me a liar?
HERMAN	I didn't use the word.

SAM	But you don't believe me.
HERMAN	This is getting us nowhere. I told you the last time we talked that it couldn't go on.
SAM	I know.
HERMAN	And I have to think about the other people in the department.
SAM	I know.
HERMAN	Sam, I'm sorry. This is your second warning. And I'm putting it in your personnel record. One more time and you're out.
SAM	O.K.
HERMAN	I'm sorry, Sam, we just can't live with surprises anymore.
SAM	I understand.
HERMAN	(*Stands and holds out his hand.*) I'm sorry.
SAM	What about unemployment?
HERMAN	What about it?
SAM	Will you let me draw it if you fire me?
HERMAN	Are you trying to be fired so you can have a summer at the beach?!
SAM	No. What about a reference?
HERMAN	If anyone called, I'd say you're a good worker, when you show up.
SAM	Is that all?
HERMAN	What else is there?
SAM	Nothing.

HERMAN   Get back to work. (*Sam exits.*)

Comments

Were the manager's objectives achieved? Only partially. He followed the company policy book and warned Sam for a second infraction. However, we don't have the sense that Herman wants to get rid of Sam for bad work, so we must assume that firing him is not really an overpowering objective.

This scene was done properly, with decorum and control. Although there is no indication that anyone else has complained about Sam, we have to assume that the department is overloaded when he doesn't show up. However, Herman had an either/or objective: to get Sam to show up on time or to put him on warning. The fundamental element missing from this scene is *communication*. Sam talked only in monosyllables. If Herman were really listening, he would have heard an inner dialogue trying to get out. Is there a way to reach Sam and find out if there are any problems and try to induce better work habits?

The Dialogue—Example 2 (continued)

HERMAN   Sam, what do you think I ought to do?

SAM   I don't know. Fire me. I guess.

HERMAN   Do you want to be fired?

SAM   No.

HERMAN   Do you like it here? Do you like the work?

SAM   Yes.

* ACTION ASTERISK

If Herman has listened carefully, he has realized that Sam has talked only in monosyllables throughout the interview. This can either make him impatient or he can try to break through Sam's reserve and try to reach an understanding.

HERMAN   Sam, come on. Let's talk. You know that we like you here. You know I like you. I like your work. I like your cooperativeness and your good nature. But something has happened this summer. Let's talk about it.

SAM	Nothing's happened. I've just been late a few times.
HERMAN	Stop it! Just cut it out! I've known you over a year, and I tell you, you're behaving differently! Now, talk to me about it. If there's a problem, maybe I can help. Is everything all right at home?
SAM	Everything's fine.
HERMAN	Is your girl O.K.?
SAM	Sure.

* ACTION ASTERISK

Will Herman persist? The answer lies in his department's current and future needs. If Sam really *is* a good member of the departmental team, if he has a future in the company, growth prospects, and if his departure would unnecessarily burden the rest of the staff, Herman should probably persist.

HERMAN	I'm going to level with you because I'd like to keep you. I was young once. And I was dating a really terrific gal, and it was summer, and we were in love. And it sure was hard to go back to work every Monday. And we loved the beach, and Friday seemed like a great day to be there, because there were fewer people. And I worked at a company bigger than this, and they weren't quite so understanding. And they fired me. And I took the rest of the summer off and got a terrific tan. But you know something?
SAM	What?
HERMAN	I had a hell of a time explaining what I'd been doing for two months when I went out looking for another job.
SAM	Two months isn't long to be out of work.
HERMAN	It is in the computer business. There are so many jobs, *no* one should be out of work. But those who succeed give their whole time and energy. They don't lay back or goof off and let others do the job.

SAM	I'm not goofing off!
HERMAN	Sam, level with me. I'm trying to tell you that I'm here to understand. I don't want to pry and I don't want to get personal. But *something* has made you change.
SAM	It's summer! I love the beach. I love my girl. We don't have much time together. We like to be together, we lose track of time, we go out, we swim, we dance, we party with friends. We don't know where home will be soon.
HERMAN	What do you mean?
SAM	My family's been thinking of retiring to Florida. My girl is going to college in Pennsylvania. I want this job. I want a college degree. I want it all! And we've been trying to grab as much time as possible. I don't know what we're going to do. I want us to have a future. A good future. But there's nowhere to turn. And we won't be together too much longer. And my folks may be gone, and...

* ACTION ASTERISK

Herman's persistence, sharing of some personal experiences, and shouting have broken the dam of Sam's reserve. He is letting it all pour out. Now the manager's problem is to find a solution which will be helpful to the young man and to the company. It is a dreadful thing to get an employee to "confess" and then have no solutions to the problems once he or she has done so.

HERMAN	How much vacation time do you have left?
SAM	None.
HERMAN	Do you want to work here?
SAM	I love working here! The people are great. The pay is good. I love college. We want a better life...than our folks...
HERMAN	Everybody wants that, Sam. It's the American dream. And the American way is to work for it. And that's what

	you've been doing. But you've endangered your future. I don't want that and you don't want that. We've got to solve the problem. Do you have any ideas?
SAM	I don't know. I can't think. It all seems to be crashing in around me. My folks may leave. She'll be gone. I just can't seem to get it sorted out.
HERMAN	Sam, I'll make you a deal. It's Tuesday. Do your work today. Then take the next two weeks off without pay. I need time to rearrange the work for that brief period. And it will give you time to go to the beach, go to Florida, be with your girl, get your head together, do whatever it takes to decide what you're going to do about your life. What do you think?
SAM	I don't know. I really appreciate it. It's just that...well, I need this and I need her...I mean, I want it all.
HERMAN	Maybe you can have it all. But this is your last chance here. Go back to the desk. Work hard today. I'll see you back on Monday, the thirteenth at nine o'clock. If you come back, I'll expect you to buckle down and be a professional. If you're late, you're fired. If you goof off again, you're fired. Is that clear?
SAM	Yes, I know. Thanks. I appreciate it. I know you think I'm a goof-off. But thanks for believing in me. (*Sam grabs Herman's hand.*) We'll put it together and I'll be back. I promise. And I'll make you proud!
HERMAN	O.K. O.K. I believe you. Now get to work. I've got to get busy. Make this chance count, Sam. It could be a turning point.
SAM	I will. (*He leaves.*)

Summary

It is easy to interpret the above scene as a cop-out on the part of the manager. But there is every indication that Sam is a good worker with growth potential and substantial interpersonal skills. What is important is that the manager is conscious of the needs and traumas and differences of a young individual with family pressures pulling on him (the family moving away to retirement, leaving him on his own) and the pressures of losing a girlfriend for months to come. He's willing to give a *good* employee the chance to go to a comfortable environment and sort out his life. Whatever Sam's decision or behavior in the future, Herman has gone the full mile to keep him on the productive path. If he must fire him later and replace him, he has behaved in a mature, compassionate/creative manner. His staff will see him as caring—capable of doing the same for others—and work harder for him. Those employees who would mistake him as a "pushover" or "too easy" probably do so at their peril. He does not seem like the kind of person who would tolerate real goof-offs.

What about the situation if the manager were a younger man, or a woman? Could they relate as well as this mature manager? Yes. Creative concern and caring know no boundaries of age or sex. Understanding the *different* needs of each employee is a matter of curiosity and concern, not going by the book. The "book" is there to guide a manager, not to dictate his or her every action. And the real secret is *communication*, breaking the barrier of differences, to talk about the *real* things we all share. Work is not an island in a person's life: It is a part of the total crazy quilt of behavior. The good manager looks for the rest of the pieces and tries to identify with them.

This does not mean that he or she pries into the employee's personal life; quite the contrary. But it does mean that he or she realizes that behavior doesn't happen in isolation. Many things impact upon it. Enticing the best work out of an employee requires curiosity and nurturing. What we *share* is more important than how we *differ*.

4
THE OVERACHIEVER

Introduction

An overachiever in an office can be a mixed blessing, particularly for the manager in charge of his or her activities.

It is always exciting and rewarding to have an employee with boundless energy and enthusiasm, who finishes the work ahead of schedule, devotes that extra effort to getting every last detail perfect, and pitches in with ideas and assistance whenever a need arises.

But, conversely, it can be time-consuming and distressing when that assistance spills over into someone else's territory uninvited, when the work becomes excessive and unmanageable, and when other people in the department find the quickness of the overachiever a subtle, though unintended, criticism of their own work and work habits.

The thoughtful manager will try to channel those energies and abilities in productive ways, so that the overachiever does not disrupt the functions of the rest of the work force but still has ways in which his or her creativity can be tapped, not stifled.

Work patterns in the American work place seem to go in cycles. Our Puritan heritage (even though most of us aren't descended from Puritans) for centuries has influenced how we think about work. "A good day's work for a good day's pay" is not taken lightly by the majority of Americans. Hard work as a virtue is a fundamental truth in our society.

But other societal forces have brought new ideas to the work place and have fractionalized the way we think. It is safe to say that any roomfull of employees would have five or six ideas about what "good work" really is and what the employer/employee relationship really entails.

The union movement and its causes have altered the way many people regard work. People coming from union households and union traditions have a strong awareness of the adversarial relationship of employer and employee. While giant robber baron companies taking advantage of the little unprotected worker have gone the way of the dodo bird, there is still in the work place a consciousness of negotiation and *quid pro quo*.

The enormous (and inevitable) success of American business in the years after 1945 created yet another view of the work place. American business simply could not fail, and the right degrees from the right schools practically guaranteed personal success in business. There is a tradition of manifest destiny which has crept into the working environment out of this phenomenon.

The laid-back attitudes of the sixties have made their mark and the "team spirit," "cooperation," "sticking together" habits of the new immigrants and the human rights movement have affected the caldron more.

What is the result? There is *no* universally accepted attitude toward work in the American work place. Many heritages and many philosophies direct how we interact with each other and how we perceive our employment.

The astute manager will not despair. Indeed, it is more exciting and rewarding to work in an atmosphere of challenges and change than to work in a homogenous society of predictability.

Managers need not resort to nickel living room psychiatry and try to figure out where the work staff is "coming from." But the awareness that people *are* different, with different assumptions and expectations, is the first giant step toward managing them well.

Which brings us back to the overachiever. There are many ways a person can become an overachiever: the person embracing the Puritan ethic operating in a laid-back environment; the person who has always had to "prove" he or she is worthy of praise or promotion, and constantly strives to reach a personal vision of worth; the person who has found that being "better" at something than everyone else is the way to win recognition and praise; the person with boundless energy who channels that energy into work, not dissipation; and so forth.

For a manager, the reasons are not as important as the work itself. If that person is a *good* worker, efficient, thorough, creative (not flying off in all directions, like Don Quixote), then the challenge is to give him or her boundaries to work within, with an outlet for excess energy and creativity.

Use the analogy of driving a car: Overachievers should be required to drive at the speed limit; however, in order to work off their energies, they should also be sent jogging, horseback riding, or bicycling.

Soon the world will belong to the Yuppies, that great mass of twenty-four to forty-year-olds who are coming to dominate the work force. And as the acronym implies, as a group they are overachievers. They have good educations, high energy levels, and raised expectations. Woe to the manager who doesn't channel them, challenge them, and utilize them—and enjoy them.

The Situation

As Salvo has grown and its stock has increased in interest on the market, a corporate relations department has been established. Norman was hired from one of the networks as vice-president of corporate relations to create a small department to handle the requests of Wall Street analysts, prepare the annual report, write speeches and arrange appearances for the principals, and issue press releases as required.

He uses outside free-lancers for the speeches, and his staff of two handle the remaining tasks. Nancy, originally with a large PR firm, writes the press releases, and Jonathan, from a brokerage house, prepares the material for the Wall Street reviews. They join Norman, as required, in the other activities of the department.

Both of them are highly motivated and outgoing. They respect and work hard for Norman, and because of his many contacts and years of experience, they treat him almost as a father figure. They are proud of Salvo and of their part in its growth, and they never watch the clock. They work when there is work to be done, knowing that when there is slack time, they can relax and enjoy some personal time with no questions asked. They are a tight-knit little family with every reason to believe that their futures will grow with Salvo's.

The Problem

Nancy is an overachiever—there is no other word for it. She is good at her work. She is ambitious and has a high energy level that permits her to complete her own assignments rapidly, leaving her plenty of time to help other people with their tasks.

And that has become a problem. In the year she has been at Salvo, she has learned the company rapidly and is able to produce press releases in record time. She has begun to ask Jonathan for work in his investor relations area, in order to help him. She has volunteered to write a great deal of the annual report for Norman (although it requires considerable consultation on his part with the officers of the company). She has submitted speech ideas for the principals to give. And she has started typing her own material for printing, by-passing the word processing department, because they are sometimes too slow to suit her.

Norman has reluctantly decided that things are getting out of hand. The word processing supervisor has complained about the by-pass. Jonathan has forthrightly asked him if Nancy is going to take over his job. The free-lance speechwriter expressed surprise when he received a speech idea from Nancy in the mail. And Norman himself is concerned that Nancy may begin talking directly to the executive committee about the annual report.

Something must be done to put order back in the department's working procedures.

Norman has thought about the problem and realizes that he himself is very much to blame. He has run the department like a family group because he loathes the management concept of a tight ship. Because they operate together more as friends than as manager/staff, he has caused the reporting lines and the reporting procedures to be blurred.

Nancy is a good employee with fine skills and many good ideas. He doesn't want to lose her or limit her capacities. However, he also realizes that he is losing control of the department and may lose Jonathan, as well as the executive committee's respect, if things continue as they are.

He has decided to call Nancy in to talk.

Manager's Objectives

To initiate some procedures in the department to channel the work flow of everyone in an orderly way.

To keep a good employee productive, but keep her from treading into other people's territory.

The Dialogue—Example 1

Nancy comes into the office.

NANCY   Hi! How are you today?

NORMAN   Good. There are some things we need to talk about. Are you free for lunch?

* ACTION ASTERISK

Remember, bad news and food don't always mix well. The informal atmosphere of a restaurant is not necessarily the best place for employee discipline.

Nancy leaves. Norman asks his secretary to make a lunch reservation.

At the restaurant, they order and have a very relaxed conversation about the new game, when it will be launched, what kind of press conference they will have to introduce it. They have done this before; the group lunches out together occasionally to brainstorm ideas and to keep the relationship between them open. As they near the end of the meal, Norman approaches the subject at hand.

NORMAN	There is something I've been meaning to talk to you about. I guess today's as good a day as any.
NANCY	Oh? What's that?
NORMAN	Well, we're having problems finding you enough to do.
NANCY	Are you kidding? I'm busy all the time.
NORMAN	I know. But sometimes you're busy doing things you shouldn't be doing.
NANCY	(*She stops eating.*) What?

* ACTION ASTERISK
It is obvious that Nancy hasn't a clue that she is doing something she shouldn't. She believes that she is operating within guidelines and up to expectations.

NORMAN	Well, the word processing people are a little upset that you've been typing your own work lately.
NANCY	Good Lord, Norman. I've only done that two or three times. And I'd think they would be pleased. They were so swamped we would have waited a whole day for the material. I did it to keep us on schedule.
NORMAN	From now on, it would probably be better if you used them.
NANCY	Even if it delays us?
NORMAN	If that happens, just tell me and I'll straighten it out.

* ACTION ASTERISK
Norman is setting himself up as a traffic cop, evidently completely out of character to his usual operating style.

NANCY   Sure. I hate to bother you with details like that, but if
               that's the way you want it. (*She starts to pick at her
               food.*)

NORMAN   And Jonathan's getting a little concerned.

NANCY   About what?

NORMAN   Evidently, you've been taking over some of his work
               and he doesn't know why. (*Laughs.*) I think he's afraid
               you're going to take over his job.

NANCY   He was so swamped with requests after the
               stockholders' meeting that I pitched in to help! But we
               always help each other.

NORMAN   I know. But it's making him a little nervous. Maybe you
               should ask me before you pitch in again. That way I can
               talk to him first.

* ACTION ASTERISK

**Norman has been very unmanagerial in mentioning Jonathan's name. It
can bring conflict between Jonathan and Nancy; furthermore, it is not
the real issue.**

NANCY   If that's what you want. We always work wherever
               there's a job to be done. How could Jonathan think I'm
               after his job?

NORMAN   Oh, that's probably just a joke. He just wants to handle
               the Wall Street people himself. It keeps the lines of in-
               formation clear.

NANCY   Um-hmmm.

NORMAN   Would you like anything else?

NANCY   No, thank you.

(*Norman sees Nancy looking off in the distance and realizes that he has hurt
her feelings.*)

NORMAN   Listen, don't let any of this bother you. The real
               problem is me.

* ACTION ASTERISK
Suddenly there is a "problem." And the head of the department is taking the blame. Nancy must really be nervous now, with so many new situations coming at her at one time.

NANCY	What does that mean?
NORMAN	We've been so busy, I've let things get out of control. We've all got a job to do and I've not been doing mine.
NANCY	I don't understand.
NORMAN	Well, if I had been paying attention and not been so involved in my own work, it wouldn't have gotten out of hand.
NANCY	What's out of hand?
NORMAN	Well, nothing yet, but it could be. We're sort of tripping over each other doing the work, and you've gotten into some areas that aren't your territory.
NANCY	Norman, what are you trying to say?
NORMAN	Robert was surprised to get the speech suggestion you sent, and I was a little concerned that you did those pieces for the annual report. Don't get me wrong. They were good. But they were off target somewhat, and basically, I redid them. Of course, I have to meet with the executive committee to get the details straightened out anyway, and there is always a lot of rewriting. (*Norman sees that tears are welling up in Nancy's eyes.*) Now, don't take it like this. You're a real dynamo and everyone loves you. But we've all got to start focusing on our own responsibilities more. I'll give out the assignments and review everything. That way, nobody's feelings will be hurt.
NANCY	Have I been hurting people's feelings?
NORMAN	Of course not. It's just that you've been doing things which aren't really your job and some people have misunderstood. If you work on the assignments I give you, I'm sure everything will be all right.

* ACTION ASTERISK

Norman has become a real **WIMP: Won't Invoke Management Procedures.** He's hurt an employee and set himself up as a bottleneck besides.

NORMAN   Look, let's stop this. Let's go on back to the office and I'll review that press release you did.

NANCY   I'd like to walk a little bit, if you don't mind. I'll go now and meet you in about a half-hour.

NORMAN   Sure. That's fine.

Nancy rises and leaves. Norman signals for the check.

Comments

It is hard to imagine how this interview could have been handled more ineptly. Norman has succeeded in undermining the confidence of a highly motivated, very productive employee.

He has implied that people have complained about her behind her back. He has indicated that the work which she volunteered to do for others has been unacceptable. And he has shattered the father/daughter relationship which has been a subtle undercurrent in the way he has run the department all along.

He has stifled her self-starter nature and will see her volunteer very little from now on. She will continue to do reasonably good work, undoubtedly, but she will not be happy. She won't feel at home anymore, and will probably look for another job in the near future.

There is a more professional way to handle the eager overachiever.

The Dialogue—Example 2 (continued)

They are still in Norman's office.

NORMAN   Good. And there are some things we need to talk about.

NANCY   Sure.

NORMAN   I'm sorry Jonathan's out of the office today. I need to talk with him too. But I'll see him tomorrow.

* ACTION ASTERISK

Very casually, Norman has implied that the forthcoming discussion is for both of his staff, not just Nancy alone, therefore defusing in advance any fears she might have. It also allows him to reassure Jonathan tomorrow that everything went well and that his job is not being threatened.

NANCY What's up?

NORMAN It's like that old gag line, "Next week we've got to get organized." Well, that time has come.

NANCY It seems to me that we get out an awful lot of stuff for such a small group.

NORMAN We do. But we're falling all over each other now. And I've given it some thought and I want to see if we can't all come up with a better idea.

NANCY Like what?

NORMAN I've been toying with a calendar idea. I want to allocate your time and Jonathan's better. And I want to be better informed about who's doing what, and when. So then we'll all know what's going on and who needs help, and so on.

NANCY We all pitch in when there's a crunch.

NORMAN I know. But I'm not sure that's the best way. I've started by laying out a calendar for the year. Both you and Jonathan have things you have to handle at specific times each year. I want us to put those on the calendar, and also to put the preparation time on it, so we can block it out properly. Then I want us each, on a monthly basis, to add in those things which come up irregularly, like new acquisitions, or new programs, or new employees.

NANCY Where will it be?

NORMAN In the hallway outside. That way, we can always get to it and check it and revise it. And I'd like to have your input to it as soon as possible. This Friday should give you both time to list what you already know.

NANCY	That's a great idea. It will take away the surprises.
NORMAN	We will always have surprises. Maybe this will give us the time to handle them. I also need some other ideas about how to organize myself.
NANCY	What do you mean?
NORMAN	Well, I didn't know you were doing some of Jonathan's work until later. And I didn't know you were typing your own stuff instead of sending it to word processing.
NANCY	That was to save time.
NORMAN	I know. But we need to organize a little better. I don't want to be a bottleneck, but I need to know in advance what's happening so we can all keep on track.
NANCY	What about a regular weekly meeting? We used to do that in my other company and it kept us all informed.

* ACTION ASTERISK

Norman has kept on talking about getting organized until he has elicited an idea from Nancy. Formal staff meetings are nothing new in business, but they obviously are new to this department. And by allowing Nancy to come up with the idea, he is reinforcing her self-confidence and participation—before he disciplines her.

NORMAN	Maybe every Monday afternoon? That's a good idea. The three of us could review our work for the week and see where we have to pitch in and help.
NANCY	And then we could add it to the calendar to keep everything straight.
NORMAN	Right. Now about word processing; I'd like you to use them from now on. It keeps everybody happy and it doesn't use your time typing.
NANCY	They were stacked up for fourteen hours when I used them.
NORMAN	I'm not surprised. They're very busy. If that happens again, let me know and I'll see what I can do. With the

planning we're going to be doing, however, we can alert them in advance and be sure that we're on their schedule. That should solve the problem.

NANCY   Will we have our first meeting next Monday?

NORMAN   Yes. If I have your schedules on Friday, we can put them on the calendar Monday and then review where the free spots are. Maybe this will allow us time to do some special promotions.

NANCY   That would be great. I've got some ideas we might want to try.

NORMAN   (*Patiently.*) Write them down for the Monday meetings and we'll discuss them. If they're feasible, we can put them on the schedule.

NANCY   Sure.

NORMAN   Oh. One other thing. Robert was a little surprised to get that speech idea in the mail from you.

NANCY   Don't you remember? When we all had lunch that day, he said he needed some new ideas. So I sent him some.

NORMAN   I know. But I didn't know about it until later and I felt a little foolish.

* ACTION ASTERISK
The thrust of this conversation is slowly dawning on Nancy.

NANCY   Have I done something wrong, Norman?

NORMAN   Well, yes and no. You're so fast and you're so eager that you keep those ideas firing all the time and you pitch in with other people's work. But sometimes I don't know about it and sometimes they don't want it.

NANCY   I'm sorry.

NORMAN   Don't be sorry. It's more my fault than yours. We've grown very fast and I've run a very loose shop. I don't want to stifle our enthusiasm but I've got to get us organized. I don't want the calendar and the Monday meetings to become time-wasters. I want to know when you and Jonathan are working together and I want both of you to *want* to work together on projects. That way we'll produce more work with less confusion.

NANCY   Is Jonathan upset?

NORMAN   A little. He's not used to a free-wheeling environment. But if we plan together, we can team up when needed and work separately when it's appropriate.

* ACTION ASTERISK

Nancy's a bright woman. She's gotten the message and will follow the procedures from now on. But, happily, the procedures will allow her inventiveness to have an outlet—Norman—before it goes flying off anywhere else.

NANCY   I hope I haven't caused any problems.

NORMAN   Nothing serious. I just want to harness all that energy and know what's going on.

NANCY   I'll keep it in mind.

NORMAN   Good. Now get back to work and I'll look at those press releases this afternoon.

NANCY   Right. (*She exits.*)

Summary

The difference in the meetings should be obvious. Norman had a list of problems with Nancy, but he was sensitive enough to different personalities to know that he should look deeper into the issue.

In other words, instead of comfortably blaming the employee, he also looked at his own management style to see if it needed improvement too.

This led him to understand that *he* needed to get organized, for the good of the department and for his two staff members. The calendar and the Monday meetings will help keep everybody on track and will also allow good ideas to surface for discussion. If Jonathan needs help, Norman will assign Nancy to help him and vice versa. Neither will volunteer without authority.

He has also instructed Nancy to keep him informed of problems and ideas *before* the fact, and he is avoiding being a bottleneck in the process.

The principal difference in the two scenes, however, is that in the second example Norman took charge of events *before* the meeting. He had decided what he wished to accomplish and led Nancy through the discussion in such a way that she contributed to the solutions.

Managing overachievers can be a difficult job, because you must walk a fine line between killing their enthusiasm and keeping them from treading on others' toes. An understanding of their value to a department is a first prerequisite for managing them. But equally important is the need for a structure within which they can work. They need to know what is expected of them and they need some mechanism through which to channel their boundless energy and endless ideas. An unorganized *manager* is a disaster for an overachiever. But then, a disorganized manager is ultimately a disaster for everyone!

5 THE UNDERACHIEVER

Introduction

Underachievers are hard to identify. They may be people who are not sufficiently challenged to work at their full capacity. They may be working in an environment which does not allow them the full rein of their abilities. They may be lazy. They may be out of their depth.

Taken in reverse, if they are out of their depth (if they are the victims of the Peter Principle—promoted above their capacity to perform) then time will tell the full, terrible tale and they will either be dismissed or demoted to a position within their grasps.

If they are lazy, other recourses will be found—from dismissal to developing tasks which excite their energies.

If they are working in an environment which limits their abilities, then transfer to other areas where they can be more productive should certainly be considered.

But if they are the classic cases—people not sufficiently challenged to work at their full capacities—then a manager has a particularly ticklish task in view.

First of all, it's hard to distinguish among the four prototypes just described. Great care must be taken not to misinterpret under-performance and underachievement. And once the situation is fairly certain, a manager must go to some lengths to analyze the personality of the employee involved.

It is easy to interpret the assertive, positive, voluble personality as an achiever (although sometimes it is more smoke than fire, more hot air than substance). The more subtle problem is to recognize that the quiet, passive, plodding personality may also be a high achiever—or at least have the potential to be.

Direct challenge, confrontation, and goal-setting are not necessarily good with this type of person. They can be frightened by such tactics and retreat even farther into their shells of safety—following the rules, filling the forms, watching the clock.

We are, of course, talking about *good* employees—people who are cooperative, thorough, careful, honest, who do a good job within the boundaries of their understanding of the job.

What they lack is creativity; they do what is expected of them but rarely do they do the unexpected. They don't come up with new ideas to solve problems, new ways of doing an old task faster or better, new tasks or outlets for a department's skills. They're not *bad* employees, they are underachievers. You know that they are capable of making a greater contribution. The question is how?

1. Praise is one way. If they are regularly reassured that the work they are doing is satisfactory they will be less nervous when confronted with something new.
2. Talk with them confidentially, one-on-one. Such people have a tendency to clam up in a group, letting more assertive people have the floor.
3. Share problems and concerns on a "we" basis. Don't let them think that they are totally alone—and at risk—in the situation. It is a joint effort, each supporting the other.
4. Listen to them. Quietly and unexpectedly they will share insights and ideas when they are confident that they are respected and safe.
5. Give them small tasks to accomplish, with timely review and support along the way. Small steps of accomplishment can lead to bigger ones.

Like all managerial problems, the underachiever takes thought and effort. But the rewards are worth it in dedication and loyalty.

The Situation

Salvo makes its software sales to regional distributors, to large chains and franchises, and even to certain successful stores in large cities. Its accounts receivable is, therefore, a somewhat complicated mechanism and the process can be delayed, particularly from the distributors and franchises, because they wait to collect from the point-of-sales stores before paying their bills.

Salvo uses some enticements, such as discounts for prompt payment, but like all product-oriented companies, it constantly tries to find ways to improve its cash flow.

The Characters

Joe, the controller, is a stickler for good billing and follow-up and has tried to devise numerous ways to keep the money flowing in. He works closely with the credit/collections people to stay ahead of problems, but as an old-fashioned CPA, he believes that accurate records, timely billing, and good follow-up can account for a large percentage of cash in any business. His record has been generally good during his six years, and as the company has grown, he has built a small department of three to handle the billing and accounting of the receivables.

Mary is the manager of the group. She started as a clerk, working for Joe, when the company was small, and has grown with the company to reach the managerial level. She is in her late thirties, quiet, a graduate of a good community college, and very detail-oriented. She takes pride in her work, but is not creative in finding ways to make the cash flow faster.

Joe is looking for other ideas and wants to get her more involved in creating them as well as implementing them. He is not unhappy with her work, but feels that as a manager she should take more responsibility for forming procedures as well as in carrying them out. He has called her to his office to try to develop some new ideas.

Manager's Objective

To motivate a good employee to exercise more managerial creativity rather than simply carry out policies already in place.

The Dialogue—Example 1

Mary comes to the door.

JOE Come in. Close the door. (*She does.*) How are you?

MARY Fine. How are you?

* ACTION ASTERISK

Evidently, Joe has not told Mary what the meeting is about. He has simply called her to his office. Thus, the small talk.

JOE	I'm fine. I've been thinking about your department and I wanted to talk to you about it.
MARY	Oh? Is anything wrong?
JOE	No. No. It's just the ongoing problem. I'm trying to figure out ways to get more money in here quicker.
MARY	We're up to date on all our billing.
JOE	I know that. I check the reports. It seems that no matter what we do, some of the accounts will wait thirty or sixty days.
MARY	It's usually the same ones.
JOE	I know. They seem to live on our float. However, every time we add an account I worry that we don't develop some way to get our money quicker.
MARY	So far we've been able to keep up with the billing.

* ACTION ASTERISK

Mary continues to reiterate that her department is performing as expected. She must have fears that Joe is trying to find fault.

JOE	Oh, I know. Everything's up-to-date. Except the receipts. Last month 15 percent were thirty days behind.
MARY	We added two programs and three chains.
JOE	Right. What are we going to do? That was 4 percent higher than the month before.
MARY	What do you mean?
JOE	We're going in the wrong direction. The more we sell, the higher our percentage of delayed payments. What can we do?

MARY   Have you talked with collections?

* ACTION ASTERISK
Mary doesn't see the problem as hers. She and her department are doing their job. Can't someone else solve the problem?

JOE   They don't even get involved until it's sixty days overdue. And that's only about 5 percent, thank God.

MARY   What do you want us to do?

JOE   Do you have any ideas?

MARY   We're following the procedures. We send a bill. And then we send a follow-up after twenty-five days...

JOE   And the cash return is slipping.

MARY   I don't know what else we can do.

JOE   That's the point. We've got to come up with something. Don't you have any ideas?

MARY   We'll do whatever you say. We're very busy now, but if you want another letter, we'll put one in the works.

JOE   It's not what *I* want. It's just good business sense. You work with all these accounts. Can't you figure out some ways to get them paying more promptly?

* ACTION ASTERISK
This is a direct challenge which Mary is unprepared to handle. It is unlikely that Joe has ever treated her as anything more than a well-paid clerk. She has performed well when told what to do. But it is unlikely that she has ever been expected to *decide* what to do.

MARY   Well, I don't know. We bill and then we do follow-up and then in sixty days we turn it over to collections.

JOE   We've got to do better than that. Don't you have any ideas?

MARY   Well, no. We just keep plugging away.

JOE That's not good enough. You've got to be more creative. Come up with some other ideas. Get that department in gear. If it doesn't keep up with sales, we're
going to hear about it. It doesn't do any good to sell this
stuff if we can't get the money in the bank.

MARY I'll try. Who should I talk to?

JOE I don't know! Use some initiative. Get your thinking
cap on. Surely there are some ways you can make the
department more productive.

* ACTION ASTERISK

Joe has gone off the deep end and is mouthing cliches. He is talking to a
former clerk who is very dedicated and hardworking, but who has not
had the training or the inspiration to do other than what she is doing.
She has been an implementer and is suddenly expected to be an innovator. She must be totally unprepared for this challenge.

MARY I'll see what I can think of.

JOE Good. Get back to me in a few days and let's go over
your ideas.

MARY All right.

Comments

Was the manager's objective achieved? No.

Although he didn't intend to do so, Joe has probably terrified Mary and
made her extremely uncomfortable in her job. It is unlikely that she will
think of something innovative or meaningful in the next few days. She will
be thinking mostly about how the job has abruptly changed and how uncomfortable she is, and is going to be, in it. And this could ultimately
detract from her implementation skills because she is distracted with this
new problem of creativity.

Underachievers need training and support systems (as does everyone
else). Only when those are in place is it possible to challenge them, fairly,
to perform at a higher level of productivity. Joe let his frustration with typical business problems overrule his good judgment regarding behavior
toward a valued employee.

There are some steps he missed along the way.

The Dialogue—Example 2 (continued)

MARY   What do you want us to do?

JOE   I think we have to be a little more creative. What kind of follow-up letters do you send out?

MARY   You've seen them. They're form letters reminding the customer that the account is twenty-five days overdue.

JOE   Maybe that needs work.

MARY   What do you mean?

JOE   Maybe it needs jazzing up. Something to get their attention. I also wonder if we can start putting penalties on late payment—say 45 days.

MARY   The customers might resent it.

JOE   I know. But if they want the software, they'll keep coming back.

MARY   Sales might be a little upset if we did that.

* ACTION ASTERISK

Mary is asserting an opinion and showing an understanding of customer relations.

JOE   That's right. I wonder if they have any ideas, though. They're in touch with those people regularly. Surely there's a way they can help us.

MARY   I've talked to Mike a couple of times and he really doesn't want to get involved. He says his people can't sell and collect money at the same time.

JOE   He's right. When did you talk to him?

MARY   When we had such a hard time with the Powell chain. We finally turned it over to collections. Remember?

JOE   Yeah. I'm just wondering why we can't get some better ideas going.

MARY   Part of the problem is the credit clearance to begin
                  with. If our people would only sell to those with good
                  ratings we'd have a lot less problems.

* ACTION ASTERISK
Because the conversation is going on at a very calm and unchallenging
fashion, Mary is revealing that she knows a great deal about the
problem—and the business. The fact that she has not been assertive or
innovative before doesn't mean she's dumb or incompetent.

JOE   What can we do about it?

MARY   We can't do anything. But Mike could set some
                  guidelines for a sales staff. He could demand a credit
                  rating of a certain quality before the staff is allowed to
                  sell.

JOE   That would help. (*He makes a note.*) I don't know
                  whether he'll crack down or not. But I'll talk to him.
                  Maybe we can set some guidelines and at least get cash
                  in advance from certain customers.

MARY   That would help. And maybe we could send out a
                  different kind of letter after twenty-five days.

JOE   What do you mean, different?

MARY   We're sending out the letter Jim wrote several years
                  ago. Maybe we need something else.

JOE   Maybe we do. I'll talk to Norman. Better still, why don't
                  you talk to Norman and see if he can make it stronger so
                  it will stand out in the crowd?

MARY   O.K.

* ACTION ASTERISK
Joe is using her interest to get her to reach out to other expertise in the
company for help and innovation.

JOE   There's another idea. I got a mailing from AMA.
                  They're having a seminar here in town next month on
                  accounts receivable and collectibles. I think you should
                  go. Maybe they'll have some new ideas which will help

us. Here's the information. Why don't you register and we'll take care of it.

MARY   O.K. (*She takes the folder.*)

* ACTION ASTERISK

While some companies occasionally go overboard with training courses and seminars, in moderation, they are still the best way to motivate employees and to absorb new ideas which have worked at other companies. They also provide a subtle reward for employees; there is always the implication that if a company is willing to spend extra money in training a person they place an extra value *on* that person.

JOE   Let's meet again next week and talk again. You talk to Norman and I'll talk to Mike in the meantime. Then when you go to this seminar, you can review some of their ideas with me. Maybe we can improve this situation.

MARY   O.K.

JOE   I'll see you next week.

Summary

Was the manager's objective achieved? Yes.

By keeping the conversation low-key and nonthreatening, Joe was able to draw out some of Mary's own concerns and ideas about the problem.

It is true that she has never volunteered any solutions to the problem, but it is obvious that she is *aware* of them and that she has an understanding of their complexities. They will make small steps with a different late payment letter and a cash only concept with risky customers. They may get some other good ideas from the professional seminar.

The point is that Joe has involved her in the *solution* to the problem and has broken her from the habit of simply following procedure and habit. Only time will tell if she will become creative and assertive, but at least a good employee has not been intimidated and frightened. Her knowledge and ideas have been cultivated and, with patience, may grow to greater productivity.

6 THE MONDAY MORNING QUARTERBACK

Introduction

This chapter could just as easily have been called "Sunday morning reviewer" or "Saturday afternoon bookie." It isn't about sports, it's about nuisances, those people who are vitally interested in one particular subject, be it sports, opera, horse-racing, or cooking, and seek out other people with similar interests. Then they talk about their special interests—a lot. The only problem is, many of them choose to talk about it—a lot—at the office.

This behavior can quickly escalate from nuisance to disruptive if enough people are interested in the topic. A friendly, free and easy environment is conducive to abuse without the employees intending it to be. Most Monday morning quarterbacks are oblivious to the problems they cause, and with the rare exception, have no intention of causing a problem. They are so caught up in their favorite topic that they do not realize that they are taking time away from their work, that they are annoying some people, and that they are keeping other people from doing their work by talking with them. Their intentions are the best—to be entertaining, to be interesting, to make friends, to join in a mutual camaraderie. And because their intentions are good—and the results bad—a manager is caught in a dilemma.

How do you stop the interference with work without breaking the spirit of the employee?

It is assumed that we are talking about a *good* employee. If you're dealing with a goof-off or an incompetent, the problem is separate from the "quarterback" problem and should be dealt with through normal procedures.

In the following example you will find some ways of handling this management problem in a reasoned and effective way. But let's deal with another issue. How do you prevent the situation from developing in the first place? The most obvious answer is—by example.

If the manager is a "Monday morning quarterback," then the message is clear. It's O.K. to use up time in disruptive, extraneous conversation, because the boss does it. In that case one can only hope that the manager's boss will deal with it promptly and effectively. But if the manager is *not* a time-waster the message is equally clear. (Please don't interpret this as unfriendly and lacking in small talk. We are talking about excesses, not the exercise of common courtesy.) People tend to imitate their professional role models, in dress, in behavior, in social interchange, and the best preventive measure is a good example.

What else should a manger do? Walk the place on a regular basis (but certainly not at the same time every day). *See* what is going on, in different departments at different times of day. Be familiar with the work habits and relationships of your staff. Don't depend on memos, the open door policy, and secondhand information. The best way to keep a situation from going bad is to observe for yourself, and be a presence in your department. This does not mean to be Big Brother watching for flaws; it means knowing the people, their personalities, their informal relationships on a one-to-one basis. "Quarterbacking" really can't go on if the boss is there to ask how you are and to ask about your work.

And finally, the encouragement of a broader range of interests always gives employees more to share together and more things to talk about. This can range from company-sponsored ball teams, picnics and outings, nights at the theater, and competitions for the United Way to a company library and reading room, a company movie theater or the "adoption" of an orphanage or nursing home as a company project.

The more there is to do and learn together, the less likely it is that one topic will dominate the halls and shops of a business. Enlightened company policies can make a difference in everyone's life and, generally, also raise productivity.

One point should be made about this chapter and the difference between sexism and "quarterbacking." Sexist language, behavior, or inference can exist in the work place and be very disruptive. Such language and behavior can occasionally surface during enthusiastic sports exchanges and alter the tone of the exchanges to some of the listeners.

Sometimes sexist, demeaning, derogatory comments are intentional. But more frequently, people are not aware of how their remarks or actions can affect someone else.

The examples in this chapter are not to be confused with sexism and that should be apparent in the text.

The Situation

Like all companies, Salvo has its share of "Monday morning quarterbacks," those men and women who find it necessary to replay the Saturday and Sunday television sports events during working hours on Monday morning. There is general banter at the coat closets at nine and considerable discussion at the coffee wagon at ten-thirty (in spite of the fact that some employees in the line might wish to discuss something else, but it's too difficult over the din). But the *real* "quarterback" is Jordan, who appears to watch every sports event on television and delights in replaying all the crucial moments, from office to office if necessary—and not just on Monday mornings.

He is a delightful young man, a good tennis player, knows a great deal about sports, is full of enthusiasm, and tells a good story. But it has gotten out of hand. He spends over an hour every day, going from office to office, discussing the "great game" last night.

Several secretaries have made formal complaints to the personnel director because his visits interrupt their work and they also find it difficult to hear over the telephone while he is "performing" for their bosses. Two members of the sales staff (one male, one female) have complained to their directors because of the interruptions. And the president of the company was visiting with Herman in MIS one day and was somewhat astonished to find Jordan with some of the programmers, regaling them with power plays from the night before.

Jordan's boss, Joe, has been talked to by all three of the executives and has been asked to solve the problem—get Jordan back to work and keep him from bothering other people.

The Characters

Jordan is manager of payroll, reporting to Joe. Jordan is in his late twenties, a college graduate with an accounting degree, and he loves sports. He was a cheerleader in his university. Salvo is his second job. He is a very gregarious and efficient young man, and his staff of two work very hard for him because he is fair, pleasant, and a hard, fast worker.

Because of the basic informality at Salvo, he has been able to meet and mingle with a number of people in other departments who share his enthusiasm for sports. He runs the company pool (with the company's tacit permission) and enjoys making the payoffs every Monday morning. He's a good storyteller and enjoys entertaining people. Most people seem to enjoy his play-by-play.

He has been at Salvo for almost two years and his excessive interest in sports has grown in the last year, as he has come to know more people. He's a good worker, got a good raise after his first year and expects to be nicely rewarded at his next review.

Joe is controller and has been with the company for over six years. He's a family man, in his forties, with a degree in finance and a CPA. He is quiet, dedicated, and motivates his people through example, support, and a good sense of humor.

He enjoys Jordan's enthusiasm, and, as a lover of sports himself, has tolerated Jordan's expanded interest in the subject, simply because the work is always done on time and with little problem.

He has been surprised at the complaints voiced by the sales director, the personnel director, and the president because he had not realized that Jordan's activities had become so far-reaching in the company.

He privately realizes that it is also a reflection on his own managerial ability to have let this happen.

He has decided to call Jordan in and take care of it immediately. He called Jordan's office at nine-fifteen and the assistant told him "Jordan is out of the office." Joe left a call-back message and it came at ten-thirty. He asked Jordan to come to see him.

Manager's Objective

To stop Jordan's interference with other people, but without breaking his spirit or curtailing the good work of the department.

The Dialogue—Example 1

Jordan comes to the door and Joe motions him to a seat and closes the door.

JORDAN   Hi.

JOE   Good morning.

JORDAN   Boy, you didn't come near winning the pot today! You were off by a mile on every team.

JOE   I know. Where were you earlier?

JORDAN   What do you mean, earlier?

JOE	This morning. I called about nine-fifteen.
JORDAN	I was out paying off the winners.
JOE	How many were there?
JORDAN	Three today. Jimmy in MIS, and Gail in accounting, and...
JOE	Did it take you an hour and a half to pay three people?
JORDAN	What?
JOE	You returned my call at ten-thirty. Did it take an hour and a half to pay off three people?
JORDAN	Well, I stopped to get coffee before I went back to my office.
JOE	And talked about the game?
JORDAN	Sure. There are a bunch of us who talk about it over coffee.
JOE	So I've heard.
JORDAN	(*Pause.*) What's up, Joe?
JOE	We seem to be getting into too many sports here at Salvo. We're going to have to cool it for a while and concentrate more on our work.
JORDAN	There are a lot of sports fans here. It's a gas talking with them. I don't think it interferes with our work. Surely you don't think I'm not doing *my* work?
JOE	No, as a matter of fact, I know you do good work. But it's keeping other people from doing theirs.
JORDAN	You mean me?
JOE	I'm afraid so. We've had some complaints.

61

* ACTION ASTERISK
Immediately, Joe has shifted the conversation from himself to complaints registered by others.

JORDAN   What kind of complaints?

JOE   Well, it's like this morning. You were out of your office for an hour and a half. I don't know if anyone tried to reach you, besides me. But you were unavailable. And you were talking with other people, I'm sure. That had to have distracted the folks in those departments.

JORDAN   But they *wanted* to talk about it!

JOE   Just a minute. There's more. There are people who have complained because your visits disturb them.

JORDAN   What people?

JOE   The president, for one.

* ACTION ASTERISK
Now he has shifted the responsibility to the top of the company. That's a serious blow to any employee.

JORDAN   I've never discussed sports with the president!

JOE   No. But you were holding forth one day in MIS when he was there. He didn't particularly like what he saw. You know he's pretty square and likes to see work going on throughout the shop.

JORDAN   I'm not the only one who was talking! It takes two to make a conversation, you know.

JOE   I know, Jordan. There are a lot of people who enjoy talking with you, but these complaints are serious and I don't want to hear any more of them.

JORDAN   Who were the complainers?

JOE   I don't want to give names. Some of the girls don't like sports and they say it bothers them. You know how that is. It happens everywhere.

* ACTION ASTERISK

This crops up in speech more often than people realize. If "the girls" don't like it, it's a nuisance but not a serious business problem. Though Joe probably doesn't realize it, he has trivialized both the problem and the people who have complained. He has also found another cop-out for not taking control of the situation and managing it. Many people consider the use of the word "girls" in the work place sexist. Although the speaker may not *intend* to trivialize or demean, the words do so; as it is a simple behavior pattern which can be changed, managers should become conscious of its effect on others and alter the words to "the women" (just as they would describe "the men" in the work place, not "the boys").

JORDAN	I sure wish I knew who had complained about me. They did it behind my back. Why couldn't they just tell me to my face? Now I'll be suspicious of everybody.
JOE	There's no need for that. You know who your real friends are. We'll all stick together.
JORDAN	What do you want me to do?
JOE	Well, the first thing is for you guys to kind of keep it down at the coffee wagon. I guess all the sports talk disturbs some people.
JORDAN	Oh?
JOE	Yeah. Just hold it down and don't carry on so much. That should help.
JORDAN	That will be nice and dull.
JOE	And then when you go to do the pool payoffs every Monday, you'd better speed it up. Don't hang out so much with the guys who have won. This morning you were gone from your desk an hour and a half. And that's just too much. You'll have to do it a lot quicker. Be back at your desk promptly.

* ACTION ASTERISK

These are ridiculous, imprecise instructions. How can an employee follow them? How much time is "quicker"?

JORDAN	I can do it at coffee break.

63

JOE	O.K. Just so it doesn't stretch out too long. And don't go into MIS except on business. Obviously, the president stops by in there sometime, and I wouldn't want him to get any wrong ideas.
JORDAN	I still wish I knew who was talking behind by back.
JOE	Forget it. Just do your job and don't let that bother you. Keep the sports talk just among folks you know enjoy it and everything will be fine.
JORDAN	I guess.
JOE	Sure it will. Now, go on back to your office and get to work. I don't want to waste any more of your time.
JORDAN	Sure. (*He rises.*)
JOE	By the way, there's a new fellow in accounts payable named George. He may want to get in the football pool.

* ACTION ASTERISK
Even Joe obviously has not understood the real problem.

JORDAN	Great. I'll stop by and see him now.
JOE	(*Laughs.*) No. I think you'd better stop by and see him at lunch or this afternoon.
JORDAN	(*Laughs.*) Yeah, you're probably right. I wouldn't want anybody complaining.
JOE	Right. See you later.
JORDAN	Yeah. Thanks, Joe. (*He exits.*)

Comments

Was the manager's objective accomplished? No, not really. Although he *succeeded* in not breaking Jordan's spirit, he did *not* succeed in accomplishing the primary goal—stopping Jordan's interference with other people at work.

Joe chose the path of least resistance. He was the understanding boss who agreed that "some of the girls" didn't like to talk about sports and that the president was a "square" who wanted to see people working all the time. In other words, he put himself on Jordan's side; sort of "us against the world," rather than taking the position of a manager who had allowed things to get out of hand and who needed to correct some errors of behavior in an employee.

Further, he did not cope with the real problem of getting Jordan back to his desk, not bothering other people, and concentrating on work, not sports. "Cut down on" the time he talks sports, "speed up" the payouts on the pool and "just talk to folks who enjoy it" are not specific guidelines for correcting an office behavior problem. They are vague, at best, and require Jordan to exercise his own judgment—which has already proved faulty. History should alert Joe that Jordan will be back into his old patterns within a matter of days—if not hours.

In matters of discipline, managers can't be "one of the boys." It's the price you pay for being a manager.

The Dialogue—Example 2 (continued)

JOE   No, as a matter of fact, I know you do good work. But it's keeping other people from doing theirs.

JORDAN   You mean me?

JOE   Well, you've sort of been the catalyst. Actually, I've been as much of a problem as you've been.

JORDAN   Have I been a problem?

JOE   Let me start at the beginning, Jordan. That's how my mind works. You love sports. A lot of people in the world love sports. And you are particularly good at remembering special moments, and telling people about them and making them exciting all over again.

JORDAN   So?

JOE   So you've become our in-house Howard Cosell.

JORDAN   Aw, come on...

JOE   (*Laughs.*) You're right. That's unfair. You're more fun than Howard Cosell!

JORDAN   (*Sarcastically.*) Thanks.

AN EXECUTIVE'S COACHING HANDBOOK

JOE   Seriously, you spend a lot of time here talking about
                  sports. Not as much as Howard Cosell, but enough.
                  You handle all our sports pools now. You entertain
                  people on the coffee line. You keep the guys posted on
                  games they've missed. You're really our one-man sports
                  department.

* ACTION ASTERISK
**While this sounds like a lot of compliments, it isn't really good office
behavior. Jordan must be getting the message that all is not well.**

JORDAN   You sound like you're leading up to something.

JOE   I'm leading up to a criticism of both of us. I love sports
                  as much as you do and I've, frankly, indulged myself as
                  much as I've indulged you. And it's gone too far. I want
                  us to get it back on the right track and back into some
                  proportion.

JORDAN   Has someone complained about me?

JOE   Well, it's become a problem to some people. And again,
                  I've apologized for it. I should have been more aware of
                  the problem.

JORDAN   So I'm a problem?

JOE   No. But sports can become a problem in any office if
                  people let it interfere with work. For that matter, anyth-
                  ing can become a problem if it becomes excessive. I had
                  an assistant once who loved the opera. I finally had to
                  persuade him to talk about it with his friends at lunch
                  and not tie up the phone. But I'd really like to get down
                  to specifics.

JORDAN   Are you unhappy with my work?

JOE   No. On the contrary, your work is very good and very
                  prompt. That's why I've been blind to the other
                  problems. It's more a matter of perception than of
                  specifics. So let's break it down and talk about it.

JORDAN   Sure.

* ACTION ASTERISK
Instead of overwhelming Jordan, and himself, Joe is trying to sort out the complaints and deal with them individually.

JOE	Take the company pool. How many people play it?
JORDAN	Nearly a hundred.
JOE	That many?
JORDAN	Yes. It's really been growing.
JOE	How long does it take you to get all the bets?
JORDAN	I don't know. Sometimes people come by my office. Sometimes I see them in the course of the day. It's never any set time. We run several pools now and different people play different ones.
JOE	Do you talk with them much when they pledge?
JORDAN	Some, I guess. I really haven't calculated it.
JOE	What would happen if we stopped it?
JORDAN	I Don't know. A lot of people would be disappointed.
JOE	Probably. It *is* gambling. And it *is* being done on the company premises. It's gotten much bigger and more widspread than I realized. In all candor, we're vulnerable legally because of it, and if there are that many people involved, it worries me. You're becomming the company bookie.
JORDAN	I never thought of it that way.
JOE	Neither had I. But I think we'd better drop it. It solves any number of problems if we do.
JORDAN	How do I do it?
JOE	I don't. Just give me the list of all the participants and I'll send a memo to them saying that the company pools

have been discontinued and wish them all the luck with their favorite teams in the future.

* ACTION ASTERISK

This should have been looked at sooner. Not only Jordan, but the company, is vulnerable in this regard. This vulnerability goes much beyond his expenditure of time. There are legal questions posed in company pools which are tacitly allowed on company property.

JORDAN	I guess that's best.
JOE	I think so. We should have looked at it more closely before this. Now, then...about the coffee wagon.
JORDAN	The coffee wagon?
JOE	Yes. It seems to have become Salvo's "sports extra." Every day is a twenty-minute replay of every game. All we need is a tailgate and a barrel of beer.
JORDAN	I don't understand.
JOE	What would happen if our departments rotated the coffee call?
JORDAN	What do you mean?
JOE	When that bell rings, everybody jumps up and goes for coffee. The department—not just yours—is practically deserted. The lines are long. The talk goes on forever. What if our departments rotated the responsibility? Each day, one person from each section would go for coffee for the whole section, and the others would stay at their desks?
JORDAN	I think it would cause problems. Everybody wants something different from the wagon.
JOE	Well, I'd like to try it. Let's start with your group. It's manageable. And we'll see how it goes. Rotate among your people and see if we can keep most people at their desks and the hallway not so cluttered.
JORDAN	O.K., if you say so. When should we start?

JOE	Why not tomorrow? As to your talking sports with the rest of us, I think that has to stop.
JORDAN	What do you mean, stop?
JOE	If you're not taking bets and making payouts, you won't have to be out in the company talking sports so much.
JORDAN	Is that the problem?

* ACTION ASTERISK

Joe has led into the fundamental issue. But it is not secret or behind-the-back. He will now talk about it directly without damage to Jordan's ego or confidence in himself.

JOE	Yes, Jordan, it is. Casual conversation at the water fountain or the elevators or in the men's room is not the issue. Talking for long periods of time in offices and the coffee line and the programmers area and the rest can be a big problem. I don't want you misunderstood in this company. You're an excellent manager with a good future. People who see you simply as a sports maven don't know that. We have to cut out any misunderstandings now.
JORDAN	Why didn't you just tell me to stop?
JOE	You love sports. You'll never stop talking about them. However, with these new plans we have, you'll talk sports a little bit here and a lot more elsewhere. And that's fine.

* ACTION ASTERISK

Joe has done enough professional stroking to put the criticism in perspective. Jordan knows now that he is respected as a professional but that he has to cut out his sports interests at the office, except in an incidental, and acceptable, way.

JORDAN	Thanks, Joe.
JOE	Thank you. We both made some mistakes. And I'm glad they could be corrected so easily. Now, go on back to your office. And I'll see you later.

JORDAN   (*Stands.*) Sure. And thanks again.

Summary

What was the difference in the way Joe handled the problem in this example?

First, he took partial responsibility for letting the "quarterbacking" get out of hand. This was not done with the "understanding boss" attitude, which takes the position of "us against them." This was a boss who admitted that he was at fault too and intended to move swiftly to get all behavior back on a professional basis.

Second, he did not trivialize the complaints or suggest that "the girls" were complaining about "the boys." Nowhere in his discussion was there a hint of sexism. (See the Appendix for recommendations for formal company policy.)

Third, no matter how much Joe likes sports, he recognizes that too much concern, particularly in-house betting pools, can get out of hand, both in time consumption and stretching legalities. It must be noted that there are thousands (if not millions) of office pools each year on sporting events. Under the strict code of law, they can be illegal, and many are in direct violation of written company policy. When there are many participants, the opportunity for fraud and other abuses is obvious. We recommend advice of counsel on continuing them, and in the absence of that, the old advice is probably best: When in doubt, don't.

Fourth, he took Jordan out of the halls and other people's offices and put him back to work. The coffee wagon ploy may not work in the long run, but it will break certain habits. Without Jordan leading the discussions, the disruption every morning will probably wither away. Further, if it continues, it will not be laid at Jordan's door. By the time he goes back to the coffee wagon, or the department gets its own coffeepot, other habits and other conversational relationships will have formed.

Joe has not broken Jordan's spirit. But he has put a very smart young man on alert to what is appropriate behavior. Sports are fun, but not in the office. Too much of *any* extraneous (nonbusiness) discussion is a bore and disruptive, because each person has his or her own personal interests. While we are not suggesting *total* and pure business discussion only, we are suggesting moderation and awareness of others. Business meetings do *not* have to commence with last night's scores. They are like the weather: boring, because they're talked about so much, you can't do anything about them, and at least half the people present don't care. Jordan—and people like him—will find other things to talk about if they read something besides the sports pages. A well-rounded business person will do that, and have a better future because of it.

One other point: Joe never mentioned that other people had complained about Jordan. It was touched upon, but he passed over it and immediately went to solutions. He took the burden of responsibility upon himself, not blaming anyone else for the reprimand. He also avoided having Jordan think there was some kind of conspiracy behind his back by doing this. Good managers don't blame other people. If a matter is worth a reprimand and correction, it is worth taking the responsibility and not shifting that burden to others.

7
THE BOOZER

Introduction

Drinking problems at the office are no joke, although many times they are treated that way. Good ole so-and-so is allowed to drink at lunch, come back soused, cause a lot of laughter and derision behind his or her back, and one day be fired because he or she screwed up something or became too much of a nuisance.

Nobody plans it that way. There is no conspiracy to hide and tolerate alcoholics until they can't be hidden anymore. In many companies, the Puritan notion still exists that excessive drinking is a character flaw. And ignorance is terribly destructive—both of people and of morale—especially in those companies where social drinking is an integral part of the work process.

There are certain businesses or departments where the business lunch is an American commercial tradition. Other industries have a teetotaler's reputation, whether earned or not. There is no hard and fast rule, except, perhaps, the obvious: When in doubt, don't drink.

Every industry, like every culture, has its own mores, its own customs, its own traditions. Not knowing those customs and not behaving within their confines can be a deadly career error for an individual.

And for the habitual drinker, the person who needs a couple of belts at lunch to calm the nerves, to persuade a buyer or seller, to loosen up with the other person, the path can be rocky indeed.

There are several things which need saying:

1. There are recognized differences between the alcoholic (the person for whom alcohol is an addiction and a poison) and the social drinker (who can have a couple of drinks or pass them up, purely as a social ice-breaker). It takes an expert to know the difference in these people, and few companies are equipped to make those judgments.
2. Because industries have their own customs, it is helpful for a company to have stated policies which can be guidelines for all employees. It all goes back to the fundamental organization plan—what is *expected* of each person? If those guidelines are sound and known, employees don't operate in a vacuum and have a better chance of performing to expectations.
3. For better or worse, the conduct of a company is set by the operating executives. If they drink at lunch, the employees will assume that it's O.K., no matter what the rules say. If the executives function without drinking during the workday, the message is clear. That is why stated policy must conform to upper management behavior and vice versa. Otherwise, the employees will know that the company rules are a sham.
4. Without the above understanding, it is difficult to make an example of or punish an employee who misfunctions because of drinking. The more enlightened course is to quietly capture that employee early on, when he or she is seen operating out of the company norm, and to help discover whether the problem is a disease (alcoholism) or merely a misunderstanding of the company's code of behavior.

Happily, many companies both large and small have quietly initiated programs for the problem drinker on the staff. Those programs range from outside counseling to full "dry out" retreats. Little is known of the success or failure rate because of the confidentiality, but the need for the programs is obvious.

Several phenomena have made it possible to bring alcoholism out of the closet and to concentrate on the cure and not on recriminations.

One is the willingness of a number of celebrities to admit their substance addictions publicly, go into special environments (such as the Betty Ford Clinic in California) for cure and then to promote treatment for others. Such celebrity advocacy can have a felicitous influence on others with a problem or on those who know people with a problem.

The second influence is the arrival of a young, nondrinking population into the work force. This takes two forms, both of which have discouraged drinking of hard liquor in the younger working population. One group is into jogging, aerobics, Perrier, skiing, and tennis. The other came from the pot-smoking, wine-drinking generation who have no real taste for hard drugs and hard booze.

The third, least heralded trend is in unions. A number of enlightened leaderships have recognized alcoholism as a problem among their membership and have quietly established funds and methods of counseling and cure. Their concern is admirable and the expansion of their efforts throughout America's union ranks should be encouraged.

Finally, the work of Alcoholics Anonymous should be cause for honors and praise in this country. Their personal commitment and support system is one of the finest examples of individuals helping other individuals achieve a laudable personal goal. While no one can be forced to seek help at AA, anyone with a drinking problem should be supported and encouraged to give it a try. They are a splendid example that great change can be made "one person at a time, one day at a time."

It is unlikely that drinking during working hours will cease in American business, particularly in the so-called white collar jobs. Too much custom and tradition is involved. And to the vast majority of American workers, drinking is not a "problem." The challenge for the manager is to deal with it, humanely and effectively, when it is a problem.

The Situation

Salvo has assured itself a good profit margin with tight cost controls including good purchasing procedures.

Jim has suspected lately that Ralph has a drinking problem. The controller, whose office is down the hall from Ralph's, mentioned seeing him come in several times, in the middle of the afternoon, after a long and obviously wet lunch. Jim called Ralph's office last week about three P.M. The assistant seemed a little flustered when she reported that Ralph was out of the office. This morning, Jim received a bill for magnetic tapes from accounts payable, questioning the amount. Their assumption was that Salvo had a 40 percent discount and the bill did not reflect that.

Jim had pulled the purchasing contract from the contract files and discovered that the date was revised, the discount was 35 percent, and Ralph's signature was practically illegible. He sat in shock for some time, trying to figure out what could have happened, and what to do about it. Then he called personnel to ask for Ralph's file. When he had reviewed it, he made a call after reading the references.

Finally, he called Ralph and asked him to come in at two-thirty and to bring the file on the tape company. When Ralph asked if there was a problem, Jim simply said that he wanted to review it.

The Characters

Jim, the vice-president of finance, is proud of those procedures, which he initiated early in the formation of the company. As the company grew, he transferred the responsibility from his office to a purchasing department, reporting to him.

Ralph is the purchasing director, hired from a large computer company, where he was in a large purchasing department. This job has given him the chance to run his own department.

He is about fifty, has three daughters in college, and works very hard at satisfying all the people he buys for. And he loves a good bargain. He reads incessantly, goes to trade shows, tests out supplies and equipment, is constantly on the lookout for the best product at the best price.

He has a purchasing agent and an administrative assistant in his department, both of whom are good with detail and keep scrupulous records.

Ralph has some trouble with paperwork and detail, so he has allocated the work accordingly: His staff handles most of it. He tests new products, visits manufacturers, negotiates purchasing agreements, and is the contact for all Salvo management. So far, the procedure has worked very well and Jim is happy with the productivity of the department.

Manager's Objectives

To discover whether Ralph really has a drinking problem and to find some way to solve it.

To guarantee that such a problem will not interfere with the company's business.

The Dialogue—Example 1

Ralph arrives five minutes late, out of breath from hurrying, with the file folders under his arm.

RALPH   Those elevators should be retired to a museum! Sorry I'm late.

JIM   Sure. Sit down, Ralph. (*Jim walks past Ralph to close the door behind him, and as he does, he smells his cigar smoke and the faint odor of sin-sin. I haven't smelled that in years, Jim thinks as he goes back to his desk.*) Did you bring the file?

RALPH   Sure did. Right here. (*He puts the folders on Jim's desk.*)

JIM	I'd like to look at your latest copy of our agreement with them. What's the deal? (*Ralph sifts through the contract file and then hands Jim a duplicate of the one he has already seen.*) Why did the deal change?
RALPH	What?
JIM	The deal. Why did it go from 40 percent to 35 percent?
RALPH	Let me see that. (*He reaches for the folder, looks at the terms, and then starts flipping through the folder.*) They tried to bring us down to 30 percent. But I worked on them and got them to 35 percent.
JIM	What do you mean you "worked on them"?
RALPH	You know. I talked with them. I did a little yelling. I did a little persuading. The usual.
JIM	Why didn't you talk with me?
RALPH	I don't usually talk with you unless I can't handle it.
JIM	We don't usually get a *worse* deal. We get a better deal. Tell me more about this.
RALPH	Well, let me review it. (*He thumbs through the folders on his lap. Jim puts out Ralph's cigar.*) Here it is. (*He puts a letter on Jim's desk.*) It's a form letter, notifying us of a change of prices and a new rate schedule.
JIM	(*Jim reviews the letter.*) It looks like our purchases this year will fall in the 40 percent bracket.
RALPH	Yeah, well, we can't be sure. And they drive a hard bargain.
JIM	There are other places to buy mag tapes.
RALPH	Well, yes. But I've always done business with them. They're the best around.
JIM	I know. Who's the agent you deal with?

RALPH	Sandy O'Connor.
JIM	Isn't that the one you play softball with?
RALPH	(*Laughs.*) Yeah. We're on the church team. He's a hell of a pitcher.
JIM	And a hell of a drinker, I understand.
RALPH	Well, yes. He can put away a few.
JIM	Where did you negotiate this contract?
RALPH	I don't understand.
JIM	Was it done in your office or his?
RALPH	I don't remember.
JIM	(*Hands him the phone.*) Call Patrice. Ask her to look at your calendar and read it to me for that date...March thirteenth.
RALPH	(*Looks at him for a moment, then dials.*) Patrice? Ralph. Could you go in and look at my calendar for March thirteenth? Yeah. Thanks. (*He hands the phone to Jim.*)
JIM	Yes? This is Jim, Patrice. Could you just read the calendar for the day? Humm. Um-hmmm. Lunch, Sandy O'Connor. Yes. Yes. Thanks very much. (*He hangs up.*) You never came back from lunch. (*Ralph stares at him.*)

* ACTION ASTERISK

Jim has alerted Ralph that he knows the salesman is a friend and that the contract is suspect, a devastating charge for someone in purchasing. Now he has made it clear that the contract was negotiated in an all-afternoon drinking spree between buddies. So the challenge and the fear have begun. An alcoholic might react to this with great defense and possibly anger.

| JIM | You signed this at lunch. You gave up a 5 percent |

	reduction for us while you were at lunch, drinking with your buddy. Your drinking has cost us a bunch.
RALPH	Listen! You can't say that!
JIM	I *can* say! Because it's true. You're half in the bag half the afternoons here. And I'm pretty sure most people are covering for you. But damn it, this time you've cost us real bucks. This is ridiculous. And it can't go on!
RALPH	Now, wait a minute! I *saved* us money on this deal! And I've saved you thousands of dollars since I've been here. How dare you say I'm costing us money?
JIM	Who knows how much you've cost us? I'll have to review every contract file to be sure you haven't screwed up some other deals.

* ACTION ASTERISK

This is a real impugnment of Ralph's professional ability and integrity. Since Jim can't really prove that Ralph is an alcoholic, it borders on slander.

RALPH	You *get* every contract I sign! If you don't like what I'm doing, why don't you read them sometime instead of making accusations against me?
JIM	Careful, Ralph. I don't have time to read everything everybody does. That's why I hire people I can trust. And I can't trust you.

* ACTION ASTERISK

Jim is now buck-passing; he *should* read all agreements involving the company's finances. And he's nearing slander again.

RALPH	I don't believe this. I turned a risky-dink purchasing effort into a smooth-running department and have saved thousands in the process, and you sit there and tell me I don't know what I'm doing?
JIM	I don't know what you're doing when you're drinking.

RALPH	How dare you?
JIM	You're a drunk, Ralph, and it's obvious that you can't think straight. We'll have to settle this immediately.
RALPH	What do you mean, settle it?
JIM	I'm letting you go. Go on home and I'll be in touch with you about severance and all the rest.

* ACTION ASTERISK

Jim's ignorance of how to deal with this problem and his anger at being "betrayed" have made him decide on the classic, knee-jerk reaction: Get rid of the problem. What this sort of action would do to the department's function hasn't even been considered, much less what it will do to Ralph.

RALPH	You can't fire me!
JIM	I just did.
RALPH	And with my record, it won't stand up. I'll claim age discrimination.
JIM	You're a drunk. And we don't need you. I don't know how many other of your drinking buddies you've made lousy deals with. But when I read the contracts over the weekend, I'll have a good idea.
RALPH	No one will support that!
JIM	No one has to. The people here know you drink. These contracts will prove you drink on the job and are incompetent. I'm sorry, Ralph, you're through. Now, go get your coat and go on home. I'll call you tomorrow about settlement.
RALPH	(*Rises.*) Half this company drinks! And it never interfered with my work! I'll have you in court in a week.
JIM	No, Ralph. You won't have us in court. Now, go on home. I'll call you. (*Ralph throws the folders down on the floor, flings open the door, and storms down the hall. Jim picks up the folders and straightens them out.*)

Comments

While the above scene may seem overly dramatic, it must be remembered that drinking or not drinking on the job is a touchy subject and goes to the most private cores of a personal or business relationship. Emotions can be too close to the surface to control, especially when a manager has no knowledge or experience in the matter.

If Jim had opted to suspend Ralph rather than fire him, the results could be very unsatisfactory. Alone and sitting at home (or in a bar), worried about the suspension and the future, Ralph is unlikely to seek help or receive help.

The damage to his own self-respect and to his family relationships is incalculable. Further, it is probable that others in the company and the industry will hear about it and his reputation will be further damaged.

Finally, the message to other employees is devastating: "It's O.K. for us, the bosses, to drink during the workday, but if anyone else does, he's fired." The least that can be lost is employee respect for the company and the most is the loss of good employees who seek a more trustworthy environment in which to work.

Jim's behavior above *could* result in a substantial lawsuit: possible age discrimination, or even defamation of character. In either case, it is a problem that a growing, visible company does not need.

There is obviously a better way.

The Dialogue—Example 2 (continued)

JIM	You never came back from lunch. (*Ralph stares at him.*) You signed this at lunch and never came back. What happened, Ralph?
RALPH	I don't understand.
JIM	The deal has to be renegotiated. That's obvious. We're going to fall into the 40 percent bracket, and we've been good customers. The first order of business is to get that changed.
RALPH	I'll get right on it and see what I can do.
JIM	No. I'll take care of it. In fact, I want to review all our new contracts this week and see if we should make any adjustments. but I want to talk to you on a personal level.

* ACTION ASTERISK

Jim has taken away Ralph's authority to revise the contracts. But he has quickly moved to a "personal matter," allowing Ralph no time to question him.

RALPH	Oh?
JIM	Yes. This contract was a shocker. It borders on the irresponsible. And I...
RALPH	Now wait a minute!
JIM	Hold on, Ralph. It's partly my fault. I've trusted you so much I haven't reviewed all your work all the time.
RALPH	Why should you?
JIM	It never occurred to me that I should. I try to hire people I can trust to do their jobs. However, this has made me think twice about what I've heard.
RALPH	What have you heard?
JIM	I've heard that you occasionally come back from lunch drunk. And I think your staff covers for you sometimes.
RALPH	I'm never drunk at work! I may be a little high sometimes, but half the people here are.
JIM	I hope not. I know we have a loose policy about drinking during working hours. In fact, we have *no* policy. But drinking which clouds the thinking of our employees and results in agreements which cost this company money goes beyond the social drinking stage.
RALPH	I haven't cost this company any money!
JIM	Ralph, I don't want to talk about this contract anymore. I said I was going to revise it. And I'm going to review the rest of them to bring myself up to date and be sure they're O.K. My concern is not the past, but the future.
RALPH	Fine. If that's what you want, I won't drink at lunch anymore.

JIM	I think that's an excellent idea. But I'm not sure you can.
RALPH	What are you talking about?
JIM	I talked to Frank Kelly today. (*Ralph looks shocked.*) You know him?
RALPH	We used to work together.
JIM	I know. Not in the same department, and he works elsewhere now. But I noticed on your application that you were there at the same time and since I know him pretty well, I called him.
RALPH	So?
JIM	He says he thinks you were fired for drinking.

* ACTION ASTERISK

Jim is taking a chance with this. It could spoil a friendship between Ralph and Frank. In order to be fair to Frank, he must follow up this revelation with good news pretty quickly.

RALPH	He's a liar.
JIM	I doubt it. He doesn't have any reason to lie. He liked you and was sorry to see you go. But the rumor was that your drinking got in the way.
RALPH	I got a better job.
JIM	Yes. And did well in it. And you're doing well here. But I think your problem has started again.
RALPH	I said I'd quit.
JIM	I think you should. But I think you need help.
RALPH	I'm not a drunk!
JIM	I hope not. But I'm no expert and I'll bet you're not

either. But there *are* experts who can help and I want us to try one.

RALPH   You going to send me to AA?

JIM   You can't send people to AA. That's a personal choice. I'm going to try something else.

RALPH   What?

JIM   I want us to help you help yourself. You're too good to lose, and this kind of mistake can't be repeated. You know I manage our corporate charitable contributions?

RALPH   Yes.

JIM   One organization that we give to is in business to do just this. They have a team of experts who work just with companies and people in business. They meet privately and confidentially with the individual, they identify the problem, and they work with the person on a program to change the habit.

RALPH   What does it cost?

JIM   Nothing. They exist on corporate contributions like ours.

RALPH   But everyone will know.

JIM   No one will know. Not even your family. You're going to meet with them during the day.

RALPH   I'm too busy!

JIM   You'll meet during your lunch hour. And you'll start tomorrow. I want us to resolve this and get on to bigger and better things.

* ACTION ASTERISK
Jim has made a decision to give Ralph a chance and he's not going to allow Ralph any elbowroom to get out of it. The alternative—termination—is not stated, but it is obviously there.

RALPH	How do I reach them?

JIM — You go on back to your office. You start making a list of all the contracts which have been signed in the past nine months, so I can pull them from my files. Have it ready for me this afternoon. When you're done, bring it back and I'll have your appointment set up for you. Cancel all lunch dates for the next two weeks. Reschedule them for your office. After that time, you should have some sort of a program worked out.

RALPH — I sure hope this works.

* ACTION ASTERISK
Ralph has agreed without agreeing. He knows he has no choice.

JIM — It has to work. You need this job and I know it. And we need you. You're good, and we want to keep you. *(he stands.)* Now go on to your office and start that list.

RALPH — I'm sorry, Jim.

JIM — Don't be. We need to work out some guidelines so no else falls into this trap. And I remember what a minister of mine used to say: "Make today the first day of the rest of your life." *(Ralph shakes his head and leaves. Jim sits and finds a telephone number and then begins to dial.)*

Summary

Organizations such as the one mentioned exist in almost every major city in the country. And in smaller communities, AA and some religious organizations have excellent volunteer counseling.

Drinking in the business environment can become a serious problem, both for the individual and for the company. Help is available and should be used. The secret is to seek that help early enough to benefit all concerned and to avoid some dreadful public gaffe or confrontation.

A "drinking problem" can become chronic alcoholism in a person susceptible to the disease. A wise company management

- Is alert to the behavior of all its employees
- Has guidelines of expected behavior which should be known by and applied to *all* employees

- Has access to organizations which can help, quickly and anonymously

Human resources are the most valuable and expensive resources any company has. Helping to keep them healthy and productive is company responsibility. Throwing them out without help is not a viable solution. It is costly in the particular instance, and it sends a terrible message of not caring to other employees.

8 THE DRUG BUST

Introduction

Each of us likely knows someone who smokes pot. And it is also likely that among our acquaintances are persons who do more exotic drugs. Drugs pervade this society, and the work place is not immune.

While the individual employee may turn his or her eyes from the phenomenon, managers in charge of departments—and officers in charge of corporations—cannot. Possession of drugs is illegal. Those who lump drug use with alcohol in the work place miss the point. As long as drug possession and use are illegal, company managements are obliged to ban it from company premises. As to the matter of *selling* drugs by an employee, the company obligation should be even more obvious. Drug pushers are, under current law, criminals. Criminals must be handled by the criminal justice system, not by an ignorant or complacent management.

More truly than in almost any other instance, drug use and sale is a matter for *absolute* company policy and the only instance (probably) where justice/company discipline must be blind. The policy must be absolute and apply to each and all without exception. To blink at an infraction in this matter is to risk credibility totally.

This sounds harsh. And it flies in the face of the compassion we have urged in most other areas of employee infraction, most notably alcohol consumption. However, drug use is a national calamity, crossing all ages and strata. Sympathy and collusion on the part of a corporation can only encourage and further the calamity.

Having said all that, one must ask, is there no place for help and compassion? Of course there is. And this brings us to the matter of policies and procedures.

It is recommended that the drug use policy of a company be written, explicit, and universal: that the use of drugs on company premises and on company business be cause for instant dismissal. (See Appendix.) However, it is recommended that, as in the case of alcoholism, the company maintain a quiet relationship with local drug rehabilitation groups, and that when an employee is dismissed, he or she is given the opportunity to participate in such a program for up to three months, at company expense.

The company policy should also read that an employee who is proven to be selling drugs, anyplace, will be dismissed and the information will be turned over to the proper legal authorities.

As indicated, this policy should be written and distributed to every employee. It should also be included in the personnel packets given to each new employee, so that there is no misunderstanding.

In fact, there are certain personnel policies which should be redistributed on a yearly basis to every employee as a reminder of the company's position. They are:

- The company's drug use and sale policy
- The company's equal opportunity policy
- The company's anti-sexual harassment policy
- The company's on-site antisolicitation policy

It's good for employees to know what kind of company they work for. And it's good to have those company policies reinforced with reminders. Further, it is good for employees to know that those policies are *enforced* and that they are enforced uniformly and equally.

And now a word about the use of "should" and "must" in this introduction. They are the strongest words one manager can use with another. And this is the only chapter in which they will appear. The reason is obvious: According to our federal health agencies, in 1985, 50 percent of all job-related accidents, absenteeism, accidents caused in the transportation industry (buses, taxis, trains, planes) are drug-related. Our country is involved in a destructive epidemic, and the damages have spilled over dramatically into the work place. It appears obvious that managers must take equally dramatic action to stem the tide.

You may ask why are we so tough on drug use while we recommend understanding and help for alcoholism? Because alcoholism is recognized as a disease; drug use is an addiction and generally self-inflicted. Both can be treated and both can be "cured." Those who use alcohol and drugs should be helped. Those who push drugs should be turned over to the proper authorities, as the law requires.

The Situation

Salvo has very specific personnel policies regarding drugs—any employee proven to have used drugs on company premises or on company business is subject to instant dismissal. Any employee proven to be selling drugs, anywhere, is subject to instant dismissal, and the facts will be reported to the appropriate legal authorities.

The operative word is "proven." Rumor and innuendo are at their most dangerous in a drug accusation. Proof is imperative. The policy is written and distributed to all employees. And the company has had a clean record so far.

Joanna, the personnel assistant, has come to Margie, director of personnel, with a rumor. Alice, the word processing supervisor, has become the subject of the office scuttlebut. The messengers who bring her work are selling drugs to her, which she is then passing on to certain employees at Salvo.

Margie is horrified and instructs Joanna to tell no one else the rumor and thanks her for the tip. She then makes an appointment with Jane, the vice-president of administration, whose responsibilities also include office services (where Alice works) and security (which would, of necessity, become a part of any search and confirmation of the rumor).

Jane is equally dismayed at the news and urges Margie to keep a lid on the rumor. After some thought, Jane decides to call in Alice and test the waters with the rumor. She feels that by broaching the subject obliquely, without going into specifics, she can sense whether or not Alice has anything to hide. If she sensed anything out of the ordinary, she will then decide whether to put the security guards on the alert at the reception area and near the word processing department.

The Characters

Jane is vice-president of administration, and in that capacity oversees the personnel department and all the service departments in the office services area. She is a seasoned professional at thirty-eight, and has enjoyed her three years at Salvo, building the service departments and codifying their policies.

Alice is a liberal arts college graduate, whose ambition is to be a writer. She is supporting herself by being a super-expert in the word processing field, and has been at Salvo eight months as a supervisor. She is in her mid-twenties, laid back and quietly self-contained. To many, she is something of an enigma.

Manager's Objective

To uncover proof that Alice is or is not pushing drugs, and to carry out company policy as it relates to such matters.

The Dialogue—Example 1

Alice comes to the door.

JANE   Alice, come in and close the door. (*She does.*) I suppose you know why I've asked you in.

ALICE   Not really. I don't think we've ever met.

JANE   Well, no. But, of course, you work in one of my departments.

ALICE   I suppose so.

JANE   And there are some problems which I want us to solve.

ALICE   Sure. What can I do for you?

JANE   It's a little more complicated than that. It's a problem you have to solve.

ALICE   Oh? What's that?

JANE   Well, we've heard some information which is very disturbing.

ALICE   Yes?

JANE   I hardly know how to discuss this. You know how it is. Where there's smoke, there's fire. So we can't really ignore it.

89

* ACTION ASTERISK
This old saw is hardly the way to conduct an interview on such a serious matter. It presumes guilt.

ALICE	What in the world are you talking about?
JANE	(*Hands her a sheet of paper.*) I'm sure you've read the Salvo drug use policy.
ALICE	Sure. It was in my packet when I was hired.
JANE	Salvo is very strict about that policy.
ALICE	So?
JANE	Have you seen anyone breaking the policy?
ALICE	What do you mean?
JANE	In your dealings with the staff—you meet most of them during the course of your work—have you noticed anything suspicious?
ALICE	Of course not. And I wouldn't rat on anybody if I did.
JANE	Why not? That would be your duty.
ALICE	My "duty" is to run the word processing department as efficiently as possible and not act as the company's spy.
JANE	We've had some indication that there may be some drug use in the company...
ALICE	How?
JANE	Some people have mentioned some suspicious happenings.
ALICE	Hearsay?
JANE	Well, yes. But we've heard it from several sources.
ALICE	Why am I here?

* ACTION ASTERISK
Good question. Unless Jane has some specific direction in the conversation, Alice could rightly accuse her of slander.

JANE	Well, some of the suspicion rests on the messengers. I know you have a lot of dealings with them, and I wonder if you've noticed anything unusual.
ALICE	No.
JANE	Has there been anything unusual around your department?
ALICE	How do you mean, unusual?
JANE	I mean, do people come there who don't have work to be done?
ALICE	Sometimes. It's a friendly company.
JANE	Yes. Well, if you see anything, let me know.
ALICE	Sure. And I hope none of us in my department is under suspicion.
JANE	Oh, no. Well, that is, we're checking several places.
ALICE	You mean everyone's guilty until proven innocent?

* ACTION ASTERISK
That's what it sounds like—unfortunately.

JANE	Oh, no! We're just trying to be careful, that's all. And we need each supervisor to be alert.
ALICE	Sure.
JANE	Well, thanks for coming in.
Alice	*rises to leave.*

Comments

It is difficult to imagine this being handled less effectively. Jane did everything wrong.

She confronted an employee on a serious matter without any proof other than hearsay. She has maligned the messengers with no proof of their guilt.

She has made Salvo look like a bumbling intruder to a relatively new employee. If the employee is innocent, she may well think about relocating. If she is guilty, she has been alerted that Salvo is suspicious and will either cease the transactions or hide them or relocate.

Pushing the problem off on another unsuspecting employer is, by the way, rotten business practice. It only spreads the disease of drug trafficking to another environment.

There is a more sensible and businesslike way of handling the rumors.

Getting the Proof

Following is one suggestion for obtaining proof in such a situation. Other suggestions are offered at the end of the chapter.

After hearing the rumors, and after much thought, Jane calls in the manager of security and instructs him to have installed videotape machines on the security camera which surveys the reception area, as well as on a security camera to be installed at the word processing area. She asks that no one be told of the installations and that they be done after hours. She further instructs him to notify the receptionist that as a part of the ongoing security measures, the receptionist is to log in all messengers, with the time of their arrival, where they are from, and the person for whom they have a package. He agrees.

The videotape is the stop/go variety used by many banks and can be viewed on a time basis each day.

Each morning, Jane checked the previous day's log and then viewed that portion of the tape when a messenger delivered a package to Alice. On three occasions Jane saw a second package, and money, change hands. She set aside those tapes and then viewed the tapes of the security camera at the word processing station. This was more tedious and involved a couple of Saturdays, because she did not know what time of day would be important to check.

Unfortunately, however, her persistence was rewarded. On four occasions, two employees, a mailroom clerk and a salesman, came to Alice's desk during lunch hour, handed Alice money, and took away a package. We say "unfortunately" because there is no enjoyment in such a discovery. Trust is destroyed, lives are broken, company fabric is frayed.

Jane reviewed the tapes with Salvo's legal counsel and agreed on a course of action.

Jane called Dorothy, for whom Alice and the mail room clerk work, and Gerald, for whom the salesman works, and showed them the tapes. They were first stunned, then angry. She calmed them and then suggested that the three employees be called in, confidentially and separately, shown the tapes, and dismissed. She agreed to handle the details. By company policy, she was also obliged to turn over the material to local drug enforcement officials. Dorothy and Gerald agreed, and also agreed to remain totally silent on the nature of their employees' dismissal. This is an appropriate procedure for all the Salvo employees who know nothing of the drug trading. For any other employees who may be involved in the trading (and who have not appeared on the tapes), the message will be clear if they hear the employees have left abruptly: Get clean or get out.

The Dialogue—Example 2

Jane is seated in the small conference room where there is A/V equipment. Alice comes to the door.

ALICE   You asked me to come up?

JANE   Yes, Alice. Please come in and shut the door. (*She does.*) How long have you been with us?

ALICE   Eight months.

JANE   When you came, were you given a packet with all our policies and procedures?

ALICE   Yes.

JANE   Did you read it?

ALICE   Yes.

JANE   Did you read this one? (*She hands her a copy of the drug use policy. Alice looks at it and looks up.*)

* ACTION ASTERISK

Jane is confirming that Alice knew what the company expected when she came to work at Salvo.

ALICE   Yes.

JANE   Good. Now I'd like to show you some tape which was made by our security camera in the reception area. (*She switches off the lights and turns on the tape.*) This one was April eighth at twelve twenty-five P.M. That's you and a messenger. He gives you two packages and you hand him—what? This one is April fifteenth at twelve forty-five P.M. It's the same messenger. He hands you two packages and you hand him money. He's counting it. This one was April twenty-first, one P.M. Same messenger, same routine. He pockets what looks like bills. (*She stops the tape and turns on the lights.*) What was in those packages, Alice?

ALICE   I don't remember.

JANE   Really? It was only last month.

ALICE   I don't remember every package that messengers bring our department!

JANE   Why did you give him money?

ALICE   I didn't give him money!

JANE   It's pretty clear on the second tape that you did.

ALICE   I don't know what you're getting at!

JANE   Maybe this next tape will clear it up. (*She puts on another tape and turns out the lights.*) This is from a security camera which has been installed over the word processing department. The first shot is April tenth at one P.M. You recognize Pat from the mailroom. You counted the money he gave you. This was April sixteenth at twelve-twenty P.M. Peter from sales handed you an envelope, you opened it and looked in it before you gave him the little package. (*She stops the tape and turns on the lights. Alice is crying.*) Do you know what we have to do?

ALICE   Fire me, I guess.

JANE	Yes. Security will take you back to your office when you leave here, to pick up your personal things. I have your check here, payable through the end of the week.
ALICE	Thanks.
JANE	But that isn't all. We have to turn these tapes over to the police.

* ACTION ASTERISK

Now comes the hard part. It is a grim business to turn over an employee to legal authorities. It is much easier at this point to fire the employee and try to forget the whole thing—out of sight, out of mind. But that doesn't solve anything; it only passes the problem on to some other unsuspecting employer. And it doesn't help the culprit break the habit.

ALICE	What?
JANE	You've read our policy. Drug pushers are turned over to the authorities.
ALICE	You can't turn me over to the police!
JANE	I can. And I will. Because I must. You've been selling drugs on these premises. And it's against our policy. It's against the law.
ALICE	I won't let you!
JANE	You have no choice.
ALICE	I won't let you! (*She runs to the door. A security guard is standing there. He quietly shuts the door.*)
JANE	Alice, I'm very sorry about this. You have such a fine career before you. But maybe all isn't lost.
ALICE	(*Sinks into a chair in tears.*) What do you mean?
JANE	I must turn this material over to the police and they will decide whether or not to prosecute, based on the evidence. But we have concerns about you personally.
ALICE	Yeah?

JANE Yes. There are a couple of drug rehabilitation organizations here in town which we help support. We've never had to use them, but we're going to now. We have to fire Pat and Peter also, but we're going to offer them the chance to get into one of those programs. We'll pick up any extra costs for three months. We'd like to do the same with you. I assume you're a user as well as a pusher?

ALICE Yes.

JANE What about it?

ALICE I don't know. I can't think of anything right now.

JANE I'm sure. But think about it. Call me tomorrow or next day. I hope you will. We'd like to help stop all this. We'd like to help get you clean.

ALICE Sure.

JANE I mean it, Alice. This is no joy for us. I wish to God it had never happened. But it did. And we have to do what's right—for everyone. Including you.

ALICE Yeah.

JANE Come on. The guard will take you to your office to get your things. Then you'll come back down here.

ALICE What for?

JANE We've called the police. I'll give them the tapes and they can take over.

ALICE Oh, God!

JANE Alice, I'm sorry. Now, come on. (*She opens the door and the guard walks away with Alice.*)

Summary

Was the objective achieved? Yes.

And it is devoutly to be wished that no manager ever has to go through such a scene. However, if it *is* necessary, it should be obvious that several elements are necessary to keep it from being an utter disaster:

1. Precise, written company policies on the issue, which are familiar to all employees.
2. Proof of any rumor, either on tape or film, or with several unimpeachable and uninvolved eyewitnesses.
3. Prompt and decisive action, based on the facts, the policy, and the law.
4. Compassion, and understanding that any of us can err and that very few people are deliberately wicked. A policy of help attached to the punishment offers some hope for the future for an employee caught in such a terrible morass. It also offers some hope and consolation to those employees who hear about the episode and wonder what kind of company they work for.

Alternate Means of Obtaining Proof

If videotape facilities do not exist and are considered too expensive for security and surveillance, there are other alternatives.

1. Place a security guard at the reception area or messenger delivery center.
2. Engage an employee, with police cooperation, to become a buyer from the suspected pusher.
3. Establish new delivery procedures so that all deliveries must go through a checkpoint and other employees.
4. Establish new service procedures which would require the work finished by the word processing department to be delivered by internal messengers, cutting off the opportunity for contact.

Whatever is established, remember that verified and irrefutable *proof* is required before any action may be taken. And *policies* must be known, published, and enforced promptly and equally. Remember, you're dealing with lives and must have great care in what you do.

9
BUILDING A JOB LADDER

Introduction

In 1972 an executive order (see Appendix) required major companies to create job ladders to ensure that all employees had equal access to opportunities for advancement, promotion, and remuneration. While this executive order resulted in a lot of reappraisal and work in a number of companies, it merely reflected what many companies—small and large—have practiced for years.

Job ladders are the practical recognition of the path which an employee may take in progressing upward in a specific career or profession. They are the logical steps an employee takes to advance in identified skills, achievements, recognition, and success. While an employee's dedication and imagination are important, most job ladders are formed by the companies themselves. The companies define the jobs, the job descriptions, and the job ladders in particular skills and professions.

In enlightened companies, new challenges, new opportunities, and new problems are dealt with by redefining job skills, performance criteria, job accomplishment, and the development of new job ladders. Astute readers will recognize MBO—Management by Objectives. This is a definition—by manager and employee—of tasks to be performed and the skills and performance standards necessary to do the job. Each job has a monitoring and reward device and each job (in the normal course of things) can lead to a better job, with more challenge and more reward.

Simplistically, that is MBO, a part of which is the creation of a job ladder—the future.

Admittedly, there are dead end jobs in some situations—those jobs which lead nowhere else. (See Chapter 18.) This can eventually cause problems, because the implied expectation in most companies is that people should move ahead. Here is an example of a conflict between this expectation and an employee's best interest.

The public relations department of a large corporation has a number of employees with a variety of professional skills. One group is the publicists—those professionals who write the press releases and make the media contacts for corporations. What is the job ladder for these people? They may move from apprentice to publicist to senior. They may even specialize in a region or a medium with staff working with them. But unless they want to move into management, eventually they reach the top of their field with nowhere to go and nothing to look forward to except cost-of-living increases and small raises within company annual guidelines.

Similar examples can be found in sales, assembly-line manufacturing, computer programming, and other areas. At a certain point an employee must decide to go into management in order to continue to move up the job ladder. Whether they really want to be managers or not. And at that juncture, beware the Peter Principle! More good sales people and other such types have foundered on the shoals of management than most companies will admit. Sales skills, publicist skills, programming skills, and assembly skills are not necessarily management skills, and vice versa. Other means must be found for keeping good employees, rewarding them, and challenging them, rather than simply making them managers or giving token raises.

One way is to *make more ladders.* If there are too many people bunched together on the rungs, heads bumping against shoe soles and frustration building because there seems to be no way up for ambitious, high performers—*split the ladder.* Fine-tune the work definitions. Divide up tasks among more people, creating more job opportunities for both professional and managerial employees.

A rapidly growing company, or a company with a changing focus are excellent places to build more job ladders, to divide the work and create more opportunity for more people. It takes the willingness to look at the company and its tasks in a new perspective, and to see people separate from tasks. A better allocation of human resources and happier employees are two of the benefits from this approach.

The Situation

As Salvo continues to grow, both in companies acquired and in product developed, it experiences internal growing pains—in products to be serviced and in the people required to perform the tasks.

This trend is very evident in the products department, which includes both development and service.

Salvo has enjoyed the reputation of having sound, exciting products from the beginning of its existence. However, it has suffered on occasion in its service reputation. That is, distribution requests sometimes are filled late, corrections and refunds are not always prompt, production is sometimes off schedule because all the packaging elements do not come together on time, and so forth.

The Characters

Don is executive vice-president of products and is one of Salvo's three founding partners. He was one of the wunderkinds on a development team of a new, successful company in the late seventies and helped create Salvo because he wanted to work in a shop where he had more control of the product and where the flights of his considerable imagination could reach completion. As Salvo has grown and as he has begun to enjoy the pleasure of being a commercial success as well as a creative success, he has matured in his outlook and has become aware that service to the customers is as important as the original product.

The department has become too large for him to oversee the details of this job with any regularity. His focus is on maintaining Salvo's leadership in the fields they have chosen—games and personal and small office business programs. Don is known in the business as a one man think tank, and the company's success is predicated on his ability to stay on the cutting edge of creativity.

He has left the day-to-day running of the products department to Tom, a vice-president. Tom is another version of Don, ten years younger. He was a hacker in college and did time in a major computer company before coming to Salvo. He has assembled some ten programmers who love what they do and work intensely hard at developing new products.

Tom also directs the several service departments, but his heart isn't in it. The procedures have been allowed to just grow, and most of the people in the departments do the best they can without much guidance. Mistakes and delays are inevitable.

George is in his late fifties and worked for many years in a fulfillment house for a major magazine chain. He tries to keep the distribution system running as smoothly as possible. Gladys worked in the complaint and refund area of Macy's for many years and tries to handle Salvo's billing and refund problems with a staff of one. Martha worked at a large public relations firm for many years before she went to a publishing house where she designed book jackets, designed and wrote album covers, and worked as head of the production department. She moved to Salvo for more authority and (she thought) a little less hassle. Because the procedures have never been set out by Tom, she does the best she can to bring the production elements (program, disc, packaging, merchandising tools) together, but without final authority, she can't always make the deadlines.

Don knows of some of these problems and has decided to do something about them. He has given thought to hiring an outside service vice-president and he has also looked at the people inside for promotion potential. He has decided to promote from inside and to make the offer to Martha. She has the experience required and has demonstrated abundant loyalty to Salvo. The promotion will make her a peer with Tom, so before he promotes her, he wants to talk with Tom about it, not so much for his consent as for his enthusiasm and concurrence.

The Manager's Objective

To promote an employee into a peer level with her current boss, while keeping his enthusiasm for the idea and for the employee.

The Dialogue—Example 1

Tom comes to the door.

TOM	Did you buzz me, Don?
DON	Yes. Come on in. Shut the door. (Shuts the door and sits down.)
TOM	What's up?
DON	I've been thinking about a lot of things and I wanted to talk them over with you. We're growing so fast we can hardly keep track of what's going on anymore.
TOM	That's the name of the game. It's never dull. And we haven't had a whopping failure yet.
DON	I agree. And I hope our luck holds. Odds are, we're due for one soon and we might as well be braced for it.
TOM	Don't say that! Don't jinx us. (*They both laugh.*)

DON   I know. There's a lot more than luck at work in our success. The work your department does is the real key.

* ACTION ASTERISK

Don is doing the right thing by praising the department. After all, there's nothing *wrong* except that there is almost too much success to handle.

TOM   Thanks. We try.

DON   Damn right. But I don't want us to get too cocky.

TOM   No danger of that. There's somebody in his den right now creating a new sensation. We all know because we were all there once.

DON   Right. And it may be tempting fate, but I really don't think we'll have any trouble on the creative side. The stuff is too good and we just keep turning it out. No, I have concerns in other areas.

TOM   Oh. What?

DON   We've got problems in our service area and I think we ought to solve them.

TOM   I give that as much time as I have, Don. Those people ought to know what they're doing by now.

* ACTION ASTERISK

An unexpected complaint about one of Tom's areas has brought a reply that refers to "those people" as if they lived in a different country. This can only confirm Don's fear that Tom is quite remote from the problems and the need to really run the area.

DON   Well, I think they *do* know what they are doing. I just don't think they always have the materials they need, or the information they need or the guidance they need to keep up with our reputation.

TOM   Are you criticizing how I run those areas?

* ACTION ASTERISK
Of course he is.

DON	Well, no, not really. I don't think you do run those areas very much. You're so busy with development that you don't have time to follow up on all the details of production and distribution and complaints, and so forth. I think they kind of run themselves. And sometimes, not very well.
TOM	I resent that.
DON	No need to. It's no surprise. We've talked about some of these problems in staff meetings. And they don't seem to get any better. We're almost too busy for them to get any better.
TOM	It sure sounds like a complaint.
DON	Well, let's look at it objectively. You were hired to develop programs and to put together a department that could be the best in the business. And you've done it. Nobody can touch us and it's because of your department.
TOM	So? What's your complaint?
DON	Tom, you've talked about it yourself. You're bored to tears with shipping problems and customer complaints. And you'd be just as happy if we mailed the programs out in paper sacks; you don't care what the packaging looks like.
TOM	That doesn't sound very complimentary.
DON	Well, I'm the same way. So I understand it. Programs are our lives and the rest of it is just tedious detail.
TOM	If we ever catch up on the programs, I'll get a handle on it.
DON	We'll never catch up on our programs. There will always be something new. So you'll never get a handle on it.

* ACTION ASTERISK

This may be true, but it's pretty blunt. He's tearing into a man who has done a good job, and has been given more departments and more detail than he probably ever anticipated.

TOM	So what are you going to do about it?
DON	I'd like to put somebody in charge of those service departments who can devote full time to them and who can work up some good procedures and free you to concentrate on development.
TOM	Who?
DON	I'd like to offer the job to Martha.
TOM	I hired her!

* ACTION ASTERISK

Now we are into territorial possession and pecking order. Tom sees a subordinate getting part of his job because he hasn't been able to manage it all. Resentment is inevitable.

DON	Well, actually, we both hired her. I found her and introduced her to you when you came aboard. She joined us about a month later.
TOM	She doesn't know anything about programs!
DON	But she knows plenty about production and production schedules. She also works well with George and Gladys. I think they'll be pleased to have somebody they can get to more readily.
TOM	Have they been complaining?

* ACTION ASTERISK

Tom now sees this as some kind of conspiracy.

DON	No. Nobody's been complaining, except some of our customers. And you know who they are as well as I do.
TOM	So when do you want me to do this?

DON   Actually, I'll be the one to do it, since it's a promotion. She'll be reporting to me, so I plan to make her the offer.

TOM   I see. Are you also going to make her a V.P.?

DON   Yes. Since she'll be heading a separate department, it's entirely appropriate.

TOM   I see. Is there anything else?

* ACTION ASTERISK

Obviously, Tom is not enthusiastic about this development nor is he likely to be cooperative. Don has caused conflict in the department rather than solving its problems.

DON   No, I guess not. I'd surely like your help and cooperation in making the transition. And I hope you're happy with the choice. I'm sure she'll do a good job.

TOM   I'm sure she will. Is there anything else?

DON   No.

TOM   Okay. I'll see you later. (*He rises and leaves.*)

Comments

Was the manager's objective achieved? No. He can go ahead and promote Martha, but it is reasonable to guess that there will be some kind of trouble down the road between Tom and Martha. Don made it a *fait accompli* without engaging Tom's ideas and suggestions.

In truth, the problem of overwork was Tom's. Under a good MBO policy, he should have been given the chance to identify the problem and help develop the solution. On the other hand, if he had a real interest in running his entire department and not just programming, he would have approached Don before this in an attempt to deal with it.

As stated earlier, there is nothing wrong with a department which is growing too fast because of success, and Don has dealt with it properly by dividing up the work, creating two job ladders where there was one (now it is products *and* service, with different skills and different opportunities) but his methods have been a disaster. With all his good intentions, he has created problems between two vice-presidents for the future.

Isn't there a better way?

The Dialogue—Example 2 (continued)

TOM   So? What's your complaint?

DON   Well, you've talked about it yourself. We're almost drowning in our own success. We turn out ideas so fast that we can't always meet the production schedules or distribution schedules. I thought we ought to talk about it some more.

TOM   Good idea. We're acquiring more products too. We may have to expand the department.

DON   As we continue to grow, there's no doubt about it. But I'm wondering if we can't get more effectiveness out of the present staff.

TOM   That's a good group, Don! They work damn hard.

DON   I know they do. But I'm hoping we can get that section to work smarter, not harder. They should be the efficient balance to your programming section. But we're not quite there yet.

* ACTION ASTERISK
So far, Don has criticized performance in a section without laying any real blame anywhere. He is leaving the topic wide open for Tom to help create solutions.

DON   Were you serious about adding more people?

TOM   Well, it may come to that. We know that it can't go on like it is much longer.

DON   What kind of people did you have in mind?

TOM   What do you mean?

DON   If you think we should add to staff, what kind of people should we add?

TOM   I don't know. I haven't given it a lot of thought. I just know that something should be done.

DON	Have you talked to Martha or George or Gladys about it?
TOM	Not lately. We've all been too busy even to get together.

* ACTION ASTERISK
Don is trying to lead Tom along a path of discovery—that he really isn't controlling the service area, nor does he particularly enjoy it.

DON	Then how do you know they need more help?
TOM	They've missed some deadlines. I'm sure it's just too big a load.
DON	Did you work out those coordinating procedures we talked about? You know, Martha really wanted to get them in place. She felt that could be a great help.
TOM	I know. But I just haven't had time. The programming work has been fierce.
DON	That was several months ago.
TOM	I can't do it all, Don. We both know that the new programming takes priority over everything if we're going to stay ahead.

* ACTION ASTERISK
There's the opening Don has been looking for. Tom has put his priorities into words. Now maybe Don can get on with the reorganization.

DON	I know. And I think we have to find some way to give you some relief so that effort can continue. Would it help if some of the service requirements were off your back?
TOM	It wouldn't hurt, I'll tell you. There are times when I really feel guilty about not addressing some of the problems. But I know where our priorities are.
DON	I think if we took fulfillment and production and customer service off your plate, it would give you more time for the programming. We've got a lot of new stuff in the oven and our acquisitions are going to take some time to digest.

TOM   Where would you put them?

DON   Oh, I'd keep them in this department. But I'd get them
               out of your hair so you'd have the time you need.

TOM   Would you want to bring someone in from outside?

*ACTION ASTERISK

Tom is getting the message. Obviously, the idea of devoting his time to
the work he loves best is very appealing to him. But he is wary of bringing
in some outside person to take over what has been "his" departments.

DON   I don't know. What would you suggest?

TOM   I'm not sure that an outsider could be much help.
               We've developed out own way of doing business. We
               just need to get it organized and functioning more
               efficiently.

DON   Maybe some new ideas from outside would be a good
               thing. We've always been open to new ideas.

TOM   But we've got good people who work right here!

DON   What do you suggest?

TOM   Well...I don't know. Martha knows the process inside
               out. She's been here almost as long as I have. We hired
               her. She gets along well with George and Gladys. She's
               very organized. I think she could whip it into shape if
               she had the authority.

* ACTION ASTERISK

Better a known quality than an unknown. Don is getting his way by letting Tom go through the exercise out loud.

DON   Should I make her the offer?

TOM   (Tom has to think for a minute. Maybe they should both
               make the offer?) Sure. Why not? It's a thankless job, but
               she's doing it already.

* ACTION ASTERISK

Tom has just been insulting—about the job, which he hasn't done well, and about Martha, who he infers is not doing anything terribly important already. It is the kind of comment one can hear often in an office as a face-saving attitude. The less said about it the better. If Martha accepts the job and if Don gives her good support as well as adequate staff, things will probably improve. And if Tom is left with his beloved programs without the nuisance of the service departments, he will be more productive and, ultimately, happier.

DON   Well, this has all been very good. Tell you what. I'll talk to Martha today to see if she has any interest in the proposition. If the answer is yes, then you and I will make it final and we will have a little meeting with the whole department tomorrow and make the announcement.

* ACTION ASTERISK

Don has assured that Tom's position will be secure with the staff by making him party to the announcement. It will appear that he got one of his own staff promoted.

TOM   Good.

DON   Let me talk to her, and I'll get back to you this afternoon.

TOM   O.K.

DON   You know, if we live long enough, we may get this place organized yet.

TOM   (*Laughs.*) Right. (*Exits.*)

Summary

Did the manager achieve his objective? Yes.

Don got what he wanted by leading Tom through a conversation which was mostly questions. He "allowed" Tom to help him make the decision to cut his department in half, create a new job ladder, and elevate a subordinate to peer level.

There is no guarantee that Tom is going to be thrilled with the arrangement. And there may even be some clashes later. But Don has taken a growing department, analyzed its strengths and weaknesses, analyzed its functions, and devised a new job ladder (services) in an otherwise "creative" department (product). Two distinctly different types of personalities and professional skills will climb those job ladders and Don has created means whereby that can happen.

One word about Tom's personality: If he were a person really in need of titles and power, and if he loved big departments more than he loved the joy of programming, this interview could have gone much differently. Don succeeded because he appealed to what turned on Tom the best: more freedom to do more creative programming. With another personality, Don would have to appeal to another turn-on button.

He has saved face for Tom and shown himself as an understanding and innovative leader of a division. None of that will be lost on the rest of the staff.

10 REWARDS—PUBLIC OR PRIVATE?

Introduction

Every employee likes reward and recognition. It is fundamental in the management of human resources to set up review and recognition procedures and a reward process. (Please note that we have not said reward and punishment. Reviews can also produce reprimands and corrective measures, but in all cases those measures should be calculated to help the employee improve performance if possible.)

Rewards and recognition are the principal means by which employees can be motivated to better performance. It goes back to Maslow's theory of the need for self-actualization in employment—that level of self-awareness, self-esteem, and happiness in work which produces dedicated and highly motivated employees. Rewards and recognition help to make that possible.

We know that rewards and recognition can take many forms. Some employees have to be satisfied with a raise in their paychecks the first week of the new year and assume that they've done good work. Other employees work at companies which have elaborate performance review processes and communicate with their managers on a regular basis. But most companies fall somewhere between these examples and employees have some knowledge of work expectations, scheduled reviews, and a degree of job satisfaction.

But in most companies there is a maverick or two, those people who are successful enough or connected well enough to run their departments as they like, with blatant disregard for the company's personnel policies and procedures.

If they are charming and indulgent of their staff, if they are "loved," it is a double-edged sword to corporate control and uniformity. Generally, their staff perform well and are loyal. However, they may be more loyal to the manager than to the company. Further, there is also some risk that the good nature of the manager allows some employees to abuse certain company policies (hours, overtime, days off, expense accounts, and so forth), which can cause some dissension among the ranks or between departments.

Obviously, if the manager's maverick ways do not contribute to an efficient department, the problem can be dealt with by performance review and behavior-change processes.

It is when the department *does* run well that complications can arise. "If it ain't broke, don't fix it" is as good a maxim for business as for politics. How do you "correct" something that gets good results? Do you want to?

The answer, typically, is no. Then the dilemma rests in the manager/staff relationship. What if some employees have trouble with an exuberant manager? What if some employees don't want to be praised or rewarded publicly? What if the "hail fellow, well met" method of managing is cloying or inhibiting to an employee?

Don't laugh! Some people don't respond well to public praise, any more than they would respond well to public criticism. What can they do about it? If the company likes the results of the manager's style, such an employee is left with little but imagination, endurance, persuasion, consensus, departure. There are no easy solutions. Obviously, an employee cannot change the personality traits of a manager. But perhaps there are techniques whereby behavioral traits may be changed—at least as they relate to the individual employee. The ultimate goal is harmony in the work place, where each person may work at peak capacity and with self-assurance and self-esteem.

The Situation

Salvo has been a success in its short life for a number of reasons, but none more important than its sales and marketing efforts. The sales representatives are "hungry tigers" on the street and are allocated territory on a regional basis. The marketing department is divided by product, and the in-house directors continue to come up with some of the most eye-catching media campaigns in the industry. The retailers love them because the campaigns can be directly correlated with heavy foot traffic into the stores.

The marketing staff is enthusiastic, creative—some say rambunctious—and from a variety of backgrounds and experiences. They play off each other very well, and each product division is fiercely competitive with the others.

The Characters

Harry is the director of personal business software and is a big teddy bear of a man whom everyone loves. He works hard, plays hard, is a devoted family man, and treats all of his staff, regardless of age, as if they were part of an extended family. He once cherished the dream of being a pro baseball player and got as far as the farm team, so his instructions and admonitions are liberally sprinkled with "team spirit" enthusiasms. He spent a number of years in the marketing department of a major home products firm, so he knows his stuff. His door is always open so everyone can hear his booming enthusiasms about a new campaign, as well as his occasional annoyances. He does a great deal of personal reinforcement: pats on the back, bear hugs, lunches for the staff, birthday parties, shouts of enthusiasm, this week's achievement award. In other words, he breaks most of the recognized office codes of conduct, and everybody loves him.

Kathy is twenty-eight and one of Harry's superstars. A Vassar graduate, she went to work for a major women's magazine and then moved to a small ad agency before coming to Salvo. She is attractive, a laid-back yuppie with proper manners and an incisive, analytical mind. She writes the best copy in the shop. She has a rapier wit and enjoys Salvo very much. But she has never met anybody like Harry before—the ex-farm boy from Indiana. At first his loudness terrified her and then she tried to avoid his bear hugs.

Now that she knows him better, she recognizes his enormous capacity for pulling creativity from a disparate crew, but now he embarrasses her. She has won the week's achievement award (an all-expense-paid trip to the local disco for one night), and he tacked her copy on the board last week with "A+" scrawled across it.

Like any young, creative person, she is restless to succeed, needs reinforcement (and rewards), and wants very much to have a good career path at Salvo, but her style is so antithetical to Harry's that she has become almost cowed in her work efforts.

Employee's Objective

To try to get the reinforcement and encouragement she requires while curbing the public enthusiasm of her boss toward her.

The Dialogue—Example 1

Harry is reading some copy at his desk.

HARRY	(*Shouts.*) This is brilliant! *People in the department look up and then at each other. He strides to his door.*
HARRY	Kathy! (*She looks up.*) Stand up! (*Slowly she does. He waves the sheet of paper.*) I want everyone to know that this is brilliant! Everybody get to work or Kathy's going to win this week's award again! (*He starts to clap. Others join in. Kathy sits down and slumps very low in her chair, her face flushed. Harry goes back to his office, the others return to their work. Kathy sits for a moment staring at her desk. Then she takes a deep breath, gets up from her chair, and goes to Harry's office.*)
KATHY	Harry, could I talk with you?
HARRY	Sure, hon. What's up? *She closes the door and sits down.*
KATHY	I don't know how to say this.
HARRY	You can tell me anything, hon. You know that. What can Uncle Harry do to help? *She realizes that he thinks she has some kind of personal problem and has come to "Uncle Harry" for help.*
KATHY	Oh, no. It's nothing like that! I mean, it's about work. I mean...
HARRY	What's the matter, kid? Pressure getting to you?
KATHY	No. Actually, I mean, I love the pressure and I love what we're doing...
HARRY	(*Very puzzled.*) So what's the problem?
KATHY	Well, I'm uncomfortable.
HARRY	About what?
KATHY	You're always telling me I'm brilliant...

HARRY   You are!

KATHY   And you keep telling everybody else.

HARRY   Keeps them on their toes. If anybody's brilliant, I tell them so. That way I build their confidence and it makes other people work harder.

KATHY   Well, it embarrasses me.

HARRY   What? Don't you want to be told when you do good work?

KATHY   Of course I do. That's one of the reasons I left the agency. We never knew where we stood.

* ACTION ASTERISK

This is a typical employee response; all of us need positive reinforcement, and when we don't get it, we get uncertain and unhappy. However, this won't help her with her current problem with Harry; this is what he thinks he's doing.

HARRY   Damn straight. I don't want that ever to happen in my shop. I want everybody to know when they're doing well.

KATHY   I know. And it's a wonderful feeling to be appreciated and encouraged. But I just can't handle some of it.

HARRY   Like what?

KATHY   Like just now. You came out and waved my copy and said I was brilliant and clapped and told everybody I was going to win again.

HARRY   So?

KATHY   I was mortified.

HARRY   You were what?

KATHY	I had a teacher in grade school once who would post our short stories on the bulletin boards with comments. She always wrote that mine were excellent. Within three months all the kids hated me.
HARRY	This isn't grade school.
KATHY	I know. But I'm still upset by it. Don't get me wrong. I *need* to know that I please you and that I'm doing well. But couldn't we do it privately?
HARRY	That's not my style.

* ACTION ASTERISK

Harry has just cut off communication. As a manager he has an obligation to listen to his employee's needs and problems. At the very least, he should hear out the conversation and determine if he needs to handle *this* employee a little differently to keep her productive. At the very most, it may be a sign that his management style, though apparently effective, may need a mojor overhaul to keep track of a changing company and growing staff.

KATHY	I know it isn't. And everyone loves you and loves to work here with you. But I really would prefer it if you could review me in private, tell me what I've done right and what I've done wrong. I really don't know how to handle all this public praise.
HARRY	Listen, Kathy, you're young. You'll get used to a lot of styles in business. I worked for several bastards in my time and I swore that if I ever ran a department I'd run it like a family—everything out in the open, everybody loving each other and working together and competing and being happy when the other guy did something great. That's the way I've run this place and it's really paid off.

* ACTION ASTERISK

This last line is dangerously close to "that's the the way I've always done it," and we all know what a trap that can be for a successful manager. Though his reasons seem perfectly admirable, lurking underneath is the simple fact that he plans to run the department *his* way, without real regard for individual needs.

KATHY   Oh, I know. It's a wonderful place to work. I've been
               very happy here. It's just that I guess I need my
               reinforcement and praise more privately than other
               people.

HARRY   (*He rises and pats her shoulder.*) Listen, Kathy. You'll
               get used to it. Everybody enjoys it because everybody
               knows what's going on and everybody's a part of the ac-
               tion. You'll get the hang of it.

* ACTION ASTERISK

**Neither we nor Harry have any evidence that "everybody enjoys it." In-
deed, Kathy may be the only one with the courage to question it. A sensitive manager would have responded to this conversation by wondering—to himself—if perhaps his style needed modification, at least on an
individual manager/employee basis.**

KATHY   (*She rises to leave.*) I guess so.

HARRY   Now, go to it! You'll win that prize again this week! (*He
               pats her on the shoulder and opens the door, and she
               leaves with a troubled little smile on her face.*)

Comments

Was the employee's goal successful? No. Kathy tried to make her discomfort known to Harry and get him to change. But he was oblivious and
impervious to her needs.

While it is likely that he is very effective with his enthusiasm and
camaraderie, it is also apparent that the behavior is troublesome to some,
at least to Kathy.

If a manager is insensitive to the effects of his or her behavior on an
employee and is unable or unwilling to change, it can pose a serious
dilemma for the employee. At one extreme it can be frustrating that the
manager is oblivious and doesn't take the hints. At the other extreme it can
be dangerous if the employee insists on change and antagonizes the
manager. What to do?

Pray for an understanding manager is the first thought. But finding a way
to force change without annoying the manager is the key. It is an awkward
situation when an employee must lead a conversation, but in this instance
there is little choice. A little psychology and gentle persuasion may be
helpful.

117

The Dialogue—Example 2 (continued)

HARRY   That's not my style.

KATHY   I know. And it's really a great place to work, don't get me wrong. But I was wondering if we could try a little experiment?

HARRY   Like what?

* ACTION ASTERISK
She's gotten his attention.

KATHY   Well, all of us try very hard to please you. And you sure let us know when we do. But there's no mystery about it.

HARRY   Mystery? I don't want anything hidden in this shop.

KATHY   Oh, I know. But now, when we do something good, everyone knows about it immediately, and I think it kind of takes the edge off the competition.

HARRY   You think so, huh?

KATHY   If we didn't know how good the stuff on the next desk was we might push a little harder—that extra effort—to be sure ours was the best we could make it.

* ACTION ASTERISK
Now she's appealing to the sportsman in him, "pushing" with that "extra effort."

HARRY   I don't know. It might backfire.

KATHY   I remember when I was at the agency we had a drive for the United Way, and when you gave to the fund you were given a pin to wear. The idea was to get everyone to wear them as a sort of advertisement for the fund drive and to remind everyone else to give.

HARRY   So?

KATHY   Well, the really neat part was that the company had spotters and nobody knew who they were. So, if you were wearing your button an employee might come up to you unexpectedly and "spot" you and give you a little prize.

HARRY   Like what?

KATHY   Oh, a record or a movie ticket, or something like that, which had been promoted.

* ACTION ASTERISK

Kathy is working very hard keeping up her enthusiasm and coming up with ideas and trying to convince Harry that there are better ways of rewarding people than his very public way.

HARRY   But how does any of that apply to us, hon?

KATHY   Oh, I'm sorry. Don't you see? We would all work doubly hard because we'd never know when we were going to be singled out. You'd see all our work, of course. And you could write comments on it, like "This is trash," or "A+." You know.

HARRY   (*Smiles.*) Like last week?

KATHY   Yeah. But that would be just between us. Then maybe once a week, or once a month, you'd find a really good piece and you'd give a big, public award. And we'd all be thrilled and we'd knuckle down to work even harder!

* ACTION ASTERISK

Kathy is trying very hard to imitate Harry's own enthusiasm and bring him along with her idea. While she undoubtedly knows that she can't change him completely, she is trying to shift a part of his behavior pattern to see if she can change, at least, his behavior toward her.

HARRY   Well, I don't know. Do you really think it would work?

KATHY   It would for me!

HARRY   Yeah. Well, I don't know about everybody else.

KATHY   Would you like to just try it? Maybe for a week? And see what happens?

HARRY	Oh, O.K., Kath. What the hell? We can try something new. Anything to keep everybody on their toes.
KATHY	Great! (*She rises to leave.*)
HARRY	Thanks, Kathy. And keep up the good work.
KATHY	Sure. (*She exits smiling.*)

Summary

Was the employee's objective satisfied? Only time will tell. Kathy convinced Harry to change his behavior for a week. Who knows if it will affect the work of the staff or whether he will be comfortable behaving in a different way?

The main point to be made is that Kathy tried to understand Harry's personality and then mimic it to make him change his mind. She captured his enthusiasm and then used it to spark his interest in trying something new. She avoided challenging him and antagonizing him. And by so doing, she has effected some change which will make her own life more palatable. If she's lucky, the change will become permanent. But if it isn't, she has demonstrated both loyalty and resourcefulness. Undoubtedly, she'll come up with another idea if she has to.

And who knows? Even though Harry may revert to his old ways with others, this conversation may sink in during the next week and he may realize that Kathy—and perhaps others—need different motivational techniques. Anything can happen. Meantime, instead of confrontation, Kathy used psychology and inventiveness to cope with her manager/employee problem.

11 YOUNG AND RESTLESS (Reinforcement)

Introduction

Just as some people find it difficult to say thank you or express their generosity, some managers find it hard to praise employees and supply them with the reinforcement they need for continuing good work.

Some managers are totally task-oriented and have difficulty working within the guidelines of Management by Objectives. Mutual goal-setting and periodic reviews are activities they have to get through in order to conform to company policy. But they are not comfortable with the procedure and, at best, go through the motions.

While setting tasks and giving monetary rewards for jobs well done works for some employees, there are others who need the interaction and reinforcement of reviews, conversation, encouragement. While the willing practice of MBO generally makes for a more productive work place, it must be said that the other, task-oriented kind of management *can* get results. It is not recommended, but it is not "bad"—except for the employees who require something more. They can suffer very badly under the totally task-oriented manager who does not communicate.

In the worst case, lack of feedback will cause them to leave. But if they truly like their jobs or the company, or need the work, they must find some other way.

Principally, they must learn to communicate with their managers through the *tasks* themselves. This is obviously the manager's paramount interest, and while he or she certainly does not wish to be bothered on every detail, the employee should keep the manager informed in advance of problems and be sure to communicate good solutions or good results. This provides the fundamental basis on which other communication may occur. Surely, even the most reticent, task-oriented manager will say well done when a good result is achieved.

Second, the employee must develop secondary support/information systems. This is not to be confused with backstair gossip. But in every company and in every department it is possible to share information (of a noncritical or nonconfidential nature) on the understanding that other information will be shared in return. This allows the employee to keep abreast of the feeling of the manager toward the productivity of the department in general and toward the employee in particular.

Care must be exercised in this regard. There is little more despicable or more destructive in a business environment than employees who gossip behind each others' backs and share personal and professional information—real and imagined—which is not directly related to the work and the workers involved.

Third, the employee must develop, in the absence of guidance from the manager, his or her own objectives, agenda, and strategies for attaining them. From the job description (which should be in existence) and the instructions given periodically by the manager, an employee should be able to fashion the goals, activity lists, and agenda which will organize his or her time, set achievement and satisfaction levels, and provide tools for monitoring success and reward.

If the boss won't do it for you, do it for yourself! Reinforcement is wonderfully conducive to good work. All of us respond affirmatively to a thank you and "That was well done."

But in the absence of that, take charge of your own life. Set your own goals, define your own achievement levels, identify your own rewards, be good to yourself. Remember, ultimately, no matter what anyone says, your own respect for and appreciation of yourself is the ultimate reward and reinforcement.

The Situation

Salvo tries, as much as possible, to work on Management By Objectives: Managers and employees cooperate to set goals and objectives which are monitored on a regular basis. Personal advancement and salary increases are based on the employee's achieving the objectives. Super achievers earn bonuses and those who fall short of the goals are reappraised and helped in resetting the goals and developing work habits to achieve them.

This is a companywide process, but its implementation is left in the hands of each manager. As in all things, some managers do it better than others. Some find it a useful mechanism whereby they can stay in touch with the employees' work without hovering; others find it hard to do and at best go through the motions, giving it short shrift.

The Characters

Tom is one of those managers. As V.P. of product development, he is dynamo, creative, hyperactive, demanding, excited about his work. He sets a high personal standard for his staff and fights for good pay and good bonuses for them. But he rarely hands out personal praise or encouragement. He assumes that they know they're doing good work by the amount of money they're paid and the success of the company.

Tim is one of the young geniuses in Tom's department. He came to Salvo directly from Princeton, where he excelled in math, statistics, and computer hacking. He is a quiet young man who develops some of the more glitzy, esoteric (and successful) games that the company sells. In his two years at Salvo he has conceived no fewer than three successful game packages. He is paid well and has gotten two handsome bonuses. But Tom has never *told* Tim that he is good. Tim needs the reinforcement and knows that he needs it. While a lot of his work is done in a team environment, he also does a lot of private thinking and development. He needs more than money to reassure him that he is doing well and that his future is bright.

He has decided that the next time he has a conference with Tom, he will confront him and ask for an evaluation.

Employee's Objective

To lead his boss into a discussion of his work and an evaluation of his future.

The Dialogue—Example 1

Tom is in his office and reaches for the buzzer on his desk.

TOM   Tim? Could you come in a minute? And bring the
                Catbird material. (*He continues reading until Tim
                appears at the door.*) Come on in. Have you finished
                Phase II yet?

TIM   Nearly. There is one more puzzle to develop.

TOM	When will it be done?
TIM	I hope today. I'm working on it now.
TOM	Good. We'll set up the team testing for tomorrow.
TIM	I'd like to hold off until I'm sure it works.
TOM	Come on! You said it would be done today. Let's get on with it.
TIM	I said I *hoped* to have it done today. If I don't get it finished I'd just waste the schedule time tomorrow and inconvenience the team.
TOM	Would a little midnight oil help?

* ACTION ASTERISK
Tom is pushing Tim to work late to finish a phase of the project. So far we have no indication that he is behind schedule, so the urging for overtime borders on the presumptuous. Tom is obviously what is known in some offices as a slave driver.

TIM	Midnight oil isn't the solution. I've got to think it through and creativity isn't always on call when you want it.
TOM	You're smart enough. Just hunker down and stick to it.
TIM	Am I?
TOM	Are you what?
TIM	Smart enough.
TOM	What's that supposed to mean?
TIM	I wonder sometimes if I'm smart enough to handle this. The feedback is kind of slim.

* ACTION ASTERISK
Tim has blurted out his concerns and is criticizing both himself and Tom. That's no way to get an honest evaluation—or respect.

TOM	What's going on with you? You're one of the best-paid designers in the department. You got a bigger bonus than anyone last year.
TIM	I know. I mean, I guess I know. But...
TOM	But what?
TIM	I'm just not sure of my status. You've never evaluated my work. And you seem unhappy with me now...
TOM	Tim, what's gotten into you? If I were unhappy, you'd know it. People who work hard around here and do good work get paid big. You get paid big. Have you got another offer or something?
TIM	Oh, no.
TOM	Well, it sounds like you're not happy here. I thought we had a good thing going with you.

* ACTION ASTERISK

Now Tim really has done it. He's made his insecurities sound like he's not happy. Either he'll come off as a whiner or Tom will continue to think that he's looking elsewhere. In either case, it's a disaster.

TIM	I'm very happy here.
TOM	It doesn't sound like it.
TIM	It's just that I wonder if I could have an evaluation sometime so I'd know how you feel about me and how I'm performing and what kind of future I have.
TOM	You've been performing fine. And your future will be just fine, as long as you keep up the good work. Which brings us back to Phase II. Do you want to test the game tomorrow or not?
TIM	I guess. If that's what you want.
TOM	It's not what I want. I want the thing to work. And the sooner it does, the sooner it can get on the market. You've got to tell me where it stands.

TIM   Well, I guess we can test it tomorrow. I'll try to have it ready by then.

* ACTION ASTERISK

Tim has just made a technical decision based on wish fulfillment: his and Tom's. He has no guarantee that the game will be ready for testing. If it is, he has come through, with luck. If it isn't, he can only damage his credibility even further.

TOM   Good. Notify the team. And I'll stop by tomorrow and see how it goes. (*Tim starts to exit.*) And Tim, don't worry about your performance. It will speak for itself.

TIM   Sure.

Comments

Was the employee's objective fulfilled? No.

Tim has planted some seeds of doubt in Tom's mind and has taken a technical risk which could be very damaging. Further, he has gotten nowhere in this quest for formal evaluation and reinforcement.

What did Tim do wrong?

He picked the *wrong time*. While Tom's mind is on moving another product as quickly as possible from the drawing board to the dealers' shelves, Tim has brought up his own problems, and in a derogatory manner, at that.

Although Tim had decided to broach the subject to Tom the *next time* he saw him, it simply wasn't the *right time*. He misjudged the person and his interests. He has to focus on the topic of the conversation—the game—and satisfy Tom that everything is under control. Only then can he focus Tom's attention on something else.

The Dialogue—Example 2 (continued)

TOM   You're smart enough. Just hunker down and stick to it.

TIM   Well, we've got a couple of more days. Here's the PERT chart. (*He lays it on Tom's desk.*) I have until Thursday to complete Phase II and we'll still be on schedule.

TOM   I see.

TIM	I don't think I'll need that long, but we're still not holding up anything.
TOM	Good.

* ACTION ASTERISK

Tim has quietly reminded Tom of the agreed schedule, without making any big deal of it. He has reassured him and gotten off the "midnight oil" crack.

TIM	Could I show you something?
TOM	Sure.
TIM	I've got it all worked out but one problem. It's the last escape hatch. And I'm afraid I've painted myself into a corner. (*He spreads his diagrams on Tom's desk, and Tom bends over them.*) See? I use this formula for escapes one and two.
TOM	Yeah.
TIM	Then I take it to this module and use this formula for escape number three.
TOM	That's very good.
TIM	I finished escape number four this morning by doubling the ratio.
TOM	Yeah. That's great.
TIM	But now I'm stuck.
TOM	Why?
TIM	Well, if I continue that logic it carries me out of the circle and won't work.
TOM	Let's see that. (*He scribbles some things on a piece of paper.*)

* ACTION ASTERISK

Tim has captured Tom's attention totally by involving him in the challenge of the problem. At the very least, Tom will understand that a

little "midnight oil" and a quick fix won't be sufficient. In the best case, the two will develop a closer working relationship.

TIM	You see, I'm afraid my solution to number four may throw the whole formula. Or maybe even number three.
TOM	You may be right. Why don't you backtrack to number three? You changed modules *and* formula there. Try it with only one change and then double the ratio for number four. Number five will be easier to calculate if the logic is consistent. We want to make this hard, but not impossible.
TIM	I know. But that's why I may not be able to test by tomorrow. I don't want to waste machine time.
TOM	That's O.K. You're still on schedule. That's a good game. No need to screw it up.
TIM	Thanks.
TOM	You've done very good work. At first I thought your stuff was too sophisticated, but it's got a sense of humor. The kids love the tricks you play on them.
TIM	I guess. That's what we used to enjoy at school, so I just try to do it here.
TOM	Keep doing it. Your track record is terrific. And your team seems to work well together.
TIM	Oh, yeah. We seem like a good match. We're about to learn everybody's tricks, though.
TOM	Oh?
TIM	Well, you know how it is. When you test somebody's stuff fairly often, you catch on to their favorite tricks. After a while you can almost second-guess them. I think that's why I was trying to use a different logic with this one.

TOM   That's an interesting idea. I wonder if we should rotate our teams?

TIM   I don't know. It might keep us on our toes.

* ACTION ASTERISK

Gradually, this conversation has moved from analysis of the specific problem to a brief review of Tim's performance to an analysis of the department's structure. Tim is getting a lot more than he bargained for.

TOM   I think maybe I'll do that.

TIM   That would be fun. How would you rotate us?

TOM   How? Just change the assignments as each job is finished.

* ACTION ASTERISK

Tom is making a quick judgment without thinking it through.

TIM   We're all on a different time-frame. And we all work on new ideas when we've finished a project. How would you assign us?

TOM   I'll have to work it out.

TIM   Sure. Sounds great. Maybe we could all get together and talk about it. I'll bet there are some good ideas out there.

TOM   Sure. When you get this thing tested, we'll call a meeting. Surely we're all smart enough to figure out a way to rotate you. It'll keep all of you on your toes, like you said.

TIM   O.K. Shall I call you when I work this out?

TOM   Let me know when you set up the test. I'll sit in on it.

TIM   O.K.

Summary

Was the employee's objective satisfied? Partially.

He received a brief critique of his own work and managed to focus Tom's attention on the function and productivity of the department.

Further, he managed to induce his boss into holding a staff meeting to discuss job rotation. Out of such a meeting it can be assumed that a lot more than job rotation will be discussed. This could be a breakthrough for all the members of the department—getting the time and attention of the manager on more personal issues than deadlines.

The scene progressed differently—and productively—because Tim kept his attention focused on *Tom's* agenda: getting the project finished on time. By involving Tom directly in the project and its challenges, he was able to assure that the problem was understood, as well as to engage Tom in a very easy and personal conversation. The "slave driver" was very interested and concerned, once his professional skills were challenged and engaged.

Rewards and reinforcement can come to an employee in a number of ways. While it is ideal that they be on a formal and regular basis, that is sometimes difficult for some personalities. The challenge to an employee is to understand the manager's personality and agenda, and to elicit feedback and reinforcement within the context of the manager's ability to give it.

In this example that was accomplished in the best possible way—through the work itself.

12 THE OFFICE FLIRT

Introduction

One man's secretary can be another man's Marilyn Monroe. One woman's office assistant can be another woman's Tom Selleck. Sex—and the influence of sex—has undoubtedly been a part of office life since the first woman sat down at the first Underwood and joined the formerly male world.

And sooner or later, someone in an office will be perceived as being a "flirt." Webster defines "flirt" as "to trifle or toy, one who plays at love." Obviously, none of that—either love or flirting—has any place in a business environment.

Whether fact or fiction about office flirting makes the best-seller lists, *The Wall Street Journal*, or the convention lecture platform, the simple fact is that the vast majority of workers are uncomfortable with flirting as a behavior pattern and know that it is nonproductive and disruptive.

Both men and women flirt in the work place. And while our conditioning may imply that women are the traditional flirts, experience proves otherwise. Both men and women can appear as the company flirt, and it always presents a major problem for the manager involved.

Let's be candid. One of the most difficult problems a manager encounters is flirting in the office, leading to possible complications ranging from sexual harassment charges to love affairs going on between people in the same department or company. It's difficult because of the range and depth of possible problems and because of traditional male networks and the new female networks which make confrontation awkward and difficult.

There are several things to be considered. First, is the flirting a matter of fact or a matter of gossip? We all have heard that "where there's smoke, there's fire." However, a manager's job is to separate rumor from truth. Believing and acting on rumor is not acceptable managerial behavior. Somehow, a manager must cut through rumors and hearsay to find the truth—firsthand, if possible—about flirting in the work place. Only then is any sort of sensible action possible. All means necessary should be used to confirm or reject gossip and accusations. Facts and truth are fundamental as a beginning.

Then we come to the networks. No matter how the organization chart looks, the informal networks more often than not run a company or department, set the behavior patterns (no matter how personnel policies may read), and dictate who will be believed and who will not be. A manager undoubtedly got to be a manager because of sensitivities to those invisible networks and subtle ties. (More informal support systems are formed on a commuter train or golf course or squash court than any organizational or management guide will ever admit.) But a sensitive manager will understand that written behavior codes should apply equally to all employees, no matter whose nephew or whose executive assistant it is.

Then comes the question, is it flirting or is it sexual harassment? One woman's flirt may be another woman's aggressor. But how does a manager tell the difference?

The most obvious way is by observing. Generally, a flirt performs in public; a person seeking sexual favors in exchange for raises or promotions prefers to operate in private. Think about it. The office flirt, whether male or female, typically will make remarks, touch and kiss, or offer presents in front of other people. They seem to seek or need the audience. The more insidious and demeaning (and illegal) approaches tend to be made in private, where they are more difficult to prove.

It must be stated, however, that just because something is public does not necessarily make it right. Just because the flirt makes remarks to someone in public, offers favors, or assumes that hugs and kisses can be bestowed with impunity does not mean that they are not ultimately demeaning to the recipient. Being public does not make them right.

But they are easier behaviors for a manager to change because they can be observed and evaluated.

This chapter concerns a flirt. It does not concern sexual harassment. Corporate policy and procedures for controlling harassment are suggested in the Appendix. Sexual harassment is the *intention* to intimidate, to use, to demean, to dominate. It is an ugly behavior which ignores or makes fun of the opposite sex; denies resources, advancement, recognition; does not take the career goals of a person seriously, because of sex; pressures a person to participate in social and/or sexual activities.

Our concerns in this chapter are with *unintentional* behavior which can intimidate, demean, or embarrass.

What is the difference between a very friendly employee and a flirt? It's hard to say. But probably the best guideline is to consider the feelings of the person to whom the gestures are directed. Do they demean? Do they embarrass? Do they hurt? Are they wanted? A friendly person may demean or embarrass another person without intent or without meaning to flirt. But in an office situation, the result is more important than the intention. The manager must stop it before it gets out of hand and before it sets a behavior standard which other people may see and imitate.

Friendliness and badinage and laughter and cooperation and thoughtfulness are all wonderful traits to have in an office atmosphere. Tight-lipped, "go by the book" automatons are rarely the happiest and most productive employees. That comfortable middle ground where friendliness pervades with a respect for everyone's feelings and background is the atmosphere all good managers will strive for. It is an atmosphere based on trust as well as acute observation of behavior and its results.

The Situation

Josh, one of the founding partners and executive vice-president of sales and marketing, has taken great pride in the development of his sales and marketing staffs. With an MBA in marketing and a successful career in sales at the leading computer company, he took a career risk when he helped launch Salvo. But his professionalism, enthusiasm, and ability to inspire people have made him a very successful executive, and the staff which he has assembled is recognized as one of the best in the business.

In his forties and a dedicated family man, Josh still has a love of the process of developing computer software and will still, on occasion, play with it (with his staff) to be sure everyone understands it before they go out to sell it. He is a polite man from Virginia who tends to remember birthdays and anniversaries with cards, lunches, and unexpected bottles of champagne.

Blake is the vice-president of marketing and the antithesis of Josh. He is in his mid-thirties, divorced, has an MBA from Josh's alma mater, and is the proverbial life of the party.

Josh has said of him, "For every problem, he comes up with twenty solutions at one time. Thank God, he generally picks the best one." Blake is creative, peripatetic, charming, and very successful with his marketing campaigns. As a new bachelor, he dates a lot and is very attractive to women. And he knows it. Some say he even uses it, to get past receptionists, secretaries, assistants, to see people he needs to see on Salvo business.

While this trait may be charming in Cary Grant movies and helpful to Salvo business, it has become somewhat troublesome on the Salvo premises. Frankly, Blake flirts outrageously throughout the company. He has used his charms to get into the premises after hours, to obtain certain sales information before it was his due, and to get people to cover for him when he was out of the office too long.

The mature women on the staff are on to him. They enjoy his charm and badinage, but try never to be alone with him, either in the office or out. Even though he is now a bachelor, they know better than to mingle personal attraction with a business relationship.

However, there are younger women on the staff who are somewhat awed by his position, lulled by his considerable charm, and think of him as eligible. A few tears and backstairs gossip have been the result.

Blake is known as free with his hands and hugs and kisses a lot. Candy and flowers appear on desks after a "favor," and on occasion, he has taken out a junior staffer for drinks and dinner.

Josh has decided to be more aware and observant. But it has produced little evidence of the gossip. At a recent marketing party for a new program, he *did* see Blake kiss and hug a lot of the young ladies, but it was a particularly jolly party, so he is unconvinced.

The Characters

Salvo has exhibited two major strengths in the computer software field: the ability to create or acquire some of the tantalizing product in the business, and creative marketing, which has been innovative and productive.

While facts are scarce, rumors and discomfort have been growing for some months. However, no one has had the authority—or the stomach—to confront Blake with the problem.

Finally, Mary, Josh's secretary, has taken it upon herself to tell Josh about the rumors. She assures him that there is no evidence of any affair between Blake and any of the younger staff. However, his behavior has become bolder and bolder over recent months. It has reached the point that most of the young women are becoming reluctant to be around him, especially alone, even though many of them like him very much and are secretly flattered by his attention.

Josh is dumbfounded. Such behavior is so far from his own experience that he can hardly believe it. He asks Mary for particulars and she can only supply him with gossip. But she insists on *not* giving him names. Both of them are very aware that they are dealing only with hearsay and that it is a very unfair way to judge behavior. Josh keeps saying, "I'll have to see it myself." He has also said, "How do you expect me to do anything about it if you don't give me facts?" And her answer has been, "I've told you all I've heard. You'll have to confirm the facts for yourself."

After momentary annoyance, Josh has realized Mary is right. He has been oblivious to Blake's behavior because no one has brought it to his attention until now, and he has not been in a situation where he can observe Blake firsthand.

He is in a quandary of how to deal with gossip. Blake is a man he hired and whom he has seen do a fine job for Salvo. Further, he has not seen, in person, the kind of behavior he has now heard described.

He trusts Mary implicitly and knows that she does not lie or gossip. He also knows her courage and discomfort in telling him of the problem.

Manager's Objective

To avoid succumbing to gossip about a peron's behavior, but to discover any improper circumstances and stop them immediately. The issue is to know the facts and to make office behavior conform to company policies and good etiquette.

The Dialogue—Example 1

Josh calls Miriam, one of the marketing assistants, and asks her to find Blake in the advertising design area and to ask him to come to Josh's office. He knows Blake is working on a campaign, he knows that Miriam is one of the attractive young assistants in the department, and he knows there is a long walk from the ad department to his office. After he talks to Miriam, he gets from his desk and goes to the hall toward the ad department.

As he walks down the hall, he sees Blake and Miriam coming toward him. Blake has his arm around Miriam's shoulder and is talking closely to her face. She is smiling but seems a little uncomfortable. When they see Josh, they pull apart and Blake removes his arm from Miriam's shoulder.

BLAKE   Hi, Josh.

JOSH   Hello, Blake. Thanks, Miriam, for doing the errand.

MIRIAM   (*Almost relieved.*) Sure, Josh, anytime. (*She walks on down the hall.*)

BLAKE   What's up?

JOSH   Oh, several things. Do you have a few minutes to spare?

BLAKE   Sure. I got them started on the new campaign this morning.

JOSH   Good. I look forward to seeing the whole thing. (*They are continuing to walk toward Josh's office.*) She seems like a nice girl.

BLAKE   Who?

JOSH   Miriam.

BLAKE   Oh, yeah. She's a sweetie.

JOSH   Is she good at her job?

BLAKE   I guess so. She works for Jeanette. She's good at the parties. Great dancer. (*They walk in silence, enter Josh's office. Josh shuts the door.*)

JOSH   Blake, you really shouldn't talk that way.

BLAKE   What way?

JOSH   About Miriam. I asked you about her and all you could say was that she was a sweetie and a great dancer.

BLAKE   But she is. She's all those things. What's wrong with saying so?

JOSH   And walking up the hall, you had your arm around her.

BLAKE   I put my arm around everybody.

JOSH   You don't put your arm around me.

BLAKE   You're not as cute as Miriam. (*They both laugh.*)

JOSH   Blake, this is serious.

BLAKE   It may be, but I don't know what the hell we're talking about.

* ACTION ASTERISK

Blake has the right to be puzzled. So far this interview has been conducted without any warning of what it's about. This is the first time Blake has been confronted by his boss and friend. He deserves some quick answers.

JOSH   I asked you some questions about a young woman who works in your department and you couldn't tell me anything about her. All you could talk about was her looks and her dancing.

BLAKE   She doesn't work for me.

JOSH   Of course she does! They all work for you. You should know how well they perform and what their promotion potential is and how they're doing with the department.

BLAKE   Is she in trouble?

JOSH   Of course not. I'm just disturbed at your comments about her, and putting your arm around her.

BLAKE   Has she been complaining about me?

JOSH   No. Not that I know of.

BLAKE   Then what's all this about?

JOSH   You're known around here as the happy bachelor. I think some of the men are envious of you. At least, you try to make them feel envious with some of your stories. But I don't think the women here feel quite the same.

BLAKE   I get along great with the gals! Who's been complaining?

* ACTION ASTERISK
Calling the younger staff "the gals" and "the girls" should be a flag to any serious manager that the employee may have the problem of showing less respect to the female employees than to the male.

JOSH   That's a terrific comment, Blake. You're getting me into trouble, maybe the company into trouble, and it has to stop.

BLAKE   What are you talking about?

137

| JOSH | You're too free and easy with the girls. |

* ACTION ASTERISK
Now even Josh is talking about "the girls."

| BLAKE | I haven't had any complaints. |

| JOSH | I have. |

| BLAKE | Who? That's ridiculous. |

| JOSH | You're too free with your hands. Putting your arm around Miriam is the least of it. Evidently you're a real "touchy-feely" type these days. And the girls don't even want to be in a room alone with you. |

| BLAKE | I resent that. You'd better have proof! |

| JOSH | If I need it, I can get it. But that's not all. |

* ACTION ASTERISK
Josh *does* need more proof before he makes absolute statements. He'd be better off asking questions, or concentrating on behavior that is unacceptable.

| BLAKE | Oh? |

| JOSH | Evidently you enjoy the dancing at the marketing parties we give. |

| BLAKE | I'm not the only one. You cut a pretty mean rug yourself. |

| JOSH | But I don't take any of the girls home or out to dinner afterward. |

| BLAKE | That's only happened a few times. |

| JOSH | I know. And then there are the flowers and the candy and the times you've gotten in here after hours and the material you've been given which you weren't supposed to have. |

| BLAKE | Lots of people do favors for other people. |

JOSH	These seem to be the women. You haven't given candy to any of the guys.
BLAKE	Give me a break! Why would I give candy to a guy?
JOSH	Why do you need to give anything to anybody? Why can't you go through normal channels?

* ACTION ASTERISK
Finally, maybe Josh is going to talk about office procedures.

BLAKE	Is there something wrong with my work?
JOSH	Not that I know of. It's very good. However, all this attention to the female population of Salvo is a problem I could have done without.
BLAKE	There isn't a problem unless someone makes it a problem.
JOSH	That could happen too. I don't need a sexual harassment suit on my hands. Or worse still, I don't need some office affair gumming up the works of this department.
BLAKE	I'm not having an affair in this department! How dare you? I'm friendly to people. I treat them well. When they do me a favor, I pay them back...with candy, or flowers, or drinks, or dinner. Where have you been living? Outer Mongolia? You don't get cooperation from people unless you're nice to them!

* ACTION ASTERISK
Blake has just repeated what most people in sales and marketing believe. It is difficult to look upon being nice to peolple as an error, unless there are specific guidelines for behavior.

JOSH	You're being to nice to them. Now let me tell you what's going to happen.
BLAKE	Yeah?

* ACTION ASTERISK
Blake seems to be losing respect for Josh in this very difficult and unstructured conversation.

JOSH   You're going to stop feeling up on the girls.

BLAKE   Honestly, Josh!

JOSH   Listen to me. And you're not going to take them out for drinks and dinner anymore.

BLAKE   Even when they do good work?

JOSH   They're expected to do good work. If you knew a little more about their work, maybe you wouldn't have to "reward" them so much.

BLAKE   Anything else?

JOSH   Yes, please don't bribe anybody to give you information or to give you access to the premises. We have a normal working schedule and some pretty specific procedures for that sort of thing.

BLAKE   Don't worry. I'll be a regular nine-to-fiver.

* ACTION ASTERISK
Josh has lost him. Giving orders like a sergeant major, without any proof of misconduct, is the perfect way to lose a good employee, particulary a high-energy, ego-centered person such as Blake.

JOSH   That's not what I'm saying.

BLAKE   Really? Well, that's what you're getting.

JOSH   Blake, don't threaten me.

BLAKE   Listen, you've just practically accused me of attacking the women in this company! How do you think I'm supposed to feel?

JOSH   I've done no such thing. I just want it understood what kind of company we're running around here.

BLAKE   I understand. Believe me, I understand. Gee, what a bunch of ninnies. I wish I knew who'd gotten to you.

JOSH   That's irrelevant.

BLAKE   Not to me!

JOSH   The main thing is, do you understand that you have to change your behavior?

BLAKE   I sure do. And I sure will.

JOSH   Good. Let's see how it works out.

BLAKE   Yeah. Let's see. (*He rises and exits.*)

Comments

Was the manager's objective satisfied? Of course not. Josh has succeeded in alienating Blake and will probably lose him sometime in the future. Further, he has planted seeds of distrust which will cause problems between Blake and his staff: He will wonder which of the women have complained about him.

At best, Josh set up this interview on gossip. And he tried to set up a small scene with Miriam to test the rumors; it proved successful and a means to begin the conversation.

But the conversation was conducted as if all the rumors were facts. He left no room for Blake to explain his actions, nor did he try to explain how he wished the company employees to conduct themselves.

Conversations like this are difficult, at best, to conduct. And when they are man to man, innuendo must be avoided. The reputations of the man, or the women, must not be sullied.

Let's see if there is a better way.

The Dialogue—Example 2

BLAKE   I get along great with the gals! Who's been complaining?

JOSH   That's an interesting attitude. I don't think I've ever heard it put quite so graphically.

BLAKE   Listen. I want to know who's been complaining...

JOSH   *You* listen, Blake...and listen up good. Since your divorce, you've seemed to have a pretty good time. You seem to enjoy being a bachelor. And that's fine. But we're not running a dating service here. And as far as I'm concerned, all the women who work here are off-limits.

BLAKE   Wait a minute! You can't tell me who to date and who not to.

JOSH   I can and I will. More good companies and more good careers have gotten messed up because people start dating somebody at the office. We don't need the problem here. You don't need the problem. You've got a plateful already.

* ACTION ASTERISK

To take this strong a stand, we can assume that Blake knows that company policy states that dating on company premises is frowned upon. And the thrust of his conversation regards good business conduct; so far, he has not accused Blake of anything that needs proving.

BLAKE   What kind of problems?

JOSH   Isn't it obvious? I've been trying to tell you...leave the women here alone.

BLAKE   For the record, I *don't* date anybody from here and I don't know what you're carrying on about. My God, surely you don't think I've had anything to do with Miriam! She's a kid!

JOSH   She's not a kid and I don't think you've had anything to do with *her*. That's the point. Evidently you think you can be free with *any*body.

BLAKE   I must be losing my mind. I don't understand a word you're saying.

JOSH   You're much too free and easy with the women around here and they resent it.

BLAKE	Who does?
JOSH	All of them. Or at least a lot of them. There have been complaints.
BLAKE	Could you be specific?
JOSH	Yes. You are too free with your hands.
BLAKE	What?
JOSH	You hug a lot. You kiss and pet a lot. I understand that some of the women won't be in a room alone with you now.
BLAKE	Bull!
JOSH	Listen to me! You dance with the younger staffers a lot at parties. You've taken some of them out for drinks or dinner.
BLAKE	That was to thank them for special favors.
JOSH	Take them to lunch! And take more than one. And stop bribing your way in here after hours with candy and flowers and phone calls.
BLAKE	Now, listen, Josh. That was only a couple of times when I needed some extra information for a campaign.

* ACTION ASTERISK

As Josh itemizes the offenses he's heard, Blake is confirming them by trying to explain them. So Josh is more and more assured that he is on firm ground and knows that the gossip was true.

JOSH	You're not listening. I'm telling you in words of one syllable that this stuff has to stop. Some of the women in this company have become upset enough about your behavior to talk to me about it. And seeing how you behaved with Miriam and the things you have said, I tend to agree with them.
BLAKE	Are you charging me with sexual harassment?

JOSH	No.
BLAKE	Have they?
JOSH	No. Not yet.
BLAKE	Well, I think it's ridiculous.
JOSH	Maybe you do. But I don't. And neither, obviously, do some other people.
BLAKE	Are you going to let a bunch of women run your company?

* ACTION ASTERISK
Blake is throwing down a gauntlet at the foot of Josh's authority. How will he behave toward this last, desperate effort?

| JOSH | I never think of this company as "bunches of women" or "bunches of men." I think of us all as professionals who like to work here and who like to work together. How is it I'm not getting through to you? What is it that you don't understand? |
| BLAKE | I guess it just all seems so trivial. I've taken a few girls out for drinks or dinner to thank them. I've brought flowers and candy for the same reason. I dance with them at parties. I'm friendly with them at the office. Where is any of that wrong? |

* ACTION ASTERISK
There! There's the confession. Now Josh can get on with the business of stopping the flirting and keeping Blake as a productive employee.

JOSH	Taken separately, none of it is. Added together, you come off as the office flirt, and as a departmental director, you can't afford that. It's damaging your reputation. And ultimately, it will damage ours.
BLAKE	I can't change. I'm basically a friendly guy.
JOSH	Don't change that. Just treat the women like you treat the men.

BLAKE	You must be kidding.
JOSH	No, I'm not.
BLAKE	I'm damned if I'll dance with the boys at the next staff party. (*They both laugh.*)
JOSH	Well, no. I'm not suggesting that. However, I suggest that if you dance, you don't kiss. And you sure don't take one of the girls home.
BLAKE	O.K. That's a deal.

* ACTION ASTERISK

Josh's persistence has made Blake realize that he has to change. And as a methodical, creative man, he now is listening to Josh list, item by item, what he has to do.

JOSH	And keep your hands off the women. No more "touchy-feely." No more hugs.
BLAKE	That will be harder...but I'll do it.
JOSH	Save the lunches for people who *really* do good work—the men and the women.
BLAKE	Yeah.

* ACTION ASTERISK

Now Blake is really getting into it.

JOSH	And no more drinks and dinner.
BLAKE	Except in groups?
JOSH	*Mixed* groups.
BLAKE	Oh, well. More's the merrier.
JOSH	And no more bribery with candy and flowers.
BLAKE	Those aren't bribes, they're thank-yous.
JOSH	Check with me before you send them again.

BLAKE	(*Pause.*) O.K.
JOSH	Blake, I hope you understand how serious I am about all of this. You do a terrific job for Salvo and you've put together a good team. We've had a lot of good times and I know what good company you can be. However, since you and Nancy have parted, your life has been a little different. You're a bachelor again, but this isn't college. This could become a serious matter and I don't want that to happen.
BLAKE	Neither do I. I appreciate your candor and I appreciate the advice. I'm going to take it.
JOSH	So there's no misunderstanding, this meeting is going in your private record.

* ACTION ASTERISK

Yes. Even though this has been man to man between friends and colleagues, it has also been a discipline interview of a boss with an employee. It has to be in writing.

BLAKE	Oh?
JOSH	Yes. I'm going to make a note of the things we agreed would stop. So there's no misunderstanding. Ever.
BLAKE	Do you have to do that?
JOSH	Yes. It's not going into the personnel file. But it will be in our private review files. This is serious to me and I want it to be serious to you.
BLAKE	It is. And thanks. (*They rise and shake hands.*)
JOSH	Thanks, Blake. See you later. (*He exits.*)

Summary

Was the manager's objective satisfied? Yes.

How? By a little preplanning (he did set up a situation where he could observe Blake's behavior for himself). By showing respect—with firmness—in the interview. And by talking about the way the company expected its employees to behave, and leading Blake to reveal himself. In revealing himself, Blake confirmed his behavior, but, moreover, in talking about it, he set up conditions where they could *both* arrive at ways to change it.

In a high-powered office, with high-powered, interesting people, flirting happens. Beware of gossip. But don't ignore it.

We have no evidence that Blake is a sexist or that his *intention* was sexual harassment—the intention to demean or intimidate or use. However, had the situation continued unchecked, this behavior could have eventually been misunderstood and a harassment charge made against him. A manager's responsibility is to keep that from happening (using guidelines similar to those found in the Appendix).

For all practical purposes, Josh nearly let this go on too long. The gossip was around and growing, and he was oblivious to it. If his secretary had not come forward, this situation could have gotten totally out of control, resulting, at the least, in a demoralized staff and, at the worst, the filing of a harassment charge by some employee. Josh should have been more sensitive and observant of his direct report. However, when he *did* know, he acted quickly to bring everything under control. Find out the facts and deal with flirting in a quiet, realistic, firm way. In the final analysis, good office morale is better than the heightened "fun" of indulging the flirting.

13 THE MARINE SERGEANT

Introduction

The great majority of American companies are based on military concepts and military organizational structure. The most casual analysis of business will verify that assumption:

Two very interesting quotes will hammer home the point:

> Among other things I am now reading Clausewitz's *On War*. A strange way of philosophizing but very good on his subject. To the question whether war should be called an art or a science, the answer given is that war is most like trade.
>
> Friedrich Engels

and

> War is the trade of kings.
>
> John Dryden

Military language and concepts permeate American business. The organization chart of a typical company resembles most closely the organization chart of a military establishment, with a lot of little squares reporting up to some larger squares which report to a few large squares which report to one big square. Notice that we use the phrase "report up," and even the term "CEO" is derived from the military.

We use the words "strategy" in our planning, "troops" to describe our group of employees; we talk about "outflanking" our competition and "assaulting" our marketplaces.

In our military schools our young warriors are taught the principal duties of staff command:

G-1 personnel
G-2 intelligence
G-3 operations and planning
G-4 supply and transport

In our business schools our young would-be managers are taught the fundamentals of good corporate management:
administration and personnel
marketing research and product development
operations, production, and marketing
finance, purchasing, and transportation

No wonder young people who have served as officers in the military have had little trouble succeeding in American corporate life! And no wonder they were so sought after in the go-go days of the sixties and early seventies.

Strict military structure no longer keeps America's productivity as a beacon to the world. Part of that is due to the change of the mix in the work place. There are more people at work today who have *not* served in the military than there are those who have. The World War II veterans are retiring and Korea's and Vietnam's vets are outnumbered by the baby boomers who did *not* go into the military. So a work place permeated with military jargon and orders to obey is foreign to a majority of workers.

But another phenomenon has had more impact. America is no longer a smokestack, manufacturing country. The growing future industries will be industries of *communications*—the world of information and ideas. And a business environment whose success is based on ideas, creativity, open channels of exchange, team effort, and cooperation will not function well with a military structure or a direct order mentality.

It can be successfully argued that a battlefield is the last place you need consensus: A commander doesn't want to take a vote before the assault is made. That commander wants to give an order and know that it will be obeyed.

However, the days of giving orders and having them obeyed is well on its way to oblivion in the last quarter of the twentieth century in American business.

This is not to decry the values and virtues of military training. From it have come men and women of daring, integrity, honor, and profound dedication. We hope those traits will always find a place in American business

It is *methods* that have changed.

Inevitably, military and nonmilitary personalities will find themselves in the same company or department. And with luck, the clashes will be few or nonexistent. But when those clashes of style and method do occur, it behooves the sensible manager to analyze *what* the chief products of the department are (products? ideas? services?) and to determine the best working environment and procedures to make that task successful.

Chances are, these days, the nonmilitary way will be best and that managers must counsel with those employees who have to learn a new behavior mode and attitude. Obviously you will want to do this without breaking their spirit, dampening their enthusiasm, or causing a loss of face. It can be tricky, but it must be done. The smooth function of the enterprise is at stake as well as the career success of the affected employees.

War is hell, but work and the work place should be a rewarding experience.

The Situation

Although Salvo is a rapidly growing company with occasional overcrowding, longer working hours for some departments, and so forth, it is still a company where courtesy is the norm and order is preferred to disorder.

It is very much a people-oriented place, with birthday parties occurring regularly in all departments, and major holidays a time of general well-wishing.

Its employees know that there is a time and place to play and a time and place to work. There is a good intercom system in the company so that the work areas have the quiet hum of working voices but never the loud sounds of people trying to make themselves heard.

That is, all areas but one department in MIS.

The Characters

Darryl is director of games development in the MIS department. He and his staff test the games of the companies up for acquisition and also develop new ones for market testing. They are all very good at their jobs and have the necessary "free spirits" to develop video computer games competitive in a highly faddish market.

Darryl is a computer school graduate. Before coming to Salvo, he was an Air Force lieutenant in the programming section of one of the computer installations. He is going to night school to get his college degree in computer science. As a lifelong hacker and player of video games, he has been in his element at Salvo. Generally, his staff share his enthusiasm and enjoy working on the projects.

He has one trait, however, which is disturbing both to them and to the departments surrounding them.

Darryl conducts his duties like a Marine drill sergeant. He never asks opinions or says please; he gives orders. And those orders are given in a loud voice, through an open door. He also has the military symptom of "going through channels."

He calls out the door for a particular project leader; when that person arrives in his office, he or she is left standing while Darryl gives the orders for the job or activity. Everyone in the shop (and some adjoining areas) hears the orders. The project leader is expected to return to the team, issue the orders, and get the work done.

This drill sergeant conduct has reached a crescendo. Complaints among staff have now reached other departments, and finally, two project leaders have gone to Herman, director of MIS, to voice their complaints.

Herman is disturbed by the situation. He is in his forties and has been in computers all of his life. He served in the Army in Korea as a teenager, got his degrees on the GI Bill, and has worked for a university and a major computer manufacturer before coming to Salvo. He is a quiet and brilliant computer whiz. As the three partners have said, "He has the most disorderly desk in the company, and the most orderly mind."

He listens, observes, encourges, challengers, and loves a staff which uncovers more problems to slove. It would be hard to remember when he had ever given an *order* (except "Turn of the lights when you leave, but not the air conditioner").

He has pondered this new problem and tried to develop a way to solve it. Finally, he thinks he has a solution.

Manager's Objective

To stop Darryl from behaving like a drill sergeant and to conduct himself in a professional way with his staff, gaining their confidence and cooperation, while keeping his own enthusiasm and control.

The Dialogue—Example 1

Herman walks from his office over to Darryl's door.

HERMAN   Darryl!

DARRYL   (*Looks up.*) Yes?

HERMAN	Come to my office.

Herman walks away to his own office. Darryl sits for a minute at his desk, overcome with surprise. All work in the project area has stopped, while Herman makes his way back to his office and Darryl leaves his desk and hurries after him. Everyone stares after them. Herman sits at his desk and Darryl enters the office. The guest chair has been pushed near the conference table so that Darryl has no place to sit without moving furniture. He stands awkwardly in front of Herman's desk.

HERMAN	Where do we stand on the Firestorm project?
DARRYL	It's in the final test stage now. We should have a report by Friday.
HERMAN	Who's working on the project?
DARRYL	Ken and Janet and Sam.
HERMAN	Are they doing anything else?
DARRYL	They each have some other project programs, but...
HERMAN	Then how do you know they'll be finished?
DARRYL	That's their deadline.
HERMAN	How do you know they'll be finished?
DARRYL	I don't understand.
HERMAN	Just because it's their deadline, how do you know they'll be finished?
DARRYL	They'll work as late as necessary to finish it.
HERMAN	Who set the deadline?
DARRYL	I did.
HERMAN	Why did you pick Friday?
DARRYL	It seemed long enough to do the job.

HERMAN	To whom?
DARRYL	Sir?
HERMAN	It seemed long enough to whom?
DARRYL	To me...sir.

* ACTION ASTERISK

Darryl has lapsed, unknowingly, into a military response... subordinate to superior. Herman has gained a psychological upper hand.

HERMAN	Did they agree to it?
DARRYL	Yes, sir.
HERMAN	Did you ask them?
DARRYL	Sir?
HERMAN	Did you ask them? Or tell them?
DARRYL	I analyzed the work to be done and made the assignment. They agreed to it.
HERMAN	Did they have a chance to object?
DARRYL	I'm afraid I don't understand this conversation...sir. Is there something wrong with our reports?
HERMAN	When did you get out of the Army?
DARRYL	Air Force...sir.
HERMAN	When did you get out of the Air Force?
DARRYL	Eighteen months ago.
HERMAN	Why did you leave?
DARRYL	I'd finished my second tour and wanted to move into business.

153

HERMAN   Where did you serve?

DARRYL   Mostly at Edwards...sir. But you have all that in my ...

HERMAN   Did you like the Air Force?

DARRYL   Yes, sir!

HERMAN   Did you like giving orders?

DARRYL   Sir?

HERMAN   I never did like giving orders when I was in the Army. And I sure as hell didn't like getting them. Too many of them were stupid orders from stupid people. (*Darryl doesn't say anything.*) Isn't that right?

DARRYL   With respect, sir. No, sir. Not all of them were stupid.

HERMAN   What was your rank?

DARRYL   Lieutenant, sir.

HERMAN   Did you give a lot of orders?

DARRYL   Some.

HERMAN   Did you like giving orders?

* ACTION ASTERISK

Herman undoubtedly knows the answers to all these questions. He is putting Darryl through a drill which continues to diminish Darryl's position. His boss should know all these things about him; where he has gone wrong?

DARRYL   I didn't think about it, sir. I did what was necessary.

HERMAN   Do you like giving orders here?

Darryl is, by now, extremely uncomfortable. He is very aware of the open door behind him, and the fact that he is standing almost at attention.

HERMAN   Phyllis!

154

Herman's secretary appears at the door.

PHYLLIS   Yes?

HERMAN   Get me some coffee.

Phyllis stands transfixed, eyes wide open. Seeing the tension in the room, she turns and walks away. Darryl is taken aback. He knows that the coffee wagon is not around, and he knows that most people in MIS, including Herman, take care of their own snack needs. It is not his secretary's duty.

HERMAN   You seem uncomfortable, mister.

* ACTION ASTERISK

This military use of the word "mister" is meant to snap Darryl's attention. He's been given plenty of chance to realize that giving orders and running a "spit and polish" operation is not the acceptable behavior in this office.

DARRYL   I am, sir. I don't know what this is all about.

HERMAN   It's about your conduct.

DARRYL   Sir?

HERMAN   You've been running your shop like a damn boot camp. You give orders. You shout instructions. You never use the intercom. You never ask anyone's opinion. You think you're still in the Army.

DARRYL   Air Force.

HERMAN   Don't correct me! This isn't the military! And it never *will* be the military. The success of this company depends on what goes on in people's heads. And nothing goes on in people's heads when they're given orders and yelled at and told what to do and never given the chance to think. And that's what you've been doing.

DARRYL   I'm sorry.

HERMAN   Good. I want it to stop. I want you to join this company, mister. I want you to listen to your people, to talk *with* your people, to consult with them, to get their input

155

and their cooperation. I want to know that I've got the collective intelligence of *all* the people in your department, not just yours. We're civilians here, not military, and that's the way it's going to stay. Is that clear?

* ACTION ASTERISK

This classic chewing out can only bring back memories of the military to Darryl. Herman is trying to fight fire with fire (change his behavior by duplicating it), but that can backfire. The message *could* be interpreted: "Giving orders isn't wrong; it just depends on your rank."

DARRYL   I think so.

HERMAN   Good. Now go back to your office and start running it like a department, not a boot camp.

DARRYL   Yes, sir.

Darryl exits. The people in the project area lower their eyes as he goes to his office. Somewhere, a suppressed giggle is heard. Phyllis enters with a cup of coffee. Herman motions her to shut the door.

HERMAN   Was I too rough?

PHYLLIS   It was terrible.

HERMAN   Well, it's the only thing I could think of to get his attention. If he hates it enough and realizes what he's been doing, maybe he'll change.

Comments

Will Darryl change? Was the manager's objective accomplished? Yes and no.

Darryl will change, out of fear and dismay, but his authority and self-respect have been eroded to a point of no return. Herman, indeed, succeeded in getting his attention, but in so doing, he has gone through overkill and succeeded in destroying Darryl's position with his own staff, with co-workers, and with Herman himself. While shock treatment may be the way some managers conduct a behavior-change interview, the fallout and unforeseen results are too risky to tolerate.

Herman was obviously trying to use his own medicine on Darryl, by giving him orders in front of other people. But he went too far in the measures and has damaged Darryl's credibility and authority. The damage from this miscalculation cannot be measured.

For an employee tutored in "by the book" work and militarylike orders and conduct in a business environment, two things must be considered:

1. Is this a good employee whom I want to keep, to change, and to nurture?
2. Is there a way to make my point without destroying this employee's value to the company?

We must assume that Herman would answer yes to both questions. Therefore, let's explore another way to deal with the drill sergeant.

The Dialogue—Example 2 (continued)

DARRYL   I'm afraid I don't understand this conversation, sir. Is there something wrong with our reports?

HERMAN   Close the door, please, Darryl.
Darryl goes to shut the door and Herman moves over to his small, round conference table and pulls out two chairs. He motions for Darryl to sit.

* ACTION ASTERISK
Now that Herman has gotten Darryl's attention, he is shutting the door and turning the meeting into a formal and private discussion.
HERMAN   That was uncomfortable, wasn't it?

DARRYL   Yes, sir. What was it all about?

HERMAN   It was about management styles. We all have different styles. Some work better than others. Some work in some situations and won't work in others. I'm afraid I won't win an Oscar, but I was trying to act out one kind of style.

DARRYL   Why?

HERMAN   Can't you guess?

DARRYL   I don't think so.

HERMAN   I think you can. I was trying my best to remind you of some officer you must have had in the Air Force at some time in your career.

| DARRYL | Oh? |

* ACTION ASTERISK

Darryl still hasn't made the connection that Herman is seeking. Since Darryl doesn't even suspect that his own conduct is *wrong*, he can't make any connection with Herman's sudden, peculiar behavior. Plain talk is necessary.

HERMAN	I suppose that giving orders has a place in the military. I never liked it very much but I recognized that it had its uses. But I really think it's out of place in an office. That's what I was trying to show you.
DARRYL	I guess you made your point.
HERMAN	I hope so. There are several points I wanted to make today. It may have been a little drastic but we've got some things to straighten out.
DARRYL	Don't worry. I got your message. No more giving orders. I'll ask them nicely from now on to do what we need.
HERMAN	No, Darryl, I'm afraid that's not what this is about. *Asking* someone to do what you want instead of ordering them to do it may be a little more polite. But it misses the point. We're in the idea business. And ideas don't always come on schedule or on order. The military way or the teacher's way doesn't necessarily work in this business.
DARRYL	We have to keep to a schedule. Otherwise, we're out of business.
HERMAN	I agree. But in my experience, you have a better chance of meeting that schedule if people want to work, if they enjoy the work, if they feel like they've made a contribution to that work. You never know where a good idea is going to come from. Your style just doesn't seem to work here, Darryl.
DARRYL	Am I in trouble, sir?
HERMAN	Don't call me sir. You're not in the Army.

DARRYL	Air Force.
HERMAN	(*Laughs.*) Air Force. Let's get down to facts. You spent …what was it?…six years there?
DARRYL	Yes.
HERMAN	We don't call for people through an open door here. We have an intercom system.
DARRYL	Like you did with me?
HERMAN	Glad you noticed. We don't give orders. We work in development teams and we agree on goals that everyone can reach. That way we get the best results.
DARRYL	What happens when you give me a deadline?
HERMAN	The team decides how to reach it. We don't yell out the door and tell them.
DARRYL	What about procedures? What about lines of report?

* ACTION ASTERISK

Darryl is struggling to make the transition. Many, many men go from the military to business and carry their habits with them. Working with them, coaching them, struggling with them is crucial; they must understand that deadlines and orders and disregard for individual needs and choices has no place in the modern, competitive world. Cooperation and enthusiasm make for bigger success. MBO is not old-fashioned when it is practiced properly.

HERMAN	We believe in them, to a point. But they don't work when they're run through an open door with shouts and orders, and you never talk directly with anyone else in your section.
DARRYL	That's not the way I was taught.
HERMAN	You were taught in the military. And you have to forget it. Darryl, you're good. And the work your group turns out is terrific. But we're going to lose them.
DARRYL	What?

HERMAN	Sure. These folks aren't interested in military crap. They're not going to put up with the way you handle the department. They've never been in the military and they never will be. And we don't plan to run the military here.
DARRYL	What do I need to know?
HERMAN	I'll give it to you straight. No more orders. No more calling out your door for your "next in command." You get out there and work with your people and talk with your people. You build a team. You share ideas and build consensus. You got it?
DARRYL	I guess. It will take some work. Those habits are hard to break.
HERMAN	You start today, Darryl. I'm being direct, because I know you understand. But this isn't the style we're looking for. You left the Air Force. Leave it behind you.
DARRYL	I'll try.
HERMAN	You'll do more than try. You'll succeed. You've got all it takes. You just have to realize that the discharge is final and civilian life means sharing and caring.
DARRYL	O.K.

Herman stands and walks around the table. Darryl stands. They walk out the door together and back toward Darryl's office. Herman lays his arm casually over Darryl's shoulder as they walk.

* ACTION ASTERISK

This gesture of companionship is important. It reinforces for Darryl that he is *not* an exile; that he is respected as a part of the company. It also transmits the message to the people in the department that Darryl still has Herman's confidence and that he wasn't summoned to the office to be fired.

HERMAN	(*Softly.*) Come to me if you need some advice. And I'll keep an eye on things. If I see them getting out of hand, I'll talk to you. (*Darryl looks at him. Herman laughs.*) Quietly, I promise! No more shouting through doors. By the way, why don't you have a staff meeting now and

discuss that Firestorm project? See if there are problems. Or maybe even some new ideas.

DARRYL   Good idea. I will.

HERMAN   Fine. (*Shakes his hand.*) And I'll see you Friday with the report.

DARRYL   Right.

Herman goes back to his office.

Summary

Was the manager's objective achieved? Time will tell. But a smart man like Darryl will try very hard to conform to the behavior expected of him. He wants to succeed.

In all honesty, it is doubtful that one conversation such as this would permanently change Darryl's behavior pattern; he has worked in another way for too long. However, Herman has certainly gotten his attention and has set him on the road to staff conferences and consultations.

The next step is to send Darryl to some professional management seminars on interpersonal relationships. Learning new attitudes and habits, away from the office environment and his co-workers, will strengthen his resolve to succeed and give him some new personal tools to work with.

Herman's promise to keep an eye on things and his invitation to come and talk if there are problems reinforce the behavior patterns which are expected by the company, and they make it clear to Darryl that he is not out there alone, either to run amok or to flounder.

14
THE GOOD OLE BOY/ OLD SCHOOL TIE

Introduction

We usually enjoy meeting people who are gregarious and caring, and who show an open respect and affection for family, friends, and acquaintances.

But when that trait becomes "Love me, love my friend," it can become troublesome in the work environment.

We all know the type. No matter what the job opening, they always know someone who is "just right" for the position and expect you to interview them. Inevitably, you have some difficulty explaining why you didn't hire the person. Their regard and advocacy become a very personal matter and can color working relationships.

They want you to hire their friends, they want you to buy from their friends, they want you to do business with their friends—because, of course, their friends are "the greatest."

In addition to causing some awkwardness, there is also the problem of intruding into other people's territory. By circumventing normal channels, by ignoring company procedures, by using personal contacts or leverage, they can take over certain prerogatives or responsibilities belonging to others. Many times this can cause a waste of time or money.

Of course, we are discussing people who do this *unintentionally*. We are not talking about people who deliberately and with calculation avoid procedures or use pull for their own personal gain.

Neither are we talking about people who avoid procedures or get the company to do business with friends in order to perpetrate theft or get kickbacks. That is dealt with in another chapter.

We're talking about the honest, sincere, "good ole boy" who is loyal to the "old school tie," family, and friends because that's just the way he (occasionally, she) is. They don't mean any harm. But they cause it.

And they can drive managers crazy. Yet, how do you stop them from meddling without hurting their feelings or breaking their spirit?

With honesty. With directness. With great care. It should be clear that it is not a personal assault. Neither should it appear to be a job performance criticism. It should be presented as an insistence that they follow proper company procedures, thereby allowing all the people to do their own jobs in their own ways, without interference.

Remember, this type of person is by nature helpful, outgoing, likable. They will have a hard time understanding how those traits can be criticized. Your job as a manager is to help them understand where their concept of helpfulness ends and someone else's concept of intrusion begins.

The Situation

Salvo has policies which forbid nepotism. It tries to discourage hiring family and if it does, it requires that family members do not work in the same departments.

However, there are no rules about hiring friends and, like all companies, particularly those with large sales staffs, it hires people by personal recommendation and reference. A number of people at Salvo knew each other before they worked at the company. It is accepted practice that acquaintances may be recommended for open positions, are usually interviewed, and many times are hired.

As the company has grown, the executives have tried to develop a more general outreach for new personnel, using the skills and abilities of a growing personnel department.

But some of the employees find it hard to break old habits.

The Characters

Bill is a "good ole boy" from North Carolina/Chapel Hill. He had worked in regional sales for a tool manufacturer, a soft drink firm, and a computer firm before he came to Salvo. He is tall, blond, charming, and seems to know everybody in the country. Someone said, "He's never met a stranger." He heads the main office sales team and is on the phone or on the street most of the day. If there is a typical salesman, he is it. Lunch, drinks, dinner, club dates, golf outings, cruises, alumni reunions—all are spent cultivating clients and making them happy.

He is a sentimental, compassionate man, always ready to extend a loan, find a job for a friend's child, introduce someone to someone else. He is very easy to like but some of his traits drive some people at Salvo crazy.

A job came open in MIS and he called Herman six times about his good friend (of three weeks) who had some computer experience and needed a job.

A job in the mailroom came open and he sent a friend's son directly to the supervisor rather than to personnel. That took a bit of undoing before a qualified person was hired.

His daughter graduated from college and he invited Harry to lunch with her. Not until he was there did Harry know he was expected to hire her to write product promotion copy, even though she had no experience and there was no immediate opening.

No one can dislike Bill. But they do throw up their hands in despair at his total disregard for orderly business procedures and the need for less "old school tie" behavior.

His latest effort concerns the main office sales staff "retreat" which is planned for a weekend in about two months. The staff will go to a hotel/resort for a weekend and do a shirtsleeve concentrated workout on new product and new sales techniques.

Bill has a fraternity brother who owns a small hotel/resort about forty miles away. It is a charming place designed for weekend and vacation seclusion. It has a good reputation, twenty-five rooms, a splendid dining room, a pool and tennis courts, and one meeting room used by the local Kiwanis and Rotary.

Bill has promised the deal to his buddy and has announced to Mike that he's found just the place for the retreat. Stunned, Mike has said nothing, knowing that Norman, the V.P. of corporate relations, has a list of such places which the company uses for a variety of purposes, equipped with A/V equipment, a number of sports facilities, plenty of meeting rooms—and a company discount.

Mike is an MBA from Wharton in his mid-thirties and is growing more and more impatient with what he considers these intrusions and diversions by Bill.

What to do about Bill and his promise to his friend?

Manager's Objectives

To terminate Bill's interference with the company plans for the retreat, while keeping his enthusiasm.

To temper his constant breach of company procedures and good business practices.

The Dialogue—Example 1

Bill comes to the door.

BILL   Hi. You wanted to see me?

MIKE   Yes. Come on in.

BILL   Thanks. (*He sits.*)

MIKE   I'm working out the plans for the retreat.

BILL   Yeah. That's a great idea. We haven't had one for nearly two years. It's time.

MIKE   I agree. And so much has happened to the company in two years that it's going to be very important. We're bringing in some people to do some special sessions.

BILL   Great! What's the topic? I know some terrific consultants.

* ACTION ASTERISK

Bill is enthusiastic, as always, and eager to offer a "friend" to help.

MIKE   Well, I don't think we ought to talk about it just now. It's in the development stage and I'm hoping we can make the deal.

BILL   Fine. How can I help? Have you met Chester yet? The place is really terrific.

MIKE   That's one of the things I wanted to talk about. This Chester...

BILL   Chester Scranton. He's from Chapel Hill too. It's a really beautiful place up in Sunnyvale.

MIKE	Yes, Chester Scranton. He called...
BILL	I told him to.
MIKE	Yes. Well, he called and seems to assume that we'll be meeting there.
BILL	Oh, I told him you'd have to handle the contract and arrangements and all that. But he'll bend over backward to give us the best deal. It's his off-season so it can be a real steal.
MIKE	That's something I wanted to talk to you about.
BILL	O.K. Shoot.
MIKE	We've got some problems at Sunnyvale. There's only one meeting room and almost no A/V equipment.
BILL	Oh, Chester can rent whatever we need. And we can use the dining room part of the day.
MIKE	You see, that's very awkward and not what we had in mind.
BILL	It'll be fine. Our folks work best as a team anyway, so they probably shouldn't be split up.

* ACTION ASTERISK

Bill is automatically planning the form of the meetings and Mike is in a negotiating stance with him. This doesn't solve the problem.

MIKE	And there are no health facilities and no golf course.
BILL	We can use the golf course down the road. There are privileges. And he has tennis courts.
MIKE	It's too cold to play tennis.
BILL	We'll probably be too busy for sports anyway. Right?

* ACTION ASTERISK

Bill is being very helpful, working out every problem which Mike presents. It never occurs to him that he caused the problems.

MIKE	I don't know. Norman handles all this. He has other places.
BILL	Oh? I'll talk to Norman, then.
MIKE	No, don't talk to Norman. He's in the midst of arrangements.
BILL	That's O.K. I'll call him. I'm sure we can work everything out.
MIKE	Bill, please drop it. It's not your affair.
BILL	(*Assertive.*) My team's involved in it. It's very much my affair. And when did we get so big we didn't like to get a good deal?
MIKE	Of course we're interested in a good deal. Norman always gets good prices.
BILL	Listen. I've known Ray [the president] for years. And he'd like a good deal. And he'd like to work with somebody we can depend on.

* ACTION ASTERISK

Now Bill is making clear that he's good friends with the president. And since he operates like a loose cannon, he might just call Ray and try to force the Sunnyvale place on the department. Mike can never be sure what he will do.

MIKE	I'd rather you leave it alone, Bill, and let Norman handle it.
BILL	Sure. But if he runs into any snags, just let me know. I'm sure Chester and I can work everything out. Is there anything else?
MIKE	No, not right now. Thanks.
BILL	Sure.

167

Comments

Were the manager's objectives achieved? No.

By being vague and polite, by avoiding confronting the issue directly, Mike lost control of the conversation completely. Not only was he unable to get Bill to desist from meddling in the planning of the retreat, but he never even got around to a discussion of the other problems Bill has caused.

Bill is an open, concerned, high-energy personality who ends up meddling because of his attachments to friends, family, college chums. "Love me, love my friend" doesn't always work in an office. And the only way to deal with it is to confront it directly, before it becomes an insidious, troublesome situation.

The Dialogue—Example 2 (continued)

BILL   Has Chester called?

MIKE   That's something I wanted to talk to you about.

BILL   O.K. Shoot.

MIKE   We won't be going to Sunnyvale for the retreat.

* ACTION ASTERISK
This is a little blunt, but maybe it will get Bill's attention.

BILL   What do you mean?

MIKE   Just that. The place has no meeting rooms, it has no
                health facilities, we can't play tennis in cold weather,
                and a lot of our people like to golf.

BILL   There are golf privileges with a place...

MIKE   Bill! You're not listening. We're not going there. We
                have a whole list of places we use for meetings like this
                which have A/V equipment and meeting space and
                recreation accommodations.

BILL   But Chester is an old friend! I promised him.

MIKE   You shouldn't have. Meeting planning is not your job.

And promising things other people have to deliver is a waste of everybody's time. You've done it too often.

BILL   What's that supposed to mean?

MIKE   I'll get to it. But let's settle this first. You're going to have to call your friend today and tell him that we won't be using his place because it doesn't have what we need for our meetings. Tell him you made a mistake.

* ACTION ASTERISK
It is unlikely that a personality such as Bill's would admit he had made a mistake.

BILL   I can't do that. He's looking forward to this business.

MIKE   Bill, you *did* make a mistake. This isn't your baliwick.

BILL   I think good guys help their friends. What are friends for?

MIKE   I think it's terrific when friends help friends. You're trying to get the *company* to help your friend.

BILL   All right. All right. I'll take care of it. I'll call him.

MIKE   Fine. I'll also send a letter explaining what we require and who's in charge.

BILL   Why do that? I said I'd call.

MIKE   I know. But this way he won't bother you again.

* ACTION ASTERISK
Mike knows Bill. He assumes that in his phone call he will continue to dangle hope in front of his friend, Chester. Mike doesn't want that to happen.

BILL   What about that other comment? About promising things to people?

MIKE   It happens all the time. You're the kindest guy and easiest mark I've ever known.

169

* ACTION ASTERISK
Mike is damning with faint praise or praising with faint damns.

BILL   I'm not sure that's a compliment.

MIKE   I'm not either. But it's the truth. And it gets all of us into trouble.

BILL   I don't get people into trouble!

MIKE   Sure you do. Not real trouble. Just awkward trouble. You make friends every time you go out the door. And then you try to get all of them jobs, usually here.

BILL   Since when doesn't Salvo want to interview employees' friends?

MIKE   That's not the question. It's simply that you seem to have more friends than most and that you completely ignore any formal procedures.

BILL   What do you mean?

MIKE   You went directly to Harry with your daughter when there wasn't any job. You sent your friend's son to the mailroom, instead of personnel. And Herman heard from you, I don't know how many times, about a guy you wanted to place in his department. And now this deal with your friend's hotel. It's only been a waste of time and has caused some embarrassment.

BILL   It sounds like I may be in the wrong place.

MIKE   Of course you're not! And don't get huffy. We're not the same company we were...

BILL   That's obvious.

MIKE   ...and as we've gotten bigger we've had to put in some kinds of procedures and divide up the work. Margie and her people do a very good job in personnel. If you have people you want to recommend for jobs, send them to personnel. They'll get a good hearing and go through the proper channels.

BILL   But I'll want to talk to the managers about them.

MIKE   And you will. They'll use you as a reference and the manager will call you before or after the interview.

BILL   It's not the same.

MIKE   That's not the point. It doesn't put other managers on the spot and it lets you recommend as many people as you like.

BILL   Well...I'll try.

MIKE   I'm sure you will. And when it comes to recommending things to buy and places to go and the like, you have to go to the person in charge.

BILL   But I think Sunnyvale is terrific.

MIKE   (*Patiently.*) You should have given the suggestion to Norman and he would have checked it out. That's his job. And it wouldn't have embarrassed your friend—or us.

BILL   It just seems too formal and set in stone.

MIKE   Would you like somebody to tell you who to hire on your team?

BILL   I love suggestions!

MIKE   But you wouldn't want another department head walking in with somebody and telling you that you *have* to take them because they're so terrific, even though you don't know them, or they have no real applicable experience?

BILL   No.

MIKE   I rest my case.

BILL   But it's not the same...

MIKE   Bill. Conversation over. It *is* the same. Each of us has a job to do and we don't want someone doing it for us. The procedures are there to help all of us. Please go through channels from now on.

BILL   O.K. I'll try.

MIKE   Good. Now, call your friend. And I'll send off the letter.

Summary

Were the manager's objectives achieved? Yes.

While small and medium-sized companies may see little reason for a lot of formal procedures, an employee such as Bill can wreak havoc without them. With the best intentions in the world, these people can allow their affection for "good friends," for "old school chums" to permit them to impose on other people, intrude into other departments and other people's authority, and generally make a nuisance of themselves.

Dealing with them in an honest, straightforward manner is the best thing for everyone. Make clear that the behavior being corrected has nothing to do with their own work and jobs. This is not a job-threatening situation. (It *could* become one if it becomes too persistent and too blatant.) It is a piece of extraneous behavior which must be altered. Moreover, it is necessary to have procedures in place to take care of the situation, in order to make it logical and workable. (Example: It would be ridiculous to stop Bill from recommending people directly if that were the only way that Salvo recruits employees.)

Loyalty to friends is an admirable trait. However, it is a generally accepted axiom that an employee's first loyalty is to the company, its policies, and its future.

15 LOOKING FOR A HOME (Overtime All the Time)

Introduction

Sometime in your life you will have an employee who seems to work overtime all the time. And your frustration will come because it is usually hard to find fault with the employee. There are always logical explanations. There is an excessive amount of work at periodic times, there is special work to be delegated, there is not enough staff for the work. All of these reasons can be valid, and you will hear all of them and more.

The challenge is to determine whether a department needs reorganizing, or needs additional staff, or whether your overtime employee is really "looking for a home."

As a manager who discovers excessive overtime, particularly by a department head or supervisor, you owe it to yourself and to the employee to explore the most logical reasons first. An analysis of the amount of work, the work procedures, the work flow, the performance of all department employees are obvious and initial efforts in evaluating the situation.

It is likely that a thorough examination of the department's procedures will reveal the problem and a reorganization will make the necessary difference. Sometimes people don't work smart, they work hard. That can be remedied. At other times there is quite simply a need for more personnel.

But when a reasonable effort has been made to develop efficient procedures and provide sufficient staff and there is still the "overtime all the time" person, other possibilities must be considered.

Some people are inefficient. You must honestly appraise that and determine whether or not you can live with it or must terminate it.

Some people need to keep a lot of information close to the vest and accumulate a great deal of work only for themselves (much of which could and should be done by departmental staff). This becomes a great test of you as a manager, as you will have to find a way to take away some of the work without taking away their sense of pride or sense of importance. Remember that the work which "only they can do" may be necessary to their self-esteem and to their continuing adequate performance level. (We need not delve into the reasons why this may be so. Quite simply, the esteem they receive at the office may be the only praise or value that they feel they receive anywhere in their lives. Sad, but occasionally true.) This is the "my job is my life" syndrome.

Other people simply like it at the office better than anywhere else. They may be lonely or bored or unhappy in their home lives and find the office, its challenges, its friends, its support systems to be a much more enjoyable place. This can be the most touchy of all overtime problems for a manager to solve. After all, if they're not collecting overtime pay, what harm are they doing? And you have to be careful jumping to that conclusion to begin with. Although you may suspect that they like the office better than their homes, you should never make such an inference or statement. That would be a personal intrusion of high magnitude. However, simply letting them continue to work overtime with no effort to bring them into the company policy and company tradition sets a very bad example for the other employees who may not understand.

There is one other kind of overtime employee, of course. We're all familiar with the employee who comes in early or stays a few minutes late in an effort to impress or butter up the boss. As a coworker, we can be exasperated and annoyed. As managers, we must simply be on our guard, and analyze the situation as we would any other that concerns overtime:

1. Is the work flow well organized?
2. Are procedures being followed?
3. Are the job descriptions pertinent to the department's needs?
4. Are the people filling the jobs doing all that is in the job description?
5. Is there more work than there are people to do it?
6. How should the tasks be redivided?

Just because people work overtime doesn't mean that they are terrific employees. Close inspection may prove that they are just the opposite. Keep an open mind and be objective.

The Situation

Salvo's personnel department is a microcosm of the company's "lean and mean" tradition—that is, it has a small staff and is heavily dependent on the company's computer capability to handle its records and details. The payroll, personnel records, benefits records and statements, and salary administration grade levels and guidelines are all computerized. The software has been purchased and modified for Salvo's use and the programs are run on a confidential basis under the control of the personnel department.

The department consists of a director, a benefits manager who handles all claims, a recruiter/interviewer who screens applicants for job openings, and a very good secretary/assistant. The continued growth of the company has begun to create some strains and it is obvious to all that staff additions must be made soon to ease the strain of growing staff responsibility. It has not been determined what kind of employees are required and when, but there has been talk about an assistant in benefits, another interviewer, another departmental secretary, and someone to devote full time to keeping the systems information up-to-date. This is still in the "talking" stage and no formal job requests have been made as yet. But as the staff works longer hours, and as the work falls behind schedule occasionally, Jane, the vice-president of administration, knows that the requests will come soon.

The Characters

Margie is director of personnel and has been at Salvo for over three years. She is a professional personnel manager; that is, she majored in psychology, has taken a number of courses in personnel management, and has always worked in the personnel field.

She is in her late thirties and takes pride in being the director of personnel at a young, growing company such as Salvo. She sees her future tied to a growing company with great potential and realizes that her own potential for growth is directly tied to how well she performs in a volatile and demanding environment.

Margie is a very private person. She is single, lives alone, and has a highly evolved sense of privacy, which makes her performance in personnel above reproach. She does not gossip or talk about herself very much, nor is it possible for anyone to get any information from her that is rightly private—whether it be salaries, bonuses, promotions, or any of the other information to which she is privy.

She is also a workaholic. Margie has a tendency to "do it all herself" and has trouble delegating her work, even to her small, efficient staff. Her sense of privacy has become more exaggerated as the work has grown, and she does more and more of the work herself. She is in her office by eight-fifteen in the morning, rarely goes to lunch except for business reasons, usually leaves the office about eight P.M., and at salary review time she (and the staff) are often there much later.

Jane is at a loss to know whether the overtime work is caused by excessive demands of a growing company or whether Margie is simply unorganized and masks it with her cool demeanor and her excellent knowledge of personnel departmental requirements.

Jane and Margie are about the same age and have arrived at their positions through different routes. Although Jane has done some personnel work, she has focused on administration and management and believes very strongly in letting the professionals do their jobs. She hired Margie, respects her, has been pleased with the implementation of systems in the department, and recognizes that more work may require more people.

She has become more and more aware of Margie's long hours and realized that something must be done. Either Margie isn't organized, can't delegate, or needs more help. And she wants to set up the opportunity where they can address the incipient problem and solve it.

Manager's Objective

To aid an employee in identifying an overtime/overwork problem and develop solutions.

The Dialogue—Example 1

Margie comes to Jane's door.

JANE   Hi. Come on in and close the door.
Margie does so and sits down.

JANE   You were in early this morning.

MARGIE   No earlier than usual. I'm in about eight-fifteen every day.

JANE   You must be a real morning person. I'm really not much good to anyone until after nine o'clock.

MARGIE   Well, not really. But it's quiet and I can get some of the paperwork done before the phones start ringing.

JANE   I know the problem. I find I can handle that best after five when everyone clears out.

MARGIE	That's a good time, too. I do a lot of the inputting then.
JANE	Doesn't Joanna handle most of that?
MARGIE	She's awfully busy with the phones and the paperwork. Our growth has really swamped us recently.

* ACTION ASTERISK

Margie is touching on the overwork problem and its causes. Now is the time for Jane to get to the crux of the conversation.

JANE	Maybe it's time to get someone else in the department. With so much activity on the terminal, with changes and new hires, it might be time to get a full-time processing person to handle all of that. It will free up the rest of you.
MARGIE	Well, that's one solution. But I'm not sure there's enough work for a full-time person yet.
JANE	With all the inputting that you and Joanna do, plus the benefits and claims, it must be a substantial weekly volume now.
MARGIE	It is. But so far we've been able to handle it.

* ACTION ASTERISK

Why is Margie resisting getting a new staff member? Most managers are pleased to enlarge their staffs and lighten the load.

JANE	Does Rachel still do all the benefit inputting?
MARGIE	Yes.
JANE	As well as all the claims correspondence and new hire sign-ups?
MARGIE	Yes.
JANE	It sounds to me like a pretty big load for both of you now. I'd like to see some statistics on how many personnel transactions you process in a week. Is that too much trouble?

177

MARGIE   No. We can get a run and some totals.

JANE   We'll look at it and my guess is that it's enough to keep someone occupied at least seven hours a day. That would cut down on some of the long hours also.

MARGIE   Well, not really. There is some of that material that no one else should see. I'll have to continue doing it.

JANE   How do you mean?

MARGIE   A lot of what I do is confidential. I wouldn't want someone else handling it.

* ACTION ASTERISK

That's it! It appears that Margie is a close to the vest manager and will insist on keeping some work for herself, no matter *how* burdensome it becomes.

JANE   Margie, *all* the material in personnel is confidential. We must hire only the most trustworthy people always.

MARGIE   Oh, I understand that. But a lot of the material is too sensitive to give to anyone else.

JANE   Is that why you work late at night?

MARGIE   What? I suppose so. I handle material then that I don't want to let out to anyone else.

JANE   Don't you trust the staff?

MARGIE   Of course! They're all excellent and they handle everything with confidentiality.

JANE   So why don't you split up the work differently? Or hire additional staff and divide it up even more, so everyone won't be so overworked?

MARGIE   I think it's pretty evenly divided. I can't see putting my work on somebody else.

* ACTION ASTERISK

What is Margie's definition of "my work"? This conversation keeps going around in a circle as this manager gently but politely declines to do anything about the burdens of the department. She is refusing to delegate, and furthermore, to be prepared for future growth of the company. Remember Jane's objective—to identify the overtime problems and find solutions. So far, Jane has gotten her to agree to submit a transaction analysis, which will show volume of work and work flow.

JANE   Margie, how late do you work every night?

MARGIE   I don't keep track of it. I couldn't really say.

JANE   Do you leave here before eight every night?

MARGIE   Oh, many times.

JANE   Do you work after eight very often?

MARGIE   Sometimes. There are crunch times when the hours are long, like salary review time. But I haven't complained.

JANE   I know you haven't. But I'm aware of the long hours. And it worries me.

MARGIE   Don't worry. I can handle it. I'm used to long hours.

* ACTION ASTERISK
Margie continues to deny that the department's work hours, and particularly her own, are out of the ordinary. In fact, she is "used to it." If Jane can't get her to admit there is a problem they will never be able to arrive at solutions. And at what point is Jane going to get impatient with this? Sooner or later, the department's hours are going to be a reflection on *her*.

JANE   But these are getting out of hand. You're here nearly twelve hours a day, every day.

MARGIE   Is there some problem?

JANE   That's what we're trying to find out. I just know that those kinds of hours are ridiculous.

MARGIE   Has someone complained?

JANE   Of course not.

MARGIE   Is the work done on time?

JANE   It seems to be. But we can't continue this way. Any
                more work would cripple the department. Obviously,
                it's overworked now.

MARGIE   I don't think the staff works too much overtime. It's
                only occasional for them.

JANE   Margie, you're here all the time! You never take lunch.
                You're here on the weekends sometimes. Something
                has got to give.

MARGIE   (*Stiffens.*) I take my work very seriously and I want to
                see it done properly. I don't understand the criticism.

JANE   It isn't criticism. I'm concerned that you're here all the
                time and won't get more staff to do the work. We're a
                growing company and we don't want to find ourselves
                in a bind when it's too late to cope. Don't you *want* to go
                home sometime?

* ACTION ASTERISK
**Whoops. Jane just asked an obvious question but it is too personal for
this conversation. It has been asked almost as an accusation.**

MARGIE   What do you mean by that?

JANE   I just think this has gotten out of hand. You're going to
                have to make some changes so we won't be caught by
                surprises down the road.

* ACTION ASTERISK
**Jane is being very tough and critical out of impatience. She is also giving
orders, not having a discussion. Margie could interpret this displeasure
as a threat to her job.**

MARGIE   What kind of changes?

JANE   We've got to increase the staff, as reluctant as I am to
                say so. Now, what kind of person would you like to add
                at this time?

MARGIE   As I've said, I don't think we need to make an addition
                  at this time. Maybe later.

JANE   Margie, the time is now! We've talked around the bush
                  too long. Do you want a person to do the data input? Or
                  do you want to get an assistant in benefits? What? The
                  fact is, we're *going* to put someone in there to lighten
                  the load. I can't have this go on any longer. We look like
                  slave drivers.

* ACTION ASTERISK

Jane has now made the problem a reflection on her own management style. She's been unable to get Margie to bend or to admit there is a problem.

MARGIE   I resent that. No one works as hard as I do in that
                  department.

* ACTION ASTERISK

Does that sound familiar?

JANE   I don't doubt it. But sixty hours a week every week is not
                  what we had in mind. Place two ads in the papers next
                  Sunday for a data input person and a benefits assistant.
                  We should be able to fill at least one of the jobs within a
                  month.

MARGIE   We don't even have job descriptions yet and we don't
                  know which is more urgent.

JANE   By the time we start interviewing and selecting we'll
                  have them.

MARGIE   That will take some time.

JANE   We don't have any more time. Get them to me within a
                  week and get the transaction analysis to me within ten
                  days. If you want to review any of it first, let me know.

MARGIE   Fine. (*She rises to leave.*)

JANE   Thanks.

Comments

Was the manager's objective satisfied? Only in the narrowest sense. She has taken absolute control of the situation and it is likely that she has alienated Margie in the process. Her impatience has made her take the worst possible course—hiring people without analyzing the full needs of the department. Additionally, she has put even *more* work on Margie right now—the writing of job descriptions and the analyzing of the personnel transactions.

While it is unusual to encounter a manager who likes to work overtime and *likes* to overwork the staff, it can happen. (And they are often more difficult to handle than the manager who is always constantly complaining of overwork.)

In this instance, Jane became impatient with Margie's obvious determination to control as much of the detail as possible and did not direct the conversation toward discovery and solution.

A manager must tread carefully in this situation. There are personal feelings and personal traits involved in this kind of situation. If she wishes to keep this manager, she must salvage the situation without taking over the manager's prerogatives.

The Dialogue—Example 2 (continued)

MARGIE	A lot of what I do is confidential and I wouldn't want someone else handling it.
JANE	*Every*thing the personnel department handles is confidential. I hope we trust all the staff.
MARGIE	We do!
JANE	I'm sure. And we'll hire people we can trust when we expand the department.

* ACTION ASTERISK

Jane is using the word "we," which can be construed as confidential and inclusive or as intrusive.

JANE	I'm worried about you, Margie.
MARGIE	What do you mean?
JANE	I can remember when you came here how much you

loved the theater. I'll bet you haven't been to a show in a year.

MARGIE	(*Laughs.*) Not quite that long.

JANE	How long?

MARGIE	I don't know. I saw the revival of *The King and I* and that was fun.

JANE	It sure was. But you were a regular. I don't mean to get personal, but the hours you are keeping are ridiculous.

* ACTION ASTERISK

But, of course, she *is* getting personal. And she'd better do it with care.

MARGIE	That's what happens in a company that grows as fast as Salvo.

JANE	Well, it doesn't happen to everybody. And I don't see why it has to happen to you.

MARGIE	I don't mind. It won't go on forever.

* ACTION ASTERISK

Now, what does that mean? Is she planning to quit? Or is she going to change the department, finally? Or does she think Salvo will stop growing?

JANE	At the rate we're growing it will only get worse. You know, we have to be careful we don't marry this company.

MARGIE	I'm sorry?

JANE	Oh, you know. It can happen to men or women. We get so tied up with our jobs that everything else slowly falls by the wayside. We care about our companies. We care about our jobs. We see that we have a lot to give to a company's future and before you know it we're spending more time there than with our families or the rest of our lives.

MARGIE	Are you suggesting that's what I'm doing?

| JANE | No. But I'm determined that it won't happen. We've built a good department and we're part of a terrific company. And I'm determined that we don't fall into the trap of everything for the company and nothing for ourselves. |

* ACTION ASTERISK

Jane is getting down to personal matters but continues to use "we." She is trying to make Margie understand that a manager who is "looking for a home" at the company isn't really what Salvo—and she—want.

| MARGIE | That's not a problem here. |

| JANE | And it wouldn't be fair if it became one. There has to be time to go to the theater. And time for Joanna to finish her degree. And time for Rachel to be with her husband. And time for all the work to be done. So we're going to have to divide some of the work. |

| MARGIE | I'm concerned about the confidentiality... |

| JANE | I know, Margie. And it's what makes you such a good director. But the work is there and it's going to take more than four people...now or later. Do you have job descriptions for the data inputter and a benefits assistant? |

| MARGIE | No. |

| JANE | Let's start with that. We'll analyze the number of personnel transactions and see how many are in benefits and how many are in new hires and changes. The total number will let us know if we need someone now to do the data input. And the analysis will let us predict when Rachel will need someone and when you will. When can you have it done? |

* ACTION ASTERISK

Jane is taking decisive steps, but she is involving Margie in gathering the data and making the analysis.

| MARGIE | It will take a while. We're very busy. |

JANE	Let's say a week for the job descriptions and ten days for the analysis. I'll help. Will that be sufficient?
MARGIE	I'll try.
JANE	We'll hire whatever help we need *as* we need. But we can't continue to have you use up your energies pushing paper in the morning and punching a computer at night. We want your mind, not a lot of hours.
MARGIE	I appreciate the concern. But it will be hard to change habits.
JANE	There's something I want to say so there's no misunderstanding. These additions aren't being made to take anything away from you. They're being made to add *more* to your responsibility. As Salvo grows, your department grows and your responsibility grows. And our reliance on you grows. Now, how about Thursday at ten o'clock to take a look at those job descriptions. O.K.?
MARGIE	All right. I'll have them ready.
JANE	Good. (*Margie rises to go.*) And, Margie.
MARGIE	Yes?
JANE	Leave early tonight. Go to a movie.

Margie laughs and exits.

Summary

Was the manager's goal fulfilled? Yes. There was a limited objective and it was achieved.

There are three ways in which the second example differs from the first:

1. Jane took charge of the conversation. She never lost sight of the objective—to get the necessary data on which to base the hire/no-hire decisions and to analyze the work flow in the department.
2. She kept her compassion and interest level high so that Margie would not feel too threatened by a change in her work habits and her department.

3. When she discussed the changes she used "we," subtly assuring Margie that this was a company effort to do the best thing for everyone.

People work overtime for a lot of reasons. It is reasonable to assume, at first, that it is a matter of too much work for too few people, and that is worth analyzing.

But sometimes people work overtime because they're overly protective of their jobs, or because their jobs are more interesting than the rest of their lives. This becomes difficult territory, because you, as their manager, could be dealing with their psychology.

Lesson #1: Keep the conversation on the particulars of the job and ways in which other procedures, more staff, and different work assignments can lessen the overwork. Show concern for the person and make it a joint effort: *We* have to find solutions. As a manager, your concerns are with job performance and employee self-esteem, not with amateur psychology.

16 PEER CONFLICT

Introduction

There are particular problems in the conflicts between peers. They are generally over territory, information, and agenda.

The "territorial imperative" exists not only in the jungle, it exists—and thrives—in the business environment. Transgression into another's territory—whether real or imagined—can cause an obvious problem between peers.

Then there is the stated and unstated rule in business of the "need to know." Who knows what and how does it affect his or her job and performance? While formal guidelines may exist, the informal network operates in every company and can cause severe peer conflict when one employee is informed and another is not. Then there is the complex definition of "information." How much is enough? What form is sufficient? What detail is required? It is sometimes astonishing what is acceptable information and what is not for decision-making. People in different departments at peer level may have radically different opinions about what is sufficient information on which to act. The following scene sets forth one such conflict, but each of you can supply other examples from your experience. It crosses all disciplines and all business services.

Finally, every professional has a business agenda—spoken or unspoken, written or implied. Certain things are uppermost on the list of "things to be done" and others fall farther down. It is probably unnecessary to point out that agendas vary from department to department and from person to person. But in peer conflict, it is usual that the conflict of agendas is the most serious of the conflicts. Achievement of goals is the reason for existence of most supervisory and managerial employees. We need not discuss here the development of those goals or the plans for achieving them. Whether written or implied, goals and agendas are a part of the professional progress of the serious and committed employee. On the peer level, when those personal and professional agendas come into conflict, disaster looms.

It is imperative to state that good business planning precludes this kind of conflict* because it anticipates and directs the personal and professional goals of each department and individual. But we are talking about the ideal world—those companies which engage in a formal business planning process. In those companies where planning is nonexistent and development is improvisational, personal and departmental conflict are more possible and more likely.

Managers have tools and procedures (and just good, common sense and negotiating ability) to deal with employees who have a peer conflict with other employees. The real challenge exists when two employees have a conflict and try to work it out themselves. They lack the boss/employee relationships and must use methods other than dominance to resolve the problem.

This can take many forms. Age can be used to dominate, as can tenure with a company. Connections can be used or implied. Temper and vocal volume are also used. Or they can try reason. One or both can try to understand what the other is trying to accomplish (and if possible, also determine the hidden agenda of each) and try to arrive at some common ground where both can be in a win/win or "I'm O.K., you're O.K." situation.

The last method is usually the hardest. But is is ultimately the best because it allows for resolution without rancor and direction with mutual dignity.

The Situation

The product marketing teams at Salvo are some of the most creative and aggressive in the country. They market the products with a multitude of media choices, working closely with the advertising agency for unified

---

Back to Basics/Planning, by Mary Jean Parson, with Matthew J. Culligan. New York: Facts On File Publications, 1985.

campaigns. The agency ultimately handles the usual media: print, radio, television, and point-of-sale design as well as the co-op advertising with dealers. But the marketing teams enjoy developing point-of-sale demo tapes of the games or programs for use in the dealer stores, and the dealers love them. They are filled with sound and color and clever graphics and are very successful as a sales tool. The sales staff use them as demos when they make sales calls and then leave them with the store owners when they make the sale.

The marketing people work up an outline for the tapes, based on the product content, and then submit them to a development team member in MIS to work out with displays and graphics before the sound is added and the videotapes are recorded.

It is a complex project and a complex relationship, but the results have been highly successful.

Larry has submitted an outline of a new videotape to Eric for development. He has received a memo from Eric, highly technical, explaining (he thinks) why the project won't work as presented. Larry is accustomed to working closely with his MIS counterparts and can't understand why he got a memo instead of a phone call. Furthermore, he can't understand the memo anyway. He goes to Eric's office to straighten things out.

The Characters

Larry is one of the best marketing writers in these projects, probably because he has had both marketing and advertising experience. An MBA from Stanford, he did product marketing research for a card company before he moved to an ad agency which handled a music video account. A Californian by birth, education, and inclination, he has a real flair for this work and turns out jazzy concepts that are eye-catching as well as informative.

He is in his mid-thirties, a small man with a high energy level, a good sense of humor, and a demanding taste for excellence.

He knows what a computer can do but is not a programmer or technician. He is dependent on his MIS counterpart to translate his concepts and schedules into working and exciting displays and graphics.

Eric is new at Salvo and has been assigned to Larry. He is in his late forties, one of the real academics of computer language and systems, having worked in all of them. His last two years were spent as a teacher at a university and it has been hard for him to abandon his teacher image. He spends some of his time with the other programmers teaching them the history and usage of systems and computer language (even though they may not use this information at Salvo) and he delights in developing totally new programs to process already running assignments. He talks and writes in very technical language and has great difficulty communicating clearly with nonsystems people. His attitude, more often than not, comes off as condescending, because he seems incapable of speaking English to them, preferring to discuss a problem or project in "computerese."

The Employees' Objectives

To carry out the tasks which they have been assigned by their managers, without disruptive confrontation.

The Dialogue—Example 1

Larry appears at Eric's door.

LARRY	Eric? Do you have a minute?
ERIC	What? Oh, Larry. Well, not really. I'm pretty busy.
LARRY	It's about this memo. I don't understand it.
ERIC	I'm afraid I can't be any clearer. I detailed all the problems in it.
LARRY	Maybe you did. But I don't understand it.
ERIC	I can't help that.
LARRY	What does that mean?
ERIC	I can't help it if you don't understand. All the information is there, quite clearly stated. Maybe someone else can explain it to you.

* ACTION ASTERISK

Well, there we are. The first insult. That may go over in a college coffee house, but it's pretty lethal stuff in a business office.

LARRY	Nobody *else* wrote it. You did. And I want to know what's going on. That tape has a due date.
ERIC	Well, it can't be done that way. You'll have to rework it and give me something I can use.

| LARRY | That's what I've *always* given the department! Why can't you use it? |

* ACTION ASTERISK
Although Larry's frustration is understandable, he's about to get hung up on the classic "That's the way I've always done it" rather than direct the conversation toward "What do I have to do now" to get the job accomplished.

| ERIC | I don't know what you've submitted before, but... |

| LARRY | Why don't you *look* at what we've done before? Then you'd know what you're supposed to do. |

| ERIC | (*Coldly.*) I don't have to look at other people's work to know what I'm supposed to do. The material you submitted isn't sufficient to develop into a tape. I need to write a whole new set of programs for these projects. |

| LARRY | Why don't you use the ones we've got? |

| ERIC | Because they are jerry-rigged at best. This requires a considerable amount of sophistication and I want to get started on it. But I'll need much more detailed information than what you gave me. |

| LARRY | It was good enough for the other folks. What's your problem? |

| ERIC | Perhaps I'm a little more thorough than the other folks. |

| LARRY | Or perhaps you don't know what you're doing. Listen, Eric, I don't have time to wait around while you play with formulas and slide rules. This assignment is due in two weeks and you'd better get cracking. |

* ACTION ASTERISK
Now Larry is using "you're the new boy on the block and my project takes priority so listen to me and do what I say."

| ERIC | Don't talk to me like that. I'm not interested in dealing with hypersensitive amateurs who don't know what they're doing and know nothing about systems. |

* ACTION ASTERISK
Now that we're into name-calling, it is safe to say that the conversation will proceed downhill all the way from here.

LARRY   Amateurs! Listen, buster, I don't know where you came from, but these little videotapes we turn out happen to sell product which happens to pay your salary!

ERIC   Then it stands to reason that better tapes will sell more product.

* ACTION ASTERISK
One suspects that it's a little too late in this conversation for logic.

LARRY   So suddenly you're a marketing genius?

ERIC   No. But I know *my* business. And there's a better way to do this. But I need better information from somebody who has a passing acquaintance with systems and programming.

LARRY   Listen, Eric. I don't know what you're trying to prove. But I know my job and I've been doing these videos for two years. If you can't handle it I'm sure Herman can find someone who can. But I'm not going to screw around with memos and insults and esoterica while you try to figure out what the hell we do and what you're supposed to do.

ERIC   I know what Salvo does. And I know what I do. And I know that what you gave me is insufficient to produce anything but garbage. I don't do garbage.

LARRY   Looks to me like you don't do *anything*. You write enough memos, you find enough faults, you sit around and develop enough new programs—you won't have to produce anything for months. That's a great racket, Eric.

ERIC   Did you *read* my memo?

LARRY   I sure did.

ERIC   Then what's your problem?

192

LARRY	It's all gobbledegook! I don't want a memo. I want a program and a tape!
ERIC	Then you'll have to be more accurate in your request.
LARRY	The hell you say! Those outlines have been good enough for other people. What's your problem?
ERIC	They are technically inconsistent and therefore they cannot be done.
LARRY	Why?
ERIC	Because I say so.
LARRY	(*Pause.*) My God. You sound like my father when he couldn't think of a good reason to keep me home.
ERIC	(*Coldly.*) This conversation is going nowhere.
LARRY	Oh, no, it isn't. It's going to Herman's office. You're unbelievable. Why don't you go back to the classroom? (*He turns to the door.*)
ERIC	Larry! (*Larry looks at him.*) Don't you understand? I'm here to make it better. If we have better specifications we can work on a universal program. All this improvisation will stop, and ultimately we can create more tapes faster, and probably make them better.

* ACTION ASTERISK

That's a nice speech, and it makes infinite sense. However, it should have come at the beginning of the scene, not at the end. Then Larry would have had an idea of what Eric's agenda was and perhaps they could have worked something out.

LARRY	Sure. Meantime, I've got a deadline. Thanks a lot, Eric. The next voice you hear will be that of your boss.

He storms out.

Comments

Was the peer objective achieved? Of course not. Larry and Eric are now on a collision course and the argument has moved up the ladder to Eric's boss and will probably move up to Larry's boss.

This is a classic example of conflict over territory, information, agenda.

Larry considers the videotape *his* territory because its concept and use are his responsibility. He can't understand why Eric won't defer to his judgment and direction.

Eric considers the information *his* prerogative, because his training and experience have taught him "garbage in, garbage out." If the initial specifications for a program are faulty or incomplete, history indicates that the finished product will probably be faulty. He doesn't understand why Larry does not defer to his experience and knowledge.

Both men have different agendas. Larry wants to get on with the work, just as he has done many times in the past. Eric wants to take the time to develop a proper program which can be used many times in the future.

Larry has tenure and his success at Salvo on his side. Eric has his experience and expertise, which are the reasons he was hired into the department.

Both people have the need to get this project into the win/win column. The problem is, how do they both achieve their agendas within the time frame allowed?

The Dialogue—Example 2 (continued)

ERIC   I'm afraid I can't be any clearer. I detailed all the problems in it.

LARRY   Well, I never made any pretense at being a programming whiz. And I don't understand it.

* ACTION ASTERISK
Larry is still "hanging loose." He's deprecating himself a little while he tries to find out more about this man and this problem.

ERIC   Maybe someone else can lead you through it.

LARRY   That's possible. But it isn't relevant. You and I have to work together, so *you've* got to lead me through it. And I'm going to have to lead you through it.

ERIC   I don't understand.

LARRY   (*Sits down.*) Eric, let me explain. We've been doing these tapes for two years. The sales people love them. The dealers love them. They're always done under a deadline, unfortunately. And they've always been done from my description—like this one.

ERIC   That description is totally inadequate for a workable program.

LARRY   Maybe so. But it's what I've always done, and the programmers have made them work.

ERIC   Then they've been lucky.

LARRY   Have you looked at any of the other stuff?

ERIC   No.

LARRY   Don't you think that might help?

ERIC   I don't need help in programming. Whatever was done was obviously a lot of improvising. I want to devise a program on a sound basis which we can use with a few modifications from now on and know that we'll be getting the best possible results and with very little additional effort.

LARRY   How long will that take?

ERIC   I won't know until I see your request with all the specifications spelled out. That's why I sent you the clarifying memo and then you can fill out the spec sheet.

LARRY   Eric, this is due in two weeks!

ERIC   That's impossible.

LARRY   Tell that to my boss!

ERIC   I will if I have to.

LARRY   And then he'll be on the phone to your boss.

ERIC   That still won't get a program written.

| LARRY | This is unbelievable. I've been doing this for two years and I've never had a problem. |

* ACTION ASTERISK

He may have had a problem, but none like this one. He now knows that the two agendas are widely divergent because he needs a tape in two weeks and Eric wants a perfect tape. He'd better use all his marketing skills to find a compromise.

| ERIC | I want to get a program in so we never will have another problem. |

| LARRY | Eric, we've got a real problem right now. I've got a deadline I have to meet and you're going to have to help. We simply can't reinvent the wheel in the middle of the race. |

| ERIC | I understand your problem. But I have to do it the best way I know how. I was brought in to redo a lot of the programs for more consistency in the future and that's what I have to do. |

| LARRY | Couldn't we do both at the same time? |

| ERIC | What do you mean? |

| LARRY | Let's get someone else in the department to work with us. |

| ERIC | What would that accomplish? |

| LARRY | Debbie has worked on a couple of these in the past. Let me ask Herman to loan her to us for a few days. Maybe she can help get this one done in two weeks, but she can also act as our interpreter. |

| ERIC | Our what? |

| LARRY | Our interpreter. She can explain what I need, in your language, so you can start working on an all-purpose program. And she can explain what you're trying to tell me, so I'll know what I'm supposed to be supplying to you. |

ERIC	That sounds like a waste of her time.
LARRY	Not if it gets the job done. What do you say?
ERIC	Well, it's highly unusual. I don't really think it's necessary.
LARRY	But you'll work with her if Herman will assign her for a few days?
ERIC	Of course. If it can get us started.
LARRY	Terrific! (*He rises.*) I'll go do one of my wonderful sales pitches on Herman. And on Debbie. I'll get back to you later.

Summary

Were the objectives achieved? Yes, in the matter of resolving peer conflict. Both men kept their tempers and never lost sight of their individual objectives. Who knows whether or not the project will be completed in two weeks? But if Herman and Debbie cooperate, it has a good chance of success.

Instead of fighting over their individual agendas, each man realized that an "interpreter" might be able to bring together their conflicting styles and conflicting goals. A "bridge over troubled waters" is often what's needed in peer conflict. It's easier to agree to outside help when one party does not wish to gain dominance over the other. That was the case in this scene, and the project has a chance of success with the introduction of a third party.

Perhaps more than any other confrontation, peer conflict is the place to pause, reflect, and remember. Stop before the conflict becomes emotional. Reflect on what has been said up to that point and try to analyze the signals which the other person is giving off. And remember your agenda: What is it you are really trying to accomplish? Then let your imagination search for ways to get back on that track.

17 LET'S YOU AND HIM FIGHT (Peer Conflict II)

Introduction

Even in the best of all possible worlds, people sometimes don't get along. They can disagree on the way certain tasks are to be performed. They can have so-called personality conflicts (some people simply don't have the same chemistry as other people and these differences can cause problems in the work place).

Managers must be on the lookout for conflicts among their employees—and in themselves. The best manager defuses the situation early on, not allowing the problem—whether tasks, conduct, or chemistry—to reach a level which is disruptive and affects behavior on the job.

No one is suggesting that this does not take wisdom, sensitivity, and alertness. It does. But when a company operates on basic MBO principles, the chances are lessened that conflicts can occur because emphasis is placed on goal-setting, performance, review, and reward. All employees are focused on acceptable tasks and the manager is regularly and intimately involved in the process, so surprises are rare and employees, frankly, don't have time to get into conflicts. Their energies are directed toward shared personal/company goals and there is little leeway for conflicts with other employees who are also self-directed and company-motivated.

Conflict *can* occur, however, and the most likely place is on the peer level. Two people of equal status, with personal and departmental goals, can, without regular interaction and communication, find themselves in conflict over methods or activities. Because of their peer status, both will fight (probably) for dominance and the results can be time-consuming and, occasionally, destructive.

If they are both strongly motivated for success (some would say stubborn or ambitious) they are unlikely to "give" in such a circumstance. This is where their manager must step in clearly, decisively, and quickly to defuse the conflict, make operational decisions about the work being endangered, and focus their attentions, again, on their separate tasks. Lines of communication must also be reestablished to avoid such a conflict in the future.

As we have stated before, we are talking about *good* employees. We are not talking about people who are deliberately trying to invade another person's territory or take over another person's department. We are not talking about people who are deliberately trying to make trouble for another employee for destructive purposes. Those are rotten apples in the barrel and ultimately, no good for any company.

We're talking about peer conflict between people who are dedicated, perhaps over eager, who unknowingly or unwittingly tread into another's territory and, for whatever reasons, can't retreat from their positions. This is where the manager must jump in and rectify the situation. Letting them fight it out may work fine in a boxing ring but it is ridiculous in a work situation.

There are several things for a manager to remember at this juncture:

1. Finding fault can be destructive unless it is pointed out that *both* were at fault (even the injured party can't be perfect.)
2. Finding that both were right in some regard helps to reassure and reinforce their good conduct in the past, and in the future.
3. Quietly talking to each party privately is at first the best way to try to refocus their energies on the real tasks.
4. If that fails, both should be talked with, together, and the argument must be stopped then and there, forever. It must be clear that any continuance will be laid at both doors and that both will be held responsible for the serious consequences which will follow.
5. Solutions must be immediate, achievable and important to both parties.
6. Both parties must be sent away with specific tasks to perform.
7. Apologies and handshakes are more than polite formalities. In our culture they seal bargains and cement agreements. Use them.

8. Be sure that lines of communication are *required* to be open in the future so that a repeat of the problem is impossible.

Nobody said that being a manager was easy. *Human* relationships (remember the introduction?) present its greatest problems, and its greatest opportunity for pleasure and reward.

The Situation

Salvo has achieved success in the sales and marketing of its software product through a very simple formula: It performs its market research, develops its media and merchandising campaigns, and designs its ads and product covers by *product*; it sells the product through person-to-person contact by team and by *region*.

While there is great deal of interaction at the development stage and regular and orderly feedback from the field staff to the regional managers and then to the marketing staff, the lines of responsibility are pretty clearly drawn and respected. Until now.

Josh, the executive V.P. and one of the founding partners, has gotten complaints from both department heads (Sales and Marketing) that the other is invading his territory. There have been some verbal clashes in both their offices. Their respective staffs have talked about it at lunch and at the after-hour watering holes. And Josh is startled to have complaints from two people he respects very much. In each case, he has asked them to pull back from the conflict and devote their time to business, but to no avail.

Mike, V.P. of sales, got tired of waiting for the marketing department to complete the marketing plan for a new office software package which was eagerly anticipated by a lot of the regional distributors and chains. So he wrote a sales letter to all of them, describing the product and inviting them to reserve their orders through the sales staff, in anticipation of its roll-out.

Blake, V.P. of marketing, was furious at the letter, which he felt was a slap in the face to his department, implying that they were late. And he was also annoyed because the marketing plan would focus more on individual customer sales, individual stores, and mail order, not necessarily on the big chains and franchises.

His annoyance was further compounded when the orders started rolling in as a result of the letter, because they would have to be filled when the product was manufactured. This would delay shipments to individual stores and mail order to individuals, because of the production schedule already in place.

What a mess! Josh can't believe that his two chief executives are fighting because of a product's sudden *success*. He has decided to call them in and talk with them together.

The Characters

Mike is an MBA from Wharton with a penchant for the "show biz" type of selling. His strategies are well thought out and he sells them with flair, being a particularly good wordsmith.

Blake has an MBA from Stanford (Josh's alma mater), is dynamic and very creative. His skill at targeting markets has helped make Salvo a success.

Manager's Objective

To calm the troubled waters between two peer managers and refocus their attention away from the conflict and back on their respective jobs.

The Dialogue—Example 1

Mike and Blake arrive at Josh's door at almost the same time. They nod briefly to each other and enter.

JOSH

Come in. Sit down. Close the door, please, Mike. (*They do.*) You know why you're here. I'll get right to it. This argument between the two of you has got to stop.

MIKE

I'd be glad if it did. He's been carrying on for nearly a month about one letter.

BLAKE

That one letter went to a lot of people it shouldn't have.

MIKE

They're buying software.

BLAKE

They're not the ones we should be selling to.

MIKE

Tell them that.

BLAKE

I wish I could.

MIKE

I'll bet you do. Since when do we ration software sales?

* ACTION ASTERISK

Josh is letting them go at each other without taking charge of the discussion. While it might be considered good to let them vent some pique, it should not be allowed to build into another full-scale argument.

BLAKE

Since we know what our production schedule is and who is our target market.

MIKE	Maybe there's something wrong with the target market.
BLAKE	What! We've worked on this research and plan for three months and we damn well know what we're doing!
MIKE	And we know what we're doing. We're selling software!
JOSH	Hold it. Hold it. Just stop right there. I don't believe you two guys. You sound like you work for different companies.
MIKE	I know who *I* work for. And we're selling the hell out of the product.
BLAKE	You've taken the steam out of an entire marketing campaign, is what you've done.

* ACTION ASTERISK

Josh has let the argument start up again, without taking charge.

MIKE	If the campaign had been on time we wouldn't have any problems.
BLAKE	You don't build a campaign on whim! We had to work out details.
MIKE	We have to keep our customers happy.
JOSH	Now, stop it right there. I've heard about all of this I care to. If this is the way you've conducted business for the past month, no wonder the staff is upset. Now, cool it. Mike, why did you send the letter?
MIKE	To let our distributors and dealers know the details on the new program.
JOSH	Why didn't you wait until the marketing plan was ready?
MIKE	Because it was three weeks late already and we were getting inquiries.
BLAKE	I told you that we had...

JOSH	Hold it, Blake. I'll get to you. What's happened with it?
MIKE	We've gotten about a 30 percent return. All of them with orders.
JOSH	That sounds pretty good.
MIKE	I thought so.

* ACTION ASTERISK

Josh seems amazingly uninformed about all of this. He has known about the argument but hasn't bothered getting any of the details regarding the cause or results.

JOSH	What's your problem with all this, Blake?
BLAKE	Several things.
JOSH	Like what?
BLAKE	For starters, we didn't know anything about it.
JOSH	We can fix that. What else?
BLAKE	It's selling the wrong segment of the market.
JOSH	Selling is selling. What's your problem?
BLAKE	Of course it's selling! Our research always showed that the distributors and chains would buy it. About 40 percent, in fact, so we're running close to estimate. But our real giant market will be mail order and individual specialty stores. That's where our major campaign will go.
JOSH	So what's wrong?
BLAKE	We won't have the product when we launch the campaign! The current production will be absorbed by these advance orders.
JOSH	I see.

* ACTION ASTERISK
It's about time.

JOSH   Well, this is what we're going to do. We'll use the current production to go along with the mail-order marketing plan. Then we'll fill these orders later.

MIKE   But the dealers will squawk!

JOSH   They'll get over it. You write them another nice letter and tell them it will be a little late. If they want it, they'll understand.

* ACTION ASTERISK
Josh is compounding the problem, getting Mike back in the letter-writing business again, this time about production problems.

BLAKE   We'll still have fulfillment problems with this overlap.

JOSH   I'll talk to Martha. Maybe she can hold off on one of the other programs and get the production house to double up on this one right now.

* ACTION ASTERISK
Now he's screwing up another program's production schedule and dumping part of the problem on another department.

BLAKE   That could cause some problems.

JOSH   Not for long. Now for you two. I want you to stay out of each other's business. Mike, you're to write no more letters to customers. And Blake, I want those marketing plans developed on time from now on. Is that clear?

MIKE   Clear.

BLAKE   Yes.

JOSH   Good. Let's have no more arguments. Thanks for coming in.

Comments
Was the manager's objective achieved? Only in the broadest sense. He

has probably stopped the arguments, for a time, and he has sent them back to work.

However, he has made a series of faulty business judgments regarding this incident and he has given two impossible instructions to two highly creative people:

1. He has told Mike to write "no more letters" when, in truth, Mike's ability to communicate with the customers is fundamental to his work, and he has also contradicted himself by telling Mike to write a letter to the distributors explaining the problem.
2. He has told Blake to "get the marketing plans developed on time" from now on, as if that were a creative procedure which can always fall comfortably into a set time frame.

Josh was neither prepared nor judicious in solving this conflict.

The Dialogue—Example 2 (continued)

MIKE   Maybe there's something wrong with the target market.

JOSH   Hold it! Hold it, fellas. That's the end of round ten. Fight's over, everybody wins.

MIKE   Sorry, Josh.

BLAKE   Sorry about that.

JOSH   Yes, well, let's solve this problem.

BLAKE   It may be past solving.

JOSH   People have problems, people solve problems. I want to talk about solutions.

* ACTION ASTERISK
Josh has defused the argument by shaming two managers and has told them that he wants to get at solutions, not blame or pursue the argument.

MIKE   The real problem is that we have another success on our hands.

JOSH   Well, it's a bit more than that. First of all, I've asked the two of you to stop this argument between you, but it's just kept growing.

BLAKE   Because the problem has kept growing.

MIKE   The orders have kept growing!

JOSH   I don't want any more of this! Now let's talk some specifics. Blake, the marketing plan was late. There's no need to hash it over, but I want to avoid the problem in the future. What happened?

BLAKE   The research came in with several strange trends so we had it done over.

JOSH   It was late. Who caused it? You, or the research company?

BLAKE   We had it done over because the trends were inconclusive.

MIKE   But we were promised a deadline.

JOSH   Quiet, Mike. We know that. Why didn't you change the roll-out calendar, Blake?

BLAKE   I guess we got bogged down in the details. It slipped.

JOSH   Is that going to happen again?

BLAKE   No.

* ACTION ASTERISK

Josh is working through the tedious details like a high school principal. But he has defused the argument. And it is unlikely that Blake or Mike will ever forget the discomfort of this conversation or repeat its causes.

JOSH   Mike, the letter was obviously a hell of a sales letter. We may use the idea again in the future. However, next time I'd like to know about it—in advance.

MIKE   I understand.

JOSH   I'm not sure you do. Next time—if there *is* a next time—I'd like to know about it from both of you.

MIKE   How's that?

JOSH   Offering a product to a market segment without everyone signing off on it just can't happen. Look at the problems now. If we get into a bind again, you and Blake need to work out an interim solution together. Do you understand?

MIKE   Yes.

JOSH   Good. The idea was terrific. But now we're all left to clean up the mess.

* ACTION ASTERISK
Josh has reprimanded and praised at the same time. He doesn't want to stop creative solutions to problems, but he doesn't want them done independently in the future.

MIKE   It won't happen again, Josh.

JOSH   I know. But now, what do we do with our production problem?

BLAKE   We could postpone deliveries to the distributors.

MIKE   We could get the production house to drop another line and double up on this one.

JOSH   We could make everyone mad at us.

* ACTION ASTERISK
He wants to point out that instant solutions are not necessarily the answer.

JOSH   Why don't we tell the truth? Or most of the truth?

BLAKE   What do you mean?

JOSH   Why don't we send night letters to all the distributors and chains which have ordered and tell them that the product is so popular and the demand is so great that we have trouble filling the orders?

MIKE   Great idea!

JOSH   Let's tell them that we'll fill their order in thirds and that we're putting our production house on overtime.

BLAKE   They'll love it. Maybe we can build more demand!

JOSH   Well, we *will* put the production house on overtime so they can get us out of this tank. And Blake?

BLAKE   Yes?

JOSH   Would you put a line in the mail order ad asking for thirty-day delivery? That will give us a little breathing room.

BLAKE   Right.

* ACTION ASTERISK

Now they are rolling. Everyone is enthusiastic about the solutions and the fact that they have another winner. The argument is almost forgotten.

JOSH   Mike, draft the night letter and let me see it this afternoon.

MIKE   You've got it.

JOSH   Fine. Let's get to it. (*They stand.*) And, guys. Shake hands. (*They pause and then do so.*) Let's never forget we all work for the same company. From now on, let's talk to each other—*before* we get creative. (*They laugh and leave the office.*)

Summary

Was the manager's objective achieved? Yes.

Why? Because Josh had done his homework *before* the meeting and he painstakingly led them through the *solutions* during the meeting. He didn't let them rehash the arguments. He wanted to solve the problem and prevent it from happening in the future. Their shame at this meeting will probably guarantee that.

But, most important, he never lost sight of the customers and the company's reputation.

The plans devised are designed to address those two issues. Moreover, he focused the attention of Mike and Blake on those constituencies.

There is always the possibility of residual anger and resentment when peers collide. However, by *insisting* that communication take place and creating a necessity for it, the problem can be avoided more often than not.

The thing that cannot be avoided is managerial assertiveness. Remember, you never want to kill a good idea. And you never want to stymie an employee's creativity. Don't let two employees fight it out. Bring them together and insist that they find a workable and cooperative solution. Peer conflict is a destructive element in business life. Nip it in the bud.

18 NO PLACE TO GO

Introduction

The Peter Principle has become a part of business language since Dr. Laurence J. Peter and Raymond Hull wrote their famous book in 1969. While the book covered a series of promotion blunders with wit and insight, most of us remember it for its fundamental premise—that disaster can strike when employees are promoted a step beyond their capacity to function well, to their "level of incompetence."

There is a converse situation which can be equally devastating—at least to the employee involved—and it can be called the "no place to go" syndrome. This can occur when an otherwise good employee reaches a cul-de-sac on the job ladder and is stymied from other promotions. He or she is faced with annual reviews and raises with no hope of achieving greater responsibility or substantially higher income.

This can occur for a variety of reasons. The company may be in a no-growth or stable mode with no need for departmental reorganization or promotions. The company may have little turnover, at least in the department under consideration, with no opportunities for promotions. The employee may be very good in the present spot but not qualified for openings which do become available. The employee may have reached an age when creativity and advancement are not considered by the company (many times, wrongly) to be in the best interests of the department. The manager in charge may simply be one of those people who prefers hiring from the outside rather than giving current employees a chance at a promotion.

All of these conditions, and more, can inhibit an employee's chances for advancement. If the employee is content in the current position (and happily, this condition prevails in many instances), the manager is still confronted with the necessity of developing ongoing challenges with that employee to keep enthusiasm and productivity from going stale, as well as finding ways to reward that employee with more than the year-end cost-of-living increase and modest merit bonus. Companies generally operate within pretty tight guidelines for such increases (particularly publicly held companies) and managers need to be creative in developing incentives and reward structures which can keep employees productive in the face of no promotion.

The first consideration is incentive. No matter what the company, the department, or the condition which causes the problem, there are usually some special projects which need attention. This can be as simple as planning the entertainment for the Christmas party to as complex as an analysis of departmental growth. Long-term employees with a dedication to and knowledge of the company can offer considerable insight into problems as well as ideas and suggestions for fun and profit. Open communication channels as well as specific requests and assignments give opportunities to employees in the promotional cul-de-sac to continue their active participation in the company's destiny. Remember the credo of the good planner/manager: You never know where a good idea will come from, so don't stymie communication and participation.

But good ideas should have their rewards. It may be an unnecessary reminder, but asking an employee to do some extra work, a special project, creative thinking, without a reward at the end of the exercise could simply be viewed as extra work! Reward follows incentive, as does night the day. Otherwise, all you may get is grumbling and resentment.

Those rewards can be plaques for the "idea of the month," theater or sports tickets as a thank-you for doing a task especially well, paid time off for a lot of overtime above and beyond the call, paid vacation for employee and spouse/family for a particularly successful activity, a nice bonus check for significant achievement. None of this is going to break the bank in a company, and none of it requires restructuring a department or creating a promotion which is not really a promotion.

(As a note, it is especially sad to see companies create titles and jobs for older employees which everybody recognizes as a sham. They are moved up and over and out of the way. They are rendered useless and the action is embarrassing to everyone, including the employee. Usually this occurs because a younger employee is ready to go into the slot and the older employee is "promoted sideways" to make way. Wouldn't it be better to find a *real*, useful special assignment with real incentives and real rewards in such an instance?)

Remember the triangle: A company is concerned with the public, the shareholders, and the employees. So is the manager. All of us are employees, and we should never forget that third side of the triangle. "Et tu, Brute" could ring in our own ears someday.

The Situation

Salvo's products department has provided most of the reasons for the company's growth. Recently, its development area has been separated from its services area (see Chapter 9) and Martha has been promoted from director of production to vice-president of services. One of her staff, Pat, has been promoted to the director slot and everyone is happy with the growth of the company and this recognition of two of its employees.

All except George. For three years now he has been on the same peer level as Martha and suddenly now she's his boss. Although he does not think he could have done the job of overseeing the three departments, he's not comfortable with the fact that she is overseeing his work. Further, he has seen her assistant get a promotion to his level and wonders if he too is going to get a promotion.

He has mentioned it to a couple of his buddies at Salvo and has also touched on it lightly at Martha's office party celebration. She is sensitive enough to hear the signals and has decided she needs to talk with him quickly to stop any trouble before it starts.

The Characters

Martha is in her early forties with a background in a public relations firm and a publishing house before she came to Salvo nearly four years ago to head the production department. She is organized, with good design and writing skills, and works well with people. The product services department people were happy to see her get the promotion because she has always taken time to understand their problems and help find solutions. They know they'll have a "shirtsleeves" boss with her in charge.

George is in his late fifties and has been with Salvo for three years after many years in a fulfillment house for a major magazine chain. He has liked working at Salvo because of the dynamics of the place, but Martha's promotion has shaken him up. He has never had any greater ambitions than to run his own department very well, but this had made him uneasy.

He knows he has a few years left before retirement and he's not sure whether or not he's been passed over in a reorganization of the department.

Manager's Objective

To allay the fears of an employee that his performance has been found wanting and to find challenges for him in lieu of a meaningless promotion.

The Dialogue—Example 1

Martha has called George to her office. He arrives at the door.

MARTHA   Come in, George. Sit down.

She closes the door and then sits in the chair opposite him rather than behind her desk.

* ACTION ASTERISK

This immediately takes away the boss/employee confrontational relationship and turns the conversation into an informal meeting.

MARTHA   I wanted to talk over any problems you have in your department and to see if there's anything we need to be working on.

GEORGE   Everything's fine. We're very busy, but that's nothing new.

MARTHA   That's good. Do you have any staffing problems I need to know about?

GEORGE   No. We're O.K. now. If the pressure continues, we may have to add someone, but so far we're O.K.

MARTHA   I'll need to review your personnel roster with you. Why don't we meet again next week and you can bring me their schedules and their evaluations so I can get familiar with them.

GEORGE   Sure.

MARTHA   How do you generally cover their vacation time?

GEORGE	We lay on a little overtime. And usually I take on a summer worker—usually a student—who covers for the boys while they're away.
MARTHA	I see. Does personnel find that person for you?
GEORGE	They help. But mostly we get referrals.

* ACTION ASTERISK

George is being cooperative and very precise. But the conversation is very stilted and very formal. He is obviously wary at this meeting and probably a little resentful.

MARTHA	George, I was somewhat concerned about your comment at the party the other night.
GEORGE	Oh? I'm sorry.
MARTHA	No. It's nothing to be sorry for. I mean, it bothered me that you seemed concerned about my promotion. You must know that I have the highest regard for you and I have little interest in interfering with the way your department is run. I've always thought you did a splendid job.

* ACTION ASTERISK

Martha should be careful. In trying to reassure George that he hasn't been passed over and is not in danger, she may go too far and abdicate her authority over him.

MARTHA	I'm planning to set up regular weekly staff meetings so we can keep on top of any problems.
GEORGE	Who will be at the meetings?
MARTHA	You and Gladys and Pat.
GEORGE	Pat will be there?
MARTHA	As director of the production department, now, of course. If we keep the meetings brief and to the point, we can all be aware of problems and plan for them in advance. (*George grunts noncommittally.*) I know that

you have seemed somewhat concerned about Pat's promotion. I wondered if you wanted to talk about it.

GEORGE   Oh. I'm not worried about Pat's promotion. She's worked real hard for that spot.

* ACTION ASTERISK

Martha has confronted the issue with a direct question, but it's the wrong question; she knows his concern is about *her* promotion. This circuitous question could lead either to confrontation or to lying.

MARTHA   She sure did. The fact is, this reorganization can be real good for all of us. We can concentrate on our work, set policies, develop new procedures, hire new people if we need them. It can be a very exciting time.

GEORGE   I guess it can.

MARTHA   Where's your enthusiasm? Now you've got somebody right here to talk to. You can get my attention. I don't have a hundred other things on my mind. It's what you've been talking about for over a year.

GEORGE   I guess I just wonder what you have to do around here to get a promotion.

* ACTION ASTERISK

This is a comment heard a lot in offices and more often than not it is the bleak product of no motivation, no incentive, no reward.

MARTHA   Oh, George, don't feel that way. Salvo is growing. It's constantly changing. It's never the same one month to the next. I'm sure that if things keep on at this rate there will be a promotion for you just down the line.

* ACTION ASTERISK

Now she's done it. In her eagerness to reassure an older colleague on whom she must depend to get a good job done, she has promised a promotion which doesn't exist. Either one will eventually have to be created or George will continue to become more and more despondent—and less cooperative.

GEORGE   What kind of promotion?

MARTHA   Oh, I don't know. Something is bound to develop from our growth.

GEORGE   Oh? Then there really is nothing definite.

MARTHA   Well, I wouldn't say that. With all the acquisitions we've been making, somebody is going to have to get them organized. That's bound to be worth a promotion eventually.

GEORGE   I see. More work, huh?

* ACTION ASTERISK
George isn't fooled, or thrilled, at this point.

MARTHA   Well, you know the rules. More work, more reward.

GEORGE   Whose rules are those?

MARTHA   That's just good business practice. Now, what's a good day for our staff meeting? I want to set it so it's convenient to everyone.

GEORGE   One day's as busy as another. Anytime, I guess.

MARTHA   Good. I'll send out a memo. And thanks for coming in. It's going to be exciting building this department and growing as Salvo grows.

GEORGE   Sure.

Comments

Was the manager's objective achieved? No.

In fact, she may have worsened the problem by indicating that George would have more work to do. And even though she dangled the possibility of a nonexistent promotion in front of him, he was not fooled.

Martha's major mistake in this meeting was coming to it *unprepared*. She knew that George was bothered by her promotion and although he might not feel he had been passed over, at his age he must be concerned that he had been passed by. She should have thought out the significance of that, especially because of their age differences, and have developed some way of putting him at his ease on that issue as quickly as possible.

Also, as managers, we have all had the thought, "What do you have to do around here to get promoted?" If the answer isn't apparent or the opportunity forthcoming, employees can react with despair or bitterness. In this case, Martha was rash to promise a promotion which may not exist. However, she should make George aware of opportunities, of incentives which will have rewards.

The conversation could have been handled in a more productive way.

The Dialogue—Example 2 (continued)

MARTHA   George, I was somewhat concerned about your com-
            ment at the party the other night.

GEORGE   Oh? I'm sorry.

MARTHA   There's no need to be sorry. This whole thing
            happened so quickly that it really took us all by surprise.
            Don had obviously been thinking about it for a while
            and when he moved, he moved very quickly. What it
            really means is that he has heard our pleas for more
            order and more direction and better procedures for
            service.

GEORGE   Well, that's good.

MARTHA   Indeed it is. We have the chance now to really analyze
            the problems and develop solutions to them. I feel
            certain he will back us in any reasonable
            recommendations we make.

GEORGE   Good. We've made plenty of them in the past.

MARTHA   And I wanted to talk about that. I think those
            recommendations, and the fact that few were im-
            plemented, were a sure sign that we needed more focus
            and a reorganization.

GEORGE   Probably.

MARTHA   And I want to show my appreciation for all you did in
            those.

GEORGE   It was my job.

217

MARTHA	It was more than your job. And I'm grateful for all those suggestions. Have you and your wife seen *The King and I?*
GEORGE	No.
MARTHA	Would you like to?
GEORGE	Sure.
MARTHA	Good. I'll get tickets. You let me know a good date. Maybe you could have dinner out with Neil and me before you go to the show.
GEORGE	That would be fine.
MARTHA	It's just a small thank you for all your help and encouragement since I've been here. Besides, it will be nice to see your wife again.

* ACTION ASTERISK

This gracious gesture accomplishes several things. It makes it clear to George that Martha respects and likes him and that she is trying to thank him personally for all his cooperation in the past—the assumption being that he will continue to cooperate in the future. She is inviting him and his wife to dinner with a gentleman friend and herself, but at a restaurant, not at her home. This keeps it professional but with a personal touch. Moreover, she will be the host of the evening, implicitly in charge and in the guise as his new boss.

GEORGE	I'll ask her about dates and get back to you.
MARTHA	Good. I also want to set up regular, short weekly staff meetings so the four of us can review matters and stay on top of problems. Is there any day that's particularly bad for you?
GEORGE	Things are pretty busy all the time.
MARTHA	O.K. I'll check with Gladys and Pat and then I'll let you all know when we'll meet next week. There's one other matter I wanted to talk with you about.
GEORGE	Yes?

MARTHA   It appears that Salvo is going to continue making acquisitions and, of course, every one of them will have their own fulfillment arrangements.

GEORGE   Tell me about it. We've had to deal with some of their problems already.

MARTHA   I know. And we need to have an orderly way of doing it. You shouldn't be confronted with a problem every time we buy a new company. By the same token, I don't want to make extra work for you.

GEORGE   What do you mean?

MARTHA   It seems to me that you might want to spend a couple of days in each place to figure out what they do right and what they do wrong. What should be consolidated into a larger department and what they should continue doing for themselves.

GEORGE   That could take some time.

MARTHA   Yes. And you don't have a lot of it. However, as Salvo grows, your department is going to grow. We may want all fulfillment jobs under your jurisdiction.

GEORGE   It would make more sense to consolidate some of it. We've tried to help them piecemeal, but that's no good.

* ACTION ASTERISK

Now George is getting into it. He sees the challenge of coming up with ways of saving the company money and making things more efficient. He also has been around long enough to know that if he is given more responsibility, more departments to supervise, he can probably get a promotion or at least more money.

MARTHA   Why don't you give it some thought? If we could schedule you to visit the other shops over the next few months, we'd have a better idea of what is needed. You might also think about bringing their supervisors in here for a day or two of training.

GEORGE   Good idea. I'll see if I can work it out.

MARTHA   Fine. Let me know the date for the theater. And I'll be in touch about the staff meeting.

Summary

Has the manager's objective been achieved? Yes.

Martha was prepared to stroke him and reassure him that she liked him, respected him, and depended on his continuing good work.

We can also assume that she will have a similar conversation with Gladys, the manager of complaints and refunds.

She knows that she can't succeed unless they help her. So she is making gestures which assure them that she cares for a team effort: dinner, show, weekly staff meetings, review of problems, asking their ideas and advice on future plans.

She has also given George the opportunity to improve his future. She has promised him nothing, but she has presented him with some problems with their acquisitions which he is invited to study and try to solve.

If he succeeds in making improvements, at the least, it should mean a bonus. If the department expands, it could mean a promotion—a real one. The main thing is that the opportunity has been put in his hands to help shape his own destiny. He is not simply a forgotten cog in the wheel.

19
THE COMPANY THIEF

Introduction

Theft by employees is a horrible fact of business life. Periodic news reports set the rate of employee theft at 10 to 20 percent, with the highest rate occurring at year-end holiday time.

Theft can take all forms, from the removal of company pens, pencils, and paper, to unwarranted use of photocopy equipment and supplies, to the removal of electronic equipment and software, to padding and overstating expense accounts, to deals made with suppliers to divert company purchases to other premises. Kickbacks and payoffs are not unusual and more company employees are quietly terminated and some turned over to the authorities than ever reach newspapers and trade journals.

Collusion and graft are an unfortunate part of business and seem to be increasing in American business, particularly as international trade and investment grow. "Baksheesh," the "payoff," the "bribe," are such a fundamental part of other cultures that the impact on traditional American honesty (if it ever existed outside myth and propaganda) is growing every day.

How does a manager fight it? Taken from an overview, it could appear as hopeless as bailing a sinking boat with a teacup. But the simple fact is that stealing—in any form—is wrong. It robs the company; it robs other employees; and it robs the shareholders, who are the ultimate owners of the company.

In the best companies managers are assumed to be honest. They have *become* managers because upper management trusts them to be honest caretakers of the company's resources. If they are dishonest themselves or if they blink and turn away from dishonesty which they discover, they betray that trust and join a long line of crooks in the destruction of American business and a healthy American economy.

If you find yourself in a company where everyone seems to be on the take and part of an underground, illegal conspiracy to get what they can at company expense—get out. It is unlikely that one person will be able to change anything. And in trying, that person may make enough waves, cause enough people discomfort, or tread on enough toes to be fired or ostracized anyway. Sometimes the "take what you can get" attitude permeates a company so completely that only sweeping changes from the top can make a difference.

In other companies, naivete or inattention may have allowed organized stealing to take hold. In those situations, change is possible. Locating the culprits, proving the accusations, and creating procedures which eliminate the possibility of theft are actions which an honest, concerned manager can take.

Two items are key:
- proving the accusations
- initiating procedures for eliminating the chance of theft

While it is an axiom among security people that no system can be devised which is absolutely foolproof to a determined thief, orderly procedures can make it more *difficult* to steal and, therefore, thwart the amateur or the faint-hearted. Further, the procedures should have warning systems in them which trip up the determined or persistent thief.

It's a sticky business. None of us likes the thought of doubting the integrity of one of our employees. That's why procedures, applicable to all, are so advisable. They keep the employee on an honest road, with the understanding that everyone is expected to walk that road and that the penalties can be severe.

This is another instance where a *written policy*, distributed to each new employee and redistributed once a year (with other important ones such as those relating to drug use, antisolicitation and sexual harassment), is fundamental to protecting the company's interests (see example in Appendix). The policy should state clearly what is expected of the employee and what will not be condoned.

Penalties for infraction, from reimbursement to dismissal, should be made quite clear. The policies should be enforced promptly and universally.

One more word: If upper management is *perceived* as a group of people who take all they can get from the company, who bend the rules because they are "boss," no procedures or policies will have meaning—"monkey see, monkey do." If the boss can get away with it, so can I.

Honesty is contagious. The ideal is to have an epidemic of it at your company.

The Situation

Salvo has a large office supplies department which buys, receives, and assembles all the working materials for the company. When the staff needs supplies, they make out a requisition which is filled and delivered. The requisition then becomes the tool for internal "billing" to each department for its office supplies cost each month, as each item has a standard charge based on cost.

There is normal office supply usage, and a large use of computer paper, as the company has many departments which use terminals and printers. The volume of computer paper is quite large.

No one has ever really worried about the precise use of supplies. The amount bought each month is never quite the same as the amount requisitioned and billed each month, because the inventory in the storeroom makes up the difference.

The Characters

Angelo runs the department with discipline and a great deal of flair. He bargains for good prices with Ralph, in purchasing, keeps the storeroom in spic and span shape, and is a friend to everyone. He seems to know everyone by name and is always very helpful and prompt. In his late thirties, he is a family man with two children and a snappy dresser who always has a good joke.

His clerk, Phol, is a Cambodian refugee who is intense with a ready smile and quiet efficiency. They are a very competent pair and keep a very busy place functioning very well.

Dorothy, the office services manager, is pleased with the efficiency of the place and does spot checks every two or three months to be sure that the supplies are being ordered at a good price and that the billing of the requisitions goes to accounting in a timely manner.

Imagine her dismay when Phol asks to see her one evening after work and tells her that Angelo is stealing from the company. She is dumbfounded and asks what proof he has. He says that he has none. But he has seen it and when he confronted Angelo, he was told to mind his own business or he would be fired. Since he desperately needs the job, he has come to Dorothy because he is afraid he will eventually be blamed for the thefts.

Dorothy asked how the thefts were accomplished. The answer was rather simple. Angelo ordered computer paper in bulk each month. The truck arrived at the delivery dock after six P.M. with the load. Angelo signed for the order and he and Phol took three-fourths of the order upstairs. The other one-fourth was driven away by the driver, who was in business with Angelo. He sold it elsewhere and they split the take.

The theft was difficult to catch because the stock rested in inventory between the time of purchase and the time of requisition. That float allowed Angelo to lift one-fourth of the order each month, with no one the wiser.

Discover the Proof

Without revealing that she is suspicious of any wrongdoing, Dorothy calls Harold, the manager of internal audit, to run a check on the delivery and inventory procedures to confirm that they are functioning properly.

After a couple of months, he reports back to her that the purchase order system and the requisition and bill-out system for supplies is working fine. The delivery and inventory systems seem to be O.K. but are difficult to confirm because the float between delivery and requisition makes it practically impossible to audit the inventory absolutely. He did discover some delay in the accounts payable area and has spoken to Joe, the controller, about it, initiating a "tickler" system for more prompt payment of bills.

So Dorothy is right back where she started. In an attempt to get an outside, disinterested party (internal audit) to provide proof of guilt or innocence, she has merely confirmed what she already knew: The honesty of the operation is based on the honesty of the supervisor, Angelo.

What to do?

She decided to call in Angelo and change some procedures to see if she could gauge Angelo's reactions and determine his guilt or innocence.

Manager's Objective

To discover the truth or falsity of the accusation and to cope with the problem if the employee is guilty.

The Dialogue—Example 1

DOROTHY   Come in, Angelo. Thanks for coming up.

ANGELO   How's everything going?

DOROTHY   Oh, I'm slowly getting into the swing of things.

ANGELO   Well, it's always rough in a new job.

DOROTHY   It's just a matter of getting organized and putting in some procedures which will accommodate our growth.

ANGELO   No one would have believed our growth when we started. We can sure see it in our area. I was talking to Ray [the president] about it the other day. It sure is different from the old company.

DOROTHY   Oh? What old company?

ANGELO   I came here with Ray. The other place was so stodgy compared to here. No growth. No excitement. No real autonomy in each area.

* ACTION ASTERISK
This should be a flag that Angelo is "in" with the president, Ray; in fact, Angelo seems to have been brought to Salvo by him and has known him for a long time. She now knows she must tread carefully.

DOROTHY   I'm sure. In fact, I want to talk about your area a little bit.

ANGELO   Oh?

DOROTHY   I've been working with some of the other departments to see where all of us in office services can improve our act. I've also been looking into our departments to see if we can work smarter, not harder.

ANGELO   That's a good idea. (*Laughs.*)

DOROTHY   Right. I want to help you cut down some of your own long hours. We want to set up a procedure so that all our deliveries will be made during office hours.

ANGELO   Oh, I don't mind doing that. And besides, it's easier to get the elevators after hours.

* ACTION ASTERISK
Is Angelo protesting because he's truly a dedicated employee or because this will complicate his deal? Dorothy cannot know.

DOROTHY   Well, actually, I've talked with the building management and they would prefer deliveries during business hours. That way, they don't have to keep as much staff on at night. And they've promised to give us very responsive service with the elevators.

ANGELO   That will take Phol and me away from the stockroom more during the day.

DOROTHY   Well, I've tried to help you in that regard, too.

* ACTION ASTERISK
Dorothy continues to pitch these changes as if they were to *help* Angelo. This is fundamental in getting employees to cooperate in making changes anyway, but in this case, it takes the place of appearing to make change because she is unhappy with Angelo's performance.

ANGELO   How?

DOROTHY   I've talked with Joe, and he needs the signed delivery slips as soon as possible to take advantage of discounts. So when a delivery arrives, you call accounts payable and one of them will arrive to help in the check-in.

ANGELO   How will that affect me?

DOROTHY   This way, either you or Phol can go down and do the check-in, whoever is free. Joe will get his signed P.O.'s on time and you won't have to work extra hours just to check in supplies! Everybody comes out ahead. What do you think?

*ACTION ASTERISK
Dorothy hopes that her enthusiasm for giving smething to everybody will be well accepted by Angelo.

ANGELO   Well, I don't know. I don't need help with the check-ins and I'm not sure Phol can handle it. And I'm still worried about those elevators.

DOROTHY   Well, we won't know until we try, will we? I'm happy to give Joe what he needs. And I'll be happy that you don't have to work overtime anymore.

*ACTION ASTERISK

Dorothy is refusing to hear the reluctance in Angelo's voice and continues her upbeat enthusiasm. She's determined to make these changes in procedures to try to stop any theft which may be going on.

ANGELO   I don't know...the vendors may not like it.

DOROTHY   Oh, they're used to delivery hours. I've asked Ralph to notify all his vendors by mail, so there will be no misunderstanding. He will do that this week.

ANGELO   I see.

DOROTHY   And Joe wants to start the clerks at the delivery dock as soon as possible. So let's start tomorrow. That is, if anything arrives tomorrow. Is that O.K.?

ANGELO   Sure. If that's what you want.

DOROTHY   Good. Do you have the number in accounts payable? It's 482.

ANGELO   Yeah. O.K.

DOROTHY   Terrific. And I hope this will help ease up on some of our problems. Thanks, Angelo.

ANGELO   Yeah. Sure.

Comments

Was the manager's objective achieved? She won't know for a while. She has set some procedures in motion which will make it impossible for Angelo to steal, if he has been doing so, because he can't let the truck drive off with some of the supplies as there will be a rotating series of witnesses (the clerks) on the dock. If he was stealing that way, it will stop.

If he was not stealing, the procedures are beneficial anyway. They keep Angelo from working overtime and they give Joe his accounts payable receipts in a timely way. So everyone benefits.

Like any employee, Angelo will go through some concern and dislocation because of the new procedures, instituted without his agreement. If he is guilty, this will not be the significant reaction. If he is innocent, the procedures should be reviewed in a reasonable time, and modified, perhaps.

It is unorthodox to have an accounts payable clerk on a loading dock. But in a small company, drastic and sometimes creative measures are taken to solve problems. It is unlikely that this procedure will really work as Salvo continues to grow and expand.

What Dorothy wanted was a *witness* to the receiving transaction. A security guard is used in many companies, but they are expensive and obvious. That is not necessarily a good solution for Salvo. Besides, the secret was to have someone with the authority to *read* the bill of lading and be sure that the order paid for was the order delivered. Thus, Dorothy is trying to involve other departments (accounting and purchasing) in helping to solve her problem without telling them her real motive.

This subterfuge has been used to protect the reputation of an employee while verification or refutation of the accusations are explored. While solving the theft accusations is important, the protection of an employee's reputation is paramount.

She knew two things about Angelo: His employee said he was dishonest and the president of the company trusted him because they were old friends.

Who was right?

She tried to analyze Phol's accusation. Did he dislike Angelo and want him fired? Did he want Angelo's job? Was he a troublemaker? Did he want to be in on the take? Was he already?

On the surface, none of that was true. Phol was a quiet, cooperative employee with no signs of greater ambitions. His language barrier limited his employment potential and he seemed very happy to be working at Salvo.

What to do?

Proof of any wrongdoing seemed very hard to obtain. Dorothy should move to the next level of a manager's duties: procedures. She should consider procedures whereby the crucial point—the verification of delivery—would be under another responsibility.

The Dialogue—Example 2 (continued)

ANGELO   That will take Phol and me away from the stockroom more during the day.

DOROTHY	Well, actually, it won't take you away at all. We're getting so big, with so many deliveries arriving every day, by truck and by messenger, and so on, we're going to establish a different system altogether.
ANGELO	Oh? What's that?
DOROTHY	We need to divide up the functions anyway. We need purchasing and we need supplies requisition and inventory and we need accounts payable and we need a delivery function, so we're going to add to staff.
ANGELO	Why does it have to be divided up?
DOROTHY	For starters, it's just good business practice. But I also want to cut back on overtime and get our deliveries during regular working hours.

* ACTION ASTERISK

Dorothy has just laid it on the line. "Good business practice" should make clear that there is a need for breaking up functions, particularly in the matter of office supplies, so that there is little chance for theft or collusion. Or at least, those chances are minimized because they require cooperation among several departments.

ANGELO	So we're going to hire a receiving clerk?
DOROTHY	I'll probably hire at a higher level than that. Although I see it as a one-person job right now, I'd like to have someone there who can head up a department if we grow.
ANGELO	Who will that person report to?
DOROTHY	To me.
ANGELO	Oh. So we won't be doing any delivery receiving at all.
DOROTHY	(*Brightly*.) That's right. We'll divide up the work so it's more evenly distributed. And so there are checks and balances.

229

ANGELO   Why do we need extra help?

DOROTHY   You said yourself that we were going through in-
                credible growth. The time has come to take care of it.
                And to prepare for the future.

* ACTION ASTERISK

It would be difficult for Dorothy to analyze Angelo's reaction just now.
He is obviously not happy with the new development and the removal of
some of his responsibilities. This could be the normal resentment of an
ambitious employee, or the reaction of someone who sees a good deal
frustrated. Dorothy must move forward with her plan, on the assumption that Angelo is innocent.

ANGELO   Is there anything else?

DOROTHY   No. I'll be interviewing as soon as possible, and when
                we hire somebody, we'll all work together to make the
                transition. Thanks for coming in, Angelo.

ANGELO   Sure.

Summary

Was the manager's objective achieved? To discover the truth or falsity of
the accusation and to cope with the problem if the employee is guilty?

Dorothy still does not know whether or not Angelo is guilty. But for good
business reasons she has changed the procedures, making it harder for
anyone to be on the take. Remember our suggestions in the Introduction:
Procedures can make it difficult for people to steal and can thwart most
stealing short of mass collusion.

She has protected Angelo's reputation (presumed innocent) and divided
responsibilities among a sufficient number of departments so that a continuance of the thefts (if there has been theft) is difficult, if not impossible.

Theft, or the suspicion of theft, is no fun for a manager. Coupled with
the responsibility for the company's property and resources is the necessity
to protect the reputation of the employees.

In the 1970s new government regulations required that companies
establish not only guidelines, but step-by-step procedures that, if followed,
would ensure that graft, theft, bribery, and corruption were eliminated
from company practices.

Anyone can break the law. But good policies and procedures make it
more difficult, less likely, and less attractive. While it may seem simplistic,

230

removing temptation and opportunity may be the best move a manager can make.

Dorothy may find that she must take other measures, and so might you in similar circumstances. Security guards on the delivery dock, another person double-checking the deliveries, security monitoring cameras in crucial locations—these and other ideas are applicable to security situations. It is crucial to *find* a thief if there is one, and to prove there is *no* theft, if that is true. The air must be cleared and doubts must be resolved.

If theft *is* discovered and proved, measures must be taken promptly to implement the company policy on the matter. (Refer to the Appendix.) First, there must *be* a policy and all employees must know it. Second, it must be exercised promptly and fairly, for the good of all—the employees and the shareholders.

20 THE UNWANTED ACQUISITION

Introduction

The words "acquisition" and "merger" strike more terror in the hearts of office staffs than any two other words in business language. This fear is the result of some of the mergers and acquisitions of the past twenty years which added bucks to the balance sheet but which thrust employees out on the streets with somewhat less grace than the expulsion from Eden. The career carnage, on occasion, has been notorious.

This pain has been caused, more often than not, by company directive. A company is acquired and hatchet men are sent in to cut costs by cutting people. Little is considered but the bottom line, except for occasional concerns about age or race discrimination suits and, of course, the golden parachutes written into the sales contracts for the few principal employees who are preserved from financial risk.

But it must also be stated that a number of acquisitions, mergers, and divestitures during those years have been handled with creativity, sensitivity, and generosity. People were not forgotten in the company's eagerness for growth and profit.

And today, with golden parachutes the norm rather than the exception for executives, with scrutiny by unions and an assortment of commissions, the dismissal of employees in a merger or acquisition is usually handled with a high degree of concern and fairness.

The onus of that care and concern rests with corporate management—both those acquiring and those being acquired. Negotiating those employee packages up front is (or should be) a part of the whole financial process. If a company is worth acquiring, it is logical to assume that the people working there made it attractive.

Happily, there are precedents and guidelines for decent transitions which principals can reference when they begin the process.

But what happens once the financial decisions are made? Let us assume that the packages for employees to be terminated are generous and fair. Let us assume that the financial details are in place and the transition requirements have been determined. Now we come to the crucial element in the implementation: the *person* who must transmit the information and make the companies' plans work.

The personality of that person, the behavior of that person can make or break the transition plan, both in perception and reality. *How* the plan is presented to the employees can determine how it is perceived and how cooperative they will be in a transition (if one is required).

Preparation is fundamental. The plan must be organized in detail, and ideally, should be in writing for all employees to read and to keep.

The presentation should be done quickly, directly, and honestly, and, of course, with compassion and understanding.

The positive elements of the plan should be emphasized and stated first. The time for fear and uncertainty should be limited or nonexistent. Employees should know what they're going to get. The safety net is the most important thing (for some, the only thing) they will hear.

And the expectations of the company should be clearly spelled out. Are they expected to continue working? If so, what is their reward and what is their cushion? Are they expected to leave immediately? If so, how are they to cope—financially and emotionally—with being thrown into an alien environment?

Preparation, honesty, compassion—the words keep appearing in this book. But since the book is basically about good human relationships, those are pretty good words to use as guideposts for managerial behavior.

The Situation

Salvo has finalized the acquisition of QTC Company. The negotiations have been held confidentially between the principal officers of the two companies. At Salvo, Jim in finance; Judy, the analyst; Herman in MIS, and Joe, the controller, have known about it because they have handled the analysis. At QTC, only the principals have known, because they have quietly supplied all the information to Salvo for analysis leading to the offer.

The employees at QTC have sensed that something is going on, but with no real information they have simply been nervous and anxious; they have had no real facts to go on.

Today, the deal has been finalized. The officers of the two companies have met and prepared the joint announcement with Norman in corporate relations. During the meeting, Ray, the president of Salvo, has reminded Kevin, the president of QTC, that as a part of the acquisition, certain accounting functions will be transferred to Salvo and most of the employees in the QTC accounting department will be phased out. He instructs Kevin to begin to make those arrangements so that there will be a smooth transition. Kevin agrees.

He goes back to his office and tries to decide how to tell Bob, his controller, that the department will soon be dissolved.

The Characters

Kevin is a young, self-made man. He has parlayed a knowledge of computer software programming into an eight-million-dollar business and now has managed to sell that company for a handsome profit. He will not stay with the company. His programmers and sales staff will be absorbed into the Salvo operation, if they want to go. But his accounting and office support people will be terminated, once the phase-in period is completed.

Bob got tired of doing the accounting for a local construction company, and when the chance came to be controller for an up-and-coming software company, he jumped at it. In QTC's four years of growth, Bob has been a loyal and dedicated employee. He's nearly forty and is about to lose his job, because there is no need for a man of his caliber on the Salvo staff. Further, the department of six which he has put together is going to be terminated also.

Manager's Objective

To let Bob know that he and his department are being terminated while keeping their loyalty and cooperation during the transition.

The Dialogue—Example 1

Bob has been called to Kevin's office. He arrives at the door.

KEVIN   Come in, Bob. Shut the door. (*Bob does.*) Sit down. (*He*

234

does.) This is a big day at QTC. (*Bob says nothing.*) I'm sure there have been a lot of rumors around the place over the past few weeks.

BOB   A few.

KEVIN   Well, they can stop now. The announcement will be in the papers tomorrow.

BOB   Oh?

KEVIN   Yes. We've been bought by Salvo.

BOB   I see.

KEVIN   We finalized the deal today and now we've got to get on with the transition, to develop what we want to do.

BOB   What sort of transition?

KEVIN   Well, all the department heads will be meeting with their counterparts at Salvo. We will work on making the software compatible with their systems. And, of course, the marketing people will work with their folks to see where we can get economies in our advertising and distribution.

BOB   Yes?

KEVIN   And, of course, your department will be working with their accounting people so we can make a reasonable transition of our accounts and payroll and so forth.

BOB   Will we be canceling our payroll service?

* ACTION ASTERISK
Bob is getting down to specifics because he thinks the whole operation is going to be absorbed.

KEVIN   Oh, I'm sure that will happen eventually. Salvo has very sophisticated systems which can accommodate this kind of growth. But that's what you fellows will have to work out—what needs to be transferred and when they're going to take it over.

BOB   Then I presume we'll be transferring the accounts payable and accounts receivable too?

KEVIN   Oh, yes.

BOB   Do they have space yet to accommodate all this?

KEVIN   You mean computer space?

BOB   Well, yes. But I was really thinking about office space. When we transfer all this they'll need about sixteen hundred to two thousand square feet just for us and all our files. Have they started planning for that?

* ACTION ASTERISK
Bob is being logical. He is assuming that he and his staff are a part of this acquisition.

KEVIN   I'm not sure what they've planned. The main order of business is to make the transition of material as easy as possible. I'm not clear about the space situation.

BOB   Haven't they indicated when they plan to move us?

* ACTION ASTERISK
There! He's asked the question directly. It's a valid concern and should have been addressed before this.

KEVIN   Well, actually, not all the people here will be going. Our records and programs will be absorbed, but there's no way that they will absorb all of the people. That's what I wanted to talk with you about. Obviously, we want this to go as smoothly as possible. It's a real feather in everyone's cap that in just four years we've been able to build a company which has been acquired by one of the industry leaders.

BOB   Which ones of us won't be going?

* ACTION ASTERISK
It would be understandable if Bob were a nervous wreck by now. Kevin has danced all around the issue without any personal concern for the department head sitting opposite him.

KEVIN	After the transition of information and material, they will take the programmers and marketing staffs. And then the accounting and office staffs will be phased out...
BOB	What?
KEVIN	*Phased* out, Bob. Not fired. That's a long way down the road, several months, I should think. We will gradually phase out the staffs and there will be a very generous arrangement.
BOB	You mean Salvo can't find a place for us?

* ACTION ASTERISK
It appears that Salvo is about to become the bad guy in this situation.

KEVIN	They have complete accounting and office staff as well as plenty of computer power. They don't really need to add people.
BOB	So we're getting the shaft!
KEVIN	Of course not. We have made some very handsome arrangements for everyone.
BOB	(*Sarcastically.*) Other than firing us?
KEVIN	Bob, that's not necessary. No one is being fired.

* ACTION ASTERISK
Really? It sure feels that way. So far, Kevin has given no assurance or safety net to Bob and his staff.

BOB	And you want all of us to stay around here for this "transition"?
KEVIN	Of course. It's in everyone's interest.
BOB	How do you figure that?
KEVIN	That's what I've been trying to tell you. No one has any idea how long the transition will take, but everyone's job is secure during that period.

BOB	I'll bet.
KEVIN	This sale is a bonus to everyone. All the stock which the employees own has tripled by this sale.
BOB	Oh?
KEVIN	Yes.
BOB	Can we cash them in tomorrow?
KEVIN	You can. But they'll probably be worth more if you hold them. They're being exchanged for Salvo stock.
BOB	When?
KEVIN	Immediately.
BOB	Good. There will be a lot of cashing in, I'm sure.
KEVIN	I hope not. But there's more.

* ACTION ASTERISK
Why must this come out in dribs and drabs?

BOB	What?
KEVIN	At the end of the transition, each employee phased out will be given all vacation pay due, plus a month's salary for each year worked at QTC.
BOB	That's only fair.
KEVIN	Actually, it's more than fair; it's more than the company policy. But we want to do it.
BOB	And how am I supposed to keep people working properly when they know they'll be out on the street as soon as the job is done?
KEVIN	I hope their pride will keep them working.
BOB	Pride went out the window about twenty minutes ago!

KEVIN	I hope not. Our bonus plan is a very attractive one.
BOB	What bonus plan?
KEVIN	In addition to the severance and the stock value, Paul and I have agreed to match the stock value one to four with cash for every employee who works through the transition.
BOB	Sort of a bribe, huh?
KEVIN	Bob! I'm shocked at you. And distressed. That's not what it is at all. We had no control over a lot of this. And Paul and I want to reward our people.

* ACTION ASTERISK

This "I'm not to blame" inference simply isn't fair. Salvo could not have bought a private company without the consent of the principals.

BOB	It sure sounds like it from where I'm sitting.
KEVIN	Paul and I want to use these means to thank all of you who have helped in our success. And to make your transition easier.
BOB	It will help, but I don't know how many people will stick around until the end.
KEVIN	We've sure tried to make it worth their while. I'm sure when it's explained, everyone will be happy. Now you go on out and call your people together and I'll join you to tell them about the package.
BOB	Where do you want to meet?
KEVIN	Let's meet in the conference room. I'll join you.
BOB	O.K. (*He exits.*)

Comments

Was the manager's objective achieved? No.

It is hard to imagine a worse scenario for the merger/acquisition trauma. Kevin is obviously suffering from the "I can't face it" syndrome and has not been able to face up to the personal preparation necessary to quell the fears of his employees and assure them that their futures are being protected and their past contributions are respected.

It is obvious from the discussion that the company has made generous and thoughtful arrangements for the employees who will not be absorbed into Salvo. But the presentation to Bob has been erratic, unplanned, and a disaster. QTC is a small company, but that does not mean that "chatting" about something as important as an employee's future is adequate. The presentation needs to be thorough and well planned to give confidence to the people involved.

Kevin has left the impression that he is not really in control and that there is nothing he can do about it. Indeed, that may be true. There are many sales and merger situations where the manager, or even a president, has no control. But they cannot *behave* that way. If they cannot control the actual decisions of who stays and who goes, and have no authority over the severance package (which is unlikely in this instance), they *can* control the way it is presented and the sense of security which they give their employees. They *can* control their *own* behavior. They can take charge of the mood of the situation if not the facts.

This scene was handled badly from the beginning. Let's do it over.

The Dialogue—Example 2

Bob comes to the door.

KEVIN	Bob. Come in. Shut the door. Have a seat. (*Bob does.*) This is a big day at QTC.
BOB	Oh?
KEVIN	We can put all the rumors to rest. Salvo has bought the company and at a very good price.
BOB	That sounds good.
KEVIN	It is. It's a great tribute to four years of hard effort and to our success.
BOB	When is the takeover?
KEVIN	The announcement is tomorrow and the transition will begin next week.
BOB	That's pretty fast.

KEVIN   There's no need to waste time. Salvo is a real go-go company and they want to get us integrated as soon as possible.

BOB   We'll be ready.

* ACTION ASTERISK
Kevin has been upbeat and Bob catches his enthusiasm.

KEVIN   I know. And that's what I want to talk about. I've asked Adele to call a staff meeting in a few minutes with your people and the office services people so I can review all the particulars with them. But I wanted to talk with you first.

BOB   O.K.

KEVIN   Since all of us are stockholders, everybody will be a little better off tomorrow. Our stock will be exchanged for Salvo stock and the buyout is nearly three-to-one in value.

BOB   Terrific! That's a hell of a deal.

* ACTION ASTERISK
By telling the good news first, Kevin has allowed Bob to envision more money in the bank and more security.

KEVIN   It sure is. It's a good payout for all the people who have worked so hard. And it makes me very proud that we made everyone a shareholder, no matter what their job is.

BOB   That's always been attractive here.

KEVIN   Right. And we don't know how long the transition period will be, so we want everyone to know what to expect. Some of the departments will be absorbed by Salvo, but some will not.

* ACTION ASTERISK
A cloud has appeared on the horizon. Kevin's task is to make a terrible event—the phasing out of a job/career—into something which Bob and his staff can see as fair and helpful.

| KEVIN | That's why we've built a very good package, thanks to Salvo's cooperation, and I want to go over it in detail at the meeting. |

* ACTION ASTERISK
Kevin is complimenting Salvo, not blaming anyone.

| BOB | What people will be affected? |

| KEVIN | Not quite half the company. Paul and I will be phased out, and eventually so will the accounting department and office services. |

| BOB | What? |

| KEVIN | Salvo has very complete staff and services in that area, so it is unlikely that anyone from our staff will be needed. However, the whole package is explained in this folder. (*He hands a folder to Bob.*) In addition to the stock trade, we will be paying for all unused vacations as well as a month's salary for every year worked. And, of course, benefits will continue for as long as the person is employed. |

| BOB | That doesn't give us much time. |

| KEVIN | Well, not necessarily. No one knows how long this transition is going to take. We want it to go smoothly and we want it to go right. And our people are the ones that can make that happen. |

| BOB | How can you expect us to stay? |

| KEVIN | Several reasons. In addition to the salary and benefits while you're here, and the stock trade and the severance when you leave, Paul and I have added to the package. We have hired an agency to do the outplacement work for all of you so that you'll have good jobs when you leave. We also will add to the bonus of everyone who stays during the transition. We'll pay each of you an additional one-fourth the value of your stock in cash. |

*ACTION ASTERISK
Kevin has added to the package block by block, reiterating it each time and sweetening it each time. The blow of losing a job has been softened. Further, he has handed Bob a folder which has all the information in detail.

BOB   It's still hard to believe.

KEVIN   I know. It is my great regret that we couldn't arrange that everyone would be a part of the deal. You, particularly. You've meant so much to the success of this company. But there is just no room at Salvo for all of us.

BOB   Who's going?

KEVIN   Our people in programming and marketing will be offered the opportunity. I'll be talking with them later this morning. But I wanted to talk with you and the other people first.

BOB   I appreciate that.

KEVIN   I hope you'll stay. And I hope this package will go a short way in showing you how highly we regard you.

BOB   I'll think about it.

* ACTION ASTERISK
Kevin hasn't won him completely. But he hasn't terrified him or alienated him.

KEVIN   That's all we can ask. Now, come on, let's go meet with your staff and give them these packages and tell them the news.

BOB   O.K. (*They exit together.*)

Summary
Kevin hasn't given Bob time to go off and brood or talk with anyone else. He has leveled with him and made him a party to the meeting which is about to begin.

243

Inevitably, some people will not stay at QTC for the transition; they will immediately look for jobs. But the majority will probably take advantage of the package and aid in the transition. The company has behaved honorably and generously and in an up-front manner. They will probably get loyalty and hard work in return. Most people will opt for the safety of the job while the outplacement firm helps them seek another.

The ostrich form of management will not work in this situation (or any other). The manager's head must not be in the sand. There is no hiding from a painful situation.

Plans must be made in advance and their presentation must be done with clarity and compassion and sensitivity. Kevin came prepared with a written summary of the severance package as well as a determination to give the good news first, so the bad wouldn't stop all communication even before it began.

21
THE EQUAL OPPORTUNITY HIRE

Introduction

It is a sad commentary that there is a need for a chapter on the hiring of people in the "protected classes" (age, sex, race, religion, ethnic origin, or handicap) in a management counseling book. But the equally sad fact is that problems still exist and many managers do not have the benefit of explicit company policies and procedures, sensitivity programs, or training in recruitment and interviewing.

The issues can be overwhelming for the untried, untrained manager. There are federal and state statutes to observe; there are possible company affirmative action programs, EEOC guidelines, company policy, and, of course, company traditions, unspoken and unwritten. All of these elements impact on the behavior of a manager who is in the process of hiring.

If a company has an affirmative action program in which they actually seek out, recruit, and interview women, minorities, and other "protected" individuals, managers are generally sensitized and trained in the do's and don'ts of interviewing. (See Appendix.) In addition, they are usually thoroughly acquainted with the needs of the job and the department as well as the particular desires of the company to increase its minority participation in specific job categories.

But in the absence of a formal affirmative action program, the recruitment is much more informal and managers with the best of intentions and possessing true feelings of equal opportunity in their hearts can make mistakes in an interview. Those mistakes can range from the small to the catastrophic. A manager can ask questions which will insult or alienate a prospect, alerting that interviewee that the company is insensitive to the differences which people bring to the work place. At worst, a manager could indicate during the interview that age or race or sex might limit the interviewee's chances for hiring or promotion, thus opening the way for serious discrimination charges.

One chapter in a book such as this cannot cover the gamut of appropriate and inappropriate behavior patterns in a democratic marketplace. However, we have attached an Appendix of some operative EEO guidelines as well as some suggestions for do's and don'ts in an interview. And our example is an attempt to indicate the best attitudes and behavior for such a situation.

Hiring a minority employee, at least for the first time, can be a touchy experience unless the manager recognizes some basic fundamentals. First of all, he or she must know the company for which they work. Are that company and its executives truly receptive to minority employees, or will the atmosphere be strained in spite of the credentials which an applicant may offer? This should not inhibit the hiring of minorities, but it does warn that the internal support system available to other employees must be maintained for the minority employee or that employee will surely fail. Fitting in can become impossible, and many a fine career has been smashed on the shoals of nonsupport in a hostile environment.

While attitudes and behavior will vary from company to company, it may be necessary to restate the obvious. Equal opportunity is the law of the land and it must be given more than lip service. There is simply no excuse for a managers' meeting which is all white and all male. The "cookie cutter," "someone like me" brand of hiring and management is just not acceptable anymore. Put in its simplest terms, it is blatantly un-American. President Kennedy called us a nation of immigrants; President Reagan called us a nation of nations. Our national marketplace, the people to whom we sell our goods and services, come in all shapes, colors, ages, and origins. The work place must reflect our diversity as well. In an age of universal higher education, the pool of talent, skills, and desire is limitless. When you hear a manager say, "I can't find a _____ who is qualified," your very accurate answer must be, "Then you haven't looked, and you do not see."

Being aware of how other people differ from us does not require treating them differently. It requires allowing their differences space and understanding, but not using those differences to influence how we judge their work.

While prejudice does exist, it is rarely overt and rampant in business today. (Indeed, it has become more subtle and insidious in some ways.) Minority achievers have done well in the white world because they concentrate on the job to be done and don't concentrate on their ethnicity. In so doing, they have showed their white colleagues how to forget color or race and see them as professional people doing a job. Their vision of themselves makes it possible for everyone else around them to be "color blind." It is a remarkable achievement, and when it is in effect, makes for an easy working environment.

It is regrettable that human relations, sensitivity training, and equal opportunity attitudes are not taught in business schools. It would save a lot of agony in the work place later. But enlightened companies with a dedication to training and personal achievement have taken up the challenge and are making a significant change in the American work place and, therefore, in the American way of life.

The Situation

Salvo has attempted to build orderly support departments even as its main business has grown rapidly and its sales and development departments have expanded almost chaotically.

The administration department has added staff often, just barely keeping up with the needs of the company. When the company was only ten people, one person handled the personnel and office services requirements; then others were added. Today the company numbers three hundred fifty employees and occupies two large floors in a downtown office building.

Jane started as a "one man band" and is now vice-president of administration. The personnel director and personnel department report to her, as do all the office services departments (there are six separate departments and six separate supervisors reporting). To sort out the responsibilities and prepare for the future, Jane has decided to hire an office service director to oversee these departments, allowing her to focus on her own administrative duties, space planning, and planning for the future.

She has interviewed nine candidates from the pool of answers she received from the ad, and has narrowed the field to three: a white male, thirty-five; a white female, fifty-five; and a black female, forty-five. All are college graduates and all have at least fifteen years' experience supervising or working in office services departments. She feels that any of the three could do the job but knows that it is an important position in that it requires the incumbent to relate to every level of the company—CEO to maintenance crew. She is also conscious that this is an opportunity to bring in a woman or minority on the director level, strengthening Salvo's position in its EEO policy.

She has called back each of the top three for second interviews and again, feels that the qualifications of each are quite satisfactory. The man had once owned his own business and has a real take charge attitude, something that would be needed in molding a new department. The white woman has been working for fifteen years for various companies. She started working to help put her children through school, and got serious about a career when her husband died. She is soft-spoken but has done a lot of hard problem-solving in her current position. She is eager to manage several departments.

Jane is now about to interview the black woman, Dorothy, and will then make her final decision.

The Characters

Jane is thirty-eight years old and has been at Salvo almost from its beginning. She was a liberal arts graduate at a women's college but took her first job as a media trainee in a small advertising agency. When someone was needed to buy supplies or get new cleaning people, Jane was designated. As the company grew, she slowly became more administrative than media, eventually starting a modest personnel operation, which she headed. She went to the media department of a medium-sized agency and found herself heavily into budgets and plans. She left there for a large ad agency and the second spot in a very sophisticated personnel department. She used the refund program to get an MBA, specializing in organizational planning. When the offer came from Salvo to head up her own administrative department, she jumped at it, seeing the opportunity to grow with the company. She has taken night courses in human resources management and benefits, and recently finished a real estate course in space planning.

She is personable, ambitious, and clearly a multifaceted administrative professional.

Dorothy is forty-five, black, personable, and ambitious. A college graduate, she worked as administrative assistant to the president of a small college, then moved to a larger city working in office services at a real estate firm, an accounting firm, and now a law firm. She has arrived at her current position through on-the-job training, good common sense, and the ability to get along with people. She wants greater responsibility, a larger department, some greater challenges.

She said to a friend once, "I've been black all my life. There is little that can be said or done to me that hasn't been said or done. I figure if I forget I'm black and concentrate on the job, everyone else will forget it too."

Manager's Objective

To hire the best person to oversee a variety of types of employees, who must also relate well with upper management.

The Dialogue—Example 1

JANE

Come in, Dorothy. (*Shakes her hand.*) It's good to see you again.

DOROTHY

And nice to see you.

JANE

Please sit down. (*Dorothy does so. Jane closes the door and sits behind her desk.*) Thank you for coming in again.

DOROTHY

I'm glad you asked me. I'm very interested in the job, as I told you.

JANE

I know. And It's been very interesting talking with your references. Dr. Smith at the college was full of praise even though it had been nearly thirteen years.

DOROTHY

I'm glad. Those were tough times in colleges all over the country. Students had caused problems for a while. And then the maintenance staffs caused headaches. We worked out a very good contract that year. It seemed to satisfy everyone.

JANE

How involved were you in that?

DOROTHY

As Dr. Smith's administrative assistant, I sat in on all the negotiations. As they went on, some of the staff turned to me for separate conversation because they were afraid some of their demands might be misunderstood.

JANE

Why?

DOROTHY

Everybody on the college side of the table was white. A lot of the staff were black. They saw me as a kind of interpreter.

249

JANE   Did you see yourself that way?

DOROTHY   To a degree. I had no negotiating power. But I put some of their demands in perspective for Dr. Smith and he was able to come up with some compromises that worked. Those were different times than now. A lot of white people had never even talked to a black as an equal before. There was some room for miscalculation.

* ACTION ASTERISK
Dorothy has just elaborated on something she had not discussed earlier—only after one of her references brought it up. Yet she seems proud of it. Why did she wait till now?

JANE   That's a very interesting story. Why didn't you tell it to me at our first interview?

DOROTHY   Oh, it was so long ago, I guess. And I didn't think it was particularly relevant to the office services job.

JANE   Do you find yourself counseling employees often?

DOROTHY   (*Thinking she has changed the subject.*) I think any good supervisor is available to staff for counseling, either when the employee needs it or the supervisor feels there is a need. Being available just goes with the territory.

JANE   Are you available to just one kind of employee?

DOROTHY   Excuse me? I don't understand.

JANE   Like at the college. Do you only talk to the black employees?

DOROTHY   I don't quite know what you're getting at. The college situation was one where my race was a help, but only incidentally. It wasn't planned. Nor was it necessary to repeat after the contract was signed.

JANE   So you have no problem talking with other employees who aren't black?

250

* ACTION ASTERISK

Careful! This borders on insult even though Jane needs to know it. It could probably have been phrased, "You've supervised a wide variety of employees. Do you recommend counseling with each of them on a periodic basis?"

DOROTHY   Of course not. Life being what it is, most employees at any company are not black, except at certain levels. I like to think I relate well to all of them.

* ACTION ASTERISK

Dorothy has expressed an opinion, and some criticism, of American companies in this remark. She has shown spunk and honesty; she has also expressed some positive thoughts about herself. How will Jane pick up on this?

JANE   Do you think most companies discriminate?

DOROTHY   I think companies, like people, are different from one another. Women and minorities have to make their judgments based on their own needs and experiences, and the actions of the company they're in at the moment. Don't you agree?

* ACTION ASTERISK

Dorothy has neatly turned the question back to Jane, who is also in a "protected class." She has also made a very definite but very mature and well-thought-out answer about institutionalized discrimination. Will Jane see this as a threat to a young company not tested in EEO waters or will she see it as maturity? Where do she and Salvo stand in this regard?

JANE   Yes, I do. And it's one of the reasons that working at a company like Salvo can be so rewarding. They seem especially color-blind, because computer programs don't have eyes and prejudices.

DOROTHY   How many minority managers are there?

JANE   One of our district sales managers is black: He operates out of Atlanta. Our Denver manager is Hispanic.

DOROTHY   Is there a minority manager here at the home office?

JANE   What difference would that make?

251

* ACTION ASTERISK
Dorothy is using this second interview as an opportunity to do some interviewing herself. Jane's question is out of line, even though she may be trying to find out if Dorothy needs racial support in her working environment. Or is she suddenly being defensive about Salvo?

DOROTHY	I'm not sure it would make any difference. I was just curious, since you spoke so highly of the company.
JANE	Our EEO records are really not a matter of public discussion.

* ACTION ASTERISK
While, indeed, EEO records are confidential, this is a real over reaction. Dorothy did not ask to see them and this could be a real warning to a minority interviewee that "Methinks she doth protest too much."

DOROTHY	Of course not. It was just a general question.
JANE	You seem to have a lot of experiences. I'm not sure Salvo would offer you enough variety.
DOROTHY	From what I've read, the company has a fine growth potential. I think it would offer a great deal of challenge.
JANE	Do you like challenge?

* ACTION ASTERISK
Now, this could put Dorothy on her guard. Where is the conversation leading? And Jane has ignored the fact that Dorothy has researched the company.

DOROTHY	I enjoy challenge very much. When the accounting firm relocated I found it very rewarding to coordinate all the elements. Everyone seemed pleased with the results.
JANE	Did you have help in that move?
DOROTHY	Of course! My staff was wonderful. And all the department heads were very cooperative.
JANE	Who dealt with the executives?

DOROTHY	I did.
JANE	You dealt with all the executives directly?
DOROTHY	As project coordinator it was crucial. I had to be sure that all their requirements were satisfied in the new place.
JANE	Were there any problems?
DOROTHY	There are always problems. Some picture doesn't get hung quickly. Some file cabinet goes to the wrong office. But we were straightened out within the week.
JANE	In a case like that, wouldn't it be better to allow someone who understands an executive's needs to do that?

* ACTION ASTERISK

The implication here is, "You're black and female. How do you know what an executive needs?" Boy, is that insulting!

DOROTHY	It's my job to discover everybody's needs and to try to accommodate all of them within budget and policy.
JANE	What about your staff? What sort of people have you supervised?
DOROTHY	All sorts. I've been working a long time.
JANE	Do you have any problems with the young ones?
DOROTHY	Not particularly.
JANE	Do you sort of play the mother image with them?
DOROTHY	I hope not. I try to give direction and support to everyone who works for me. Each company has its own policies and customs. If we all work within those, there are few problems.
JANE	Do the older men resent you?
DOROTHY	Not that I know of. I think respect is a two-way street. I

253

respect people who do their jobs well, and I hope it pays off.

* ACTION ASTERISK
The above questions are a roundabout way of asking, "How do people work for a middle-aged black woman?" Anyone would see through them—and be insulted by them.

JANE   Do you have any questions to ask me?

DOROTHY   Well, yes. Is it possible to tour the premises and perhaps see some of the people I might work with?

JANE   No, that's impossible. A lot of our premises are restricted.

DOROTHY   Of course. I understand.

JANE   (*Standing.*) Well, thanks for coming in. If I think of any more questions I'll call you. And you'll hear from me within the week.

DOROTHY   Thank you very much. I look forward to it. (*She exits.*)

Comments
Was the manager's objective achieved? Not really. Jane probably won't hire Dorothy because this final interview really didn't assure her of the compatibility between interviewee and company. She will have to fill the position with one of the other two candidates, neither of which is a minority person.

The above interview went wrong for two reasons:

1. Jane operates on the assumption that a black woman has trouble with staff and other management when she occupies a position of authority. As there is no indication of that in her background or references, it is a ridiculous assumption and undoubtedly based on an inner prejudice.
2. Her roundabout questions never addressed the issue of race directly: How have you coped so well and gotten so far in a prejudiced world? (The implication was there all the time and manifested itself in

gratuitously insulting questions. Again, Jane *assumed* a problem rather than dealing with the individual sitting in front of her and trying to know her better.)

Questions which *imply* race problems can only close doors to communications. And yet the interviewer must find out if the interviewee has hang-ups or is a well-balanced professional individual. Addressing the circumstances directly is the best solution. As always, honesty is the best policy.

The Dialogue—Example 2 (continued)

DOROTHY   Is there a minority manager here at the home office?

JANE   Well, no. But there are several women. And we have several minorities in the "slot," so to speak, in sales and programming and office services.

DOROTHY   That's really what matters. The *possibility* of mobility is almost as important as mobility itself. That's why I was so happy at my two other jobs and want to move from my current one. The others let me learn and grow and take on new challenges and move ahead. I know if I stay where I am now I'll be doing the same things ten years from now.

* ACTION ASTERISK
Is Dorothy too ambitious? Can Salvo give her enough challenge? Would she be unhappy here?

JANE   Do you think Salvo could offer enough variety for you?

DOROTHY   I don't doubt it a bit. I've done some research on the company since we first met and it seems to have a very exciting future according to most writers. And for someone in office services that's always good news because you know the company will be growing and you'll always have new problems to solve.

* ACTION ASTERISK
Two things have been stated here: Dorothy has done research on the company, which shows a high level of interest and initiative. And she is

255

confirming that she likes to solve problems—a good trait in any employee, particularly in office services.

JANE	Mr. Langley indicated you had quite a lot of challenge when that company relocated.
DOROTHY	(*Laughs.*) Indeed, we did! They had not expected to move for at least another two years. But the building was sold and the rent was tripled. So we accelerated our moving plans and it went off pretty well.
JANE	Were there any really big problems?
DOROTHY	There are always problems in a complete move. But we coordinated and planned each step in advance with all the department heads and paid special attention to the chief officers. Accountants are very particular people, you know. We wanted to be sure that each was happy in the new location.
JANE	Who handled all of that?
DOROTHY	I was project coordinator. With all requests coming to one person, we felt we could keep track of everything better. It worked out well.

* ACTION ASTERISK

This indicates that she worked with all department heads, from chief executive on down, and got high marks from her boss. Jane knows that the accounting firm is basically white-male, so she is reassured that this mature, black woman can relate well with others, even in stressful situations, such as a move.

JANE	So Mr. Langley said. What were the age groups there?
DOROTHY	What do you mean?
JANE	What were the ages of the people you worked with?
DOROTHY	All ages. Our mail room and print shop were mostly young men. Our cleaning staff were mostly older women. Security and maintenance were all ages. It was a well-integrated staff, I might add. Our chairman was in his sixties and my boss was in his thirties.

JANE	Did you have any problems?
DOROTHY	None that I'm aware of. Mr. Langley could answer that better than I. The real challenge was to prove that I knew how a press should be maintained and whether I could do more than change a light bulb. I respect the people who work for me and try to delegate their work in a reasonable way and provide them the staff and tools to do their jobs. I ask a lot of questions. It's the quickest way to learn something. And most people are happy to talk about their work, not just about their problems.

* ACTION ASTERISK

This is a good answer. It is confident without being arrogant and it connotes an open mind without suggesting ignorance or humility.

JANE	Do you have any questions of me?
DOROTHY	Well, yes. I may be premature, but I would like very much to see the premises here and perhaps even to see some of the people I might be working with. It might make me think of some other questions.
JANE	Actually, that's impossible, before you're hired. Many of those areas are off-limits to visitors.
DOROTHY	I understand. I guess I'm just eager to see the possibilities.
JANE	That's understandable. But there will be plenty of time for that. When could you give notice?
DOROTHY	At my current job?
JANE	Yes. When could you start with us?
DOROTHY	Within two and a half weeks! I'll give notice tomorrow and start here on Monday, the eighth.
JANE	(*Rising.*) Very good. (*Holds out her hand.*) And welcome to Salvo.
DOROTHY	Wonderful! I look forward to it. (*They shake hands.*)

JANE	Report here that Monday morning and we'll get all the paperwork done before we go to your office.
DOROTHY	Thank you. I really think it's going to be a terrific experience.
JANE	So do I. You bring what we need to the job. I look forward to working with you.
DOROTHY	Thank you. Good-bye.
JANE	Good-bye. And I'll see you the eighth at nine A.M.

Summary

Has Jane made a good decision? Without witnessing the other two interviews, it is impossible to know with certainty. However, she *did* fulfill her objective of hiring an experienced director who relates well with all levels of staff and management. And she fulfilled an implied, if not stated, objective of increasing the minority managers on the Salvo staff.

If a company is receptive to employees of all races and ethnic backgrounds, the conduct of the interviewer is crucial in the selection process. In the above example, Jane made her decision based on *business* questions. She had checked the references Dorothy had provided and found that her professional performance in a variety of situations had been excellent. So her skills and qualifications were not in question. The interview was conducted to find out how Dorothy would react to questions and situations in which her race might be an issue, but the questions were not *asked* that way. In each case, Jane brought up an incident in her background where race might have been a problem but let Dorothy discuss how she handled it. By allowing an open discussion without any *assumption* or *inference* of race in the way the question was posed, she could listen to and observe Dorothy's memory of the event and her method of working under potentially stressful situations. She asked the questions openly without subterfuge or inference. Her candor allowed the interviewee to answer with candor and to turn the questions into positive statements about herself.

While the references Dorothy provided would undoubtedly *not* discuss any racial problems, they would have found some means of saying that she did not have a "good working relationship." Since that was not the case, it is pretty obvious that Dorothy relates well in the working environment and concentrates on her job and not on her race.

And that's what it's all about. It's hard to be a minority in an interview, no matter which side of the desk you sit on. But if we all remember that we're in business in the first place to do a good job and not let our politics or our religion or our race or our sex or our age be a part of the mix, then it all becomes very simple. Prejudice is a fact of life and some people bring it to the office. But, praise be, that is becoming rarer these days. It can become absolutely extinct if we deal with the jobs people are to do and how well they can do them, rather than on issues that are better left to anthropologists and social historians.

Three little words can make all the difference in such an environment, and in such an interview: Respect, Honesty, and Trust.

Respect each other. Be honest with each other. Trust that your similarities are much more important than your differences.

22 THE EQUAL OPPORTUNITY FIRE

Introduction

Firing an employee is generally conceded to be the hardest job a manager has to do. (Indeed, there is something sick about a manager who enjoys firing someone.) But a hard job is even more difficult when it concerns an employee who is a member of a "protected class" (those covered under the Civil Rights Act—by age, sex, religion, race, national origin, or handicap).

The truth is that it should *not* be more difficult because company policies and procedures, company job descriptions, and performance expectations should apply equally to all.

But events of the past quarter century, some real, some imagined, have complicated the process and confused many managers when they are confronted with the problem. Equal opportunity has been confused with lowering the standards; affirmative action has been confused with quotas. And, let's be blunt, how many times have you heard, "You can't fire a minority"?

Well, it is impossible to deal with the entire range of EEO regulations and procedures in a book on management practices (although we do reproduce some of the pertinent guidelines in the Appendix), but it *is* possible to put some specific procedures in an example to represent both a manager's rights and an employee's rights.

We deal with EEO hiring in Chapter 21. Let us address at this juncture the firing process.

Can you fire a minority (or anyone from a "protected class")? Of course you can. And the rules are just the same as for firing any other employee. The difference is that an employee covered under civil rights legislation has recourse to Human Rights Commissions and the EEOC when it is suspected that the firing was the result of discrimination rather than for poor job performance, elimination of a job, or for cause (usually interpreted to mean stealing, fighting on the job, or an illegal activity). Those are reasons for which *any* employee may be fired.

The assumption of this author and this chapter is that we are not addressing real bigotry. It would be naive to assume that bigotry does not exist in America or in the work place. It does. However, the responsibilities of a company and its managers include removing the *manifestations* of bigotry from the work place. It is doubtful that company policy can (or should) change people's *minds*. However, fair employment practices require that it change people's *behavior*. People of all classes must be given equal access to jobs, equal treatment at the work place (free of harassment and denial of opportunities), and equal evaluation for performance.

Which brings us to the crux of the matter. It is *performance* that makes the difference when a manager decides to fire an employee, not some vague reason such as "She doesn't have the right attitude," or "He doesn't fit in." Good companies have job descriptions which detail what an employee is supposed to do. Good managers see to it that all employees have the same/equal training, support systems, and information for the same jobs. Good managers give periodic performance reviews and judge employees in the same jobs on the same criteria. And good managers keep records of those reviews, share them with the employee, and have them signed. If performance is going badly, the employee knows it and is given the opportunity to improve. Warnings are also a part of the review process if performance is going badly. Firing an employee should never come as a surprise or be misunderstood.

The Situation

As in all companies, the sales department at Salvo is of major importance to the growth and success of the company. Because of the diversity and dynamics of the company, the sales organization is divided both vertically and horizontally: that is, reporting to the vice-president of sales are four directors of product sales—games, educational, personal use, and business software. Reporting to the directors are five managers of regions in the country. In some cases, those managers have a number of sales people circulating through the regions, while in two regions there are only two or three sales people reporting to the managers in each of the product sales areas.

Salvo has found the structure very manageable in its rapid growth, allowing the flexibility necessary to add staff as new products are added and as the regions are developed by marketing. There is a great deal of mobility in the sales department: Three of the directors worked up from sales to manager to director. One, Warren, was hired from another company. All the regional managers are Salvo sales people who have worked into the managers' slots. They are aggressive, enthusiastic, like the company, and love to see it acquire new properties which they enjoy selling. There is a friendly competition among regions for sales increases, and there is highly imaginative competition among the directors who are trying to carve out a larger share of market for each of their product lines.

There are sales incentives based on share of market increase, sales increases, profit margin by office, sales per employee, and so forth. The friendly competition translates into some very substantial bonuses and trips abroad, because Salvo believes in rewarding its employees, particularly the high performers.

The Characters

Mike is vice-president of sales, and he has had more fun building his staff from within than from outside hiring. But with the rapid growth of Salvo, he has had to do both and has had considerable success. Some sales staff were absorbed through acquisitions of companies and some were hired from competitors or related fields. He uses an outside consultant to work with him in conducting a sales training seminar once a year, to keep his managers and directors on their toes, and to give a certain uniformity to the techniques and common language which all the sales people should use.

He is thirty-six, personable, a snappy dresser who loves to talk with people. With an MBA in marketing from Wharton, he came out of the videocassette sales field with a major corporation, and his love of computers from a tender age makes sales an ideal spot for him at Salvo. He believes in bringing "show biz" enthusiasm to the sale of computer software and he believes deeply that market research is fundamental to targeting Salvo's people and dollar efforts.

Knowing that he has a weakness in administrative functions, he has two very competent people on his staff to keep track of the paper flow and reporting procedures of his department. Gloria is his sales administration manager and was once an executive secretary at IBM. David is the numbers cruncher out of the research department at BBD&O.

Warren is thirty-one and a dynamo. He was the top account executive at a major computer game company by the time he was twenty-five. He loves the field and has a great rapport with the marketers and distributors around the country. He has a real affinity for the users of the product (the kids) and puts that enthusiasm to work with the buyers and distributors. He is the most successful black in this field. Mike hired him three years ago as a southern regional manager, and for the past year Warren has been the director of games sales.

They enjoy each other's company and have been known to play games together on the company computers late at night before they make a commitment to go with it. Their instincts about what will sell are legendary in the business.

The Problem

Today, Mike knows that he must fire Warren. The job of director has placed Warren totally out of his depth. He has never mastered the administrative details necessary to manage a two-million-dollar division. His reports are never on time and rarely accurate; they must be redone by Gloria and David before they are passed up the line. He takes much too long to hire new personnel when a vacancy occurs in the division, and the paperwork is always incomplete and late. Two secretaries have left him in six months because of the chaos in his office.

Complaints have come in from various distributors in the field when promised presentations don't materialize or no sales people show up when expected.

His sales staff around the country has grumbled about overwork and "not knowing what's going on" because Warren does not manage to keep them informed in a timely way.

Mike has talked with him three times in nine months, since his promotion. He has sent Warren to an administrative seminar conducted by AMA, he has assigned Gloria to his office for two weeks to aid in organizing the place, and he has had the training consultant work privately with Warren for a week.

The small improvements have not solved the problem. Mike has reluctantly concluded that he has "the wrong man in the wrong job." He has promoted one of the best sales people in the business, with a golden instinct for good games programs, into a managerial and administrative position for which he has neither the training nor the facility.

"I'm guilty of the Peter Principle," Mike has moaned to himself.

Today, he must fire Warren.

Manager's Objectives

To fire an employee who is incapable of performing the whole job.

To preserve the employee's sense of confidence and reputation so that he may find suitable reemployment as soon as possible. And to avoid a discrimination charge.

Employee's Objective

To retain his reputation and the financial security sufficient to relocate.

The Dialogue—Example 1

Warren comes to Mike's open door and Mike motions him in. Warren closes the door.

MIKE	Good morning.
WARREN	Morning. How are you?
MIKE	Only pretty good. I guess you know why I asked you to come in?
WARREN	I presume to talk about the Vintage Victors game. I tested it again last night.
MIKE	Not really.
WARREN	You should have stayed and played it. It's another winner!
MIKE	Warren, I don't know how to say this except to say it. I'm going to have to let you go. It isn't working and the competition is going to kill us.
WARREN	You've got to be kidding.
MIKE	I'm afraid not. This is one of the most painful things I've ever done, but the stakes are too high. We're terminating you today and asking for your resignation.
WARREN	That's ridiculous! I'm the best salesman you've ever had or will ever have!

* ACTION ASTERISK

Warren seems surprised at the reason for the meeting and is immediately driven to recap his superior credentials. Mike must make him understand that this is not a sudden decision and that the reasons for it have been obvious for some time. He must also make clear that he is not firing him for his performance as a salesman but for his performance as director.

MIKE	And you're the worst director. We've been over all this ground before, Warren. And it just isn't going to work.
WARREN	All that damn Mickey Mouse paperwork! What's more important to you, Mike, making sales or filling out paperwork?
MIKE	Both are important because both are necessary. At least at your level in the company they are. It's no good just making sales if we don't know how or when.
WARREN	Bull! You know soon enough. And you've got those paper pushers in your office to do that stuff.
MIKE	Those "paper pushers," as you call them, are here to do division work, not your work.
WARREN	They're here to do your work, you mean. You're as bad as I am with that stuff.

* ACTION ASTERISK

This is a slur of Mike's competence and a challenge to his authority. The conversation is heading rapidly from Warren's problems to Mike's performance as a division head.

MIKE	That's not quite true. But it's also irrelevant. I've given you three warnings in nine months. I've sent people in to help you. I've sent you to AMA. Nothing has worked.
WARREN	Things are better.
MIKE	Yes, but they're not good enough. We're getting customer complaints now. And we're getting staff complaints.

265

WARREN   Who?

MIKE   What difference does it make? You're not giving your people the kind of direction and support they need.

* ACTION ASTERISK

This sounds like some people ganged up behind his back to get Warren fired. Mike has shifted the burden from himself to others, and good leaders don't do that.

WARREN   I want to know who they are.

MIKE   Warren, I'm not going to tell you. There's no need to start some range war over complaints that people have made. Their complaints are legitimate and it only increased our problems.

WARREN   They're a bunch of bigots and they want me out.

MIKE   Warren!

WARREN   This whole company is a honky network and all of them have been trying to get me out.

MIKE   That's not true and you know it. We've got many minorities and women throughout this company. There's less discrimination here than any place I've ever seen.

WARREN   Tokens.

* ACTION ASTERISK

"Guilty until proven innocent" is as rotten in business as it is in court. Both men are now in a no-win conversation.

MIKE   You're no token! You were hired because you're the best in the business. You were promoted because you *really* know this field. You're just out of your depth in management. You're at your best when you're on the street selling.

WARREN   You needed a token and you used everything I know to build this department.

MIKE   (*Coldly.*) Warren, I needed an expert in the games field and I hired one. I also thought we had become friends. You've been in my home, my kids think you're terrific, we've traveled all over the country together...

* ACTION ASTERISK
Pulling the "some of my best friends are..." went out years ago. Real friends don't have to talk about it.

WARREN   And now that you've picked my brain, you're firing me. Well, you can't fire me.

MIKE   What do you mean?

WARREN   You haven't got a leg to stand on. Profits are up in games. We've acquired two companies in these nine months. And I'm black and I say that's why you're firing me.

MIKE   I'm firing you because you can't do the job.

WARREN   Prove it.

MIKE   I've warned you three times. I've given you help and it hasn't worked.

WARREN   Prove it.

MIKE   I have notes on all of it.

WARREN   I never saw them and I never signed them.

* ACTION ASTERISK
Bingo! Private notes in a desk drawer are *not* performance reviews. In fact, they can work *against* a company in the full light of day—or court.

MIKE   They will prove that you were warned.

WARREN   The commission won't see it that way.

MIKE   What commission?

WARREN   The commission I'm going to as soon as I leave here.

You're firing me because I'm black and because some of your honky friends have complained about me.

MIKE   I guess that ends the conversation. Your check is waiting in payroll. You'll be getting six months' severance or until you find another job. Personnel will explain your benefits. (*He stands up.*) I'm sorry, Warren.

* ACTION ASTERISK

The "or until you find another job" is a real warning flag. In this circumstance, it can only terrify or enrage an employee who sees his equity (not income) in a company being eroded with a deadline. Does he try to get a job before the six months are up? Or after? As a minority, does he have additional problems?

WARREN   Not half as sorry as you're going to be. This company had better start living in the real world. (*He leaves.*)

Comments

Were the objectives satisfied? Only one. Mike *did* fire Warren. However, he did not preserve his confidence or avoid a discrimination charge.

This scene, and variations on it, are enacted all too often in business. Department heads are faced with firing an employee who is not doing the job, who also falls under the "protected class" definition of the Civil Rights Act, and they go into the final meeting completely unprepared for the practical and emotional fallout it can bring. An unpleasant task at best becomes a confrontation. From the outset of the interview, Warren has had a growing sense of betrayal. He thinks he's doing a good job (because nothing was ever given to him in writing which had the word "warning" on it) and as the meeting progressed, the only thing that made any sense to him in this catastrophe was bigotry: Since he was doing a good job, but was being fired anyway, it must be because he is black.

Whether Warren was black or white, this termination was handled very badly. But because he *is* black, and no real businesslike procedures have been followed, he has recourse to the Human Rights Commission. That is bad for him and bad for the company. No matter who "wins" such a charge, both will be losers. They will lose time, they will lose money, and they will lose that emotional tranquillity which makes for a healthy working environment—where people are identified for their productivity and not for their race or sex.

Mike made his first mistake nine months ago and has compounded it ever since. There is a better way to terminate an employee, and it begins earlier in the working relationship.

The Dialogue—Example 2 (continued)

WARREN That's ridiculous! I'm the best salesman you've ever had and will ever have!

MIKE That's probably true, and that's why it's so painful. Let me get some details out of the way first. There is a man in the conference room who will see you after we're finished. He's the head of an outplacement firm who will work with you for up to six months to find the right spot. I frankly don't think it will take six *days* for you to relocate, but he'll work full-time with you. Second, you'll be on the payroll for six months. It's much more than corporate policy, but your contribution to the company has been so substantial, we want to do it. Your benefits will stay in effect during those six months. Third, we will have office services pack your things tonight and they will be shipped to your home tomorrow. Finally, Frank is coming into town day after tomorrow, and we ask that you meet him at the Hilton for the day to review all the projects which are currently in progress. He'll be replacing you. We're hoping this will make the transition as painless as possible and we want you to know how much we respect all that you've done. Warren, I'm sorry it had to end this way.

* ACTION ASTERISK
This long speech has allowed Warren to absorb the impact of what has happened to him. It also itemizes a long list of comforting "goodies" which can salve the wound until his ego recovers and he can really search for a job. He realizes that he's talking to friends, not enemies.

WARREN Where did I go wrong?

MIKE We both went wrong. You're the best salesman in the business. But once we took you away from sales and put you behind a desk, you never functioned at your peak again. We're the real losers.

WARREN I tried, Mike.

MIKE I know. God knows, *I* know. We've worked on it together for nine months. And every time we reviewed

269

the problem and I gave you some help, it got a little better. But now others are noticing it.

WARREN   What do you mean?

MIKE   The executive committee likes its reports on time. And Gloria and David just don't have time to redo them anymore. And some of your field staff are feeling neglected now.

WARREN   There are always complainers.

MIKE   Yes, but these complaints are valid. And some of the customers aren't getting the attention they want.

WARREN   They never do. You can never do enough.

MIKE   I know. But these are things which must be done, and they're slipping.

WARREN   Why wasn't I told?

MIKE   We touched on it at our last meeting, when you got the final warning. It's gotten worse since then. So there was no need to belabor it any more. Those warnings were important. And the help we gave you each time. That's why we had you sign them. I wanted to be sure we were both working in the same direction.

* ACTION ASTERISK

Periodic performance reviews; written reports of those reviews; signing by both parties. Agreed expectations and a final warning. Mike has gone by the book and Warren couldn't cut it. He is gently, but specifically, reminding him of all this.

WARREN   What about references?

MIKE   No question about it. The outplacement man will help you identify your strongest areas and that's what we'll support. He will stay in touch with us as well as you, so we'll be supporting your search all the way.

WARREN   You know the word will get out that I was fired because I was black.

MIKE   (*Angry.*) I'd better not hear such a rumor! It would be a damn lie.

WARREN   Just another dumb, uppity black who couldn't cut the mustard.

MIKE   Your race has never crossed our minds! This is not that kind of company—or industry—thank God.

WARREN   My reference calls may need to hear that.

MIKE   They sure as hell *will*.

WARREN   They won't ask.

MIKE   I'll tell them anyway.

WARREN   It might sound peculiar if you bring it up.

MIKE   Then I'll find a way. The counselor can help. So will personnel. Don't worry, we'll work it out. That's one nasty little rumor we'll nip in the bud.

WARREN   What are you going to tell everyone?

MIKE   That you resigned. And that you're seeking other interests. And that because of your great contribution to the company, we're helping you in that search.

WARREN   No one will believe it.

MIKE   As long as *we* believe it, it's true. We'll want you to sign a paper to that effect.

WARREN   Why?

MIKE   To keep the record straight—and complete. I have a copy of it here. Take it with you. Review it with the outplacement guy; his name is Dave Kelly, by the way. Review it with your lawyer, if you wish. We'd like it back within a week.

WARREN   Why do you need it?

MIKE	We both need it. It says we parted as friends. You owe us nothing and we owe you nothing, other than what I've outlined.
WARREN	I'm not feeling very friendly right now.
MIKE	I can understand that. I'm feeling pretty hurt myself. I don't like to fail, and I know damn well you don't.
WARREN	When do I tell the staff?
MIKE	You don't. I'm calling a staff meeting in an hour to tell them you've resigned. We'll TWX the other offices today. You go see Kelly and go on home. If you like, you can bring the letter in next week and speak to your staff then. Think about it. Meantime, go on in and see Kelly.
WARREN	(*Rises.*) O.K.
MIKE	Warren, I'm truly, truly sorry. Let's get together in a couple of weeks and see what direction you're going in.
WARREN	Sure.
MIKE	I'll call.
WARREN	Sure.
MIKE	I promise. (*He shakes Warren's hand. Warren exits.*)

Summary

There are two keys to the above interview: keeping records and being prepared.

Obviously, Mike keeps records of all his meetings with his staff, particularly when those meetings concern job performance (or nonperformance). He also has the employee read and *sign* the performance reviews, so there is no misunderstanding about what is expected to improve the employee's performance, and what will happen if this does not occur.

He came to the interview prepared to fire Warren, but also prepared to tell him about what would be done to assist him in his new job search. While the company arrangements (outplacement, six months' salary, benefits) might seem generous, they are not unusual for an employee of that status, that visibility, and that contribution to the company.

And the letter which Mike asked Warren to sign is a typical severance agreement, particularly with employees who fall under civil rights legislation (race, sex, age, religion, ethnic origin, and handicap). It ensures that the employee will receive all the severance and benefits promised, and it protects the employer from a discrimination suit later.

The main element apparent in this interview, however, was *compassion*. Mike was efficient, but humane. He did not enjoy the task or lose control of it. It is particularly easy in a sales department to make friends with the people with whom you work, because of the outgoing nature of the people attracted to the field. Firing a friend can be a devastating emotional experience. Mike will probably suffer from this encounter, but not as much as he might have, because he has handled it humanely. His primary concern was for Warren's future and well-being, once the difficult decision had been made on the facts. And he was more than fair. That will give him personal comfort in the future. And his other employees will feel safer and more loyal, knowing that they work for a caring boss.

Moreover, the major problem of a possible discrimination suit was completely avoided, simply because race was never a part of the reason for firing Warren, and the records proved that.

APPENDIX

![black bar]

Summaries of Title VII, Civil Rights Act; Executive Order on Affirmative Action

Equal Employment Opportunity

Title VII of the Civil Rights Act of 1964, with changes approved in 1972 and 1978, prohibits discrimination on the basis of race, sex, nationality, religion, age, or handicap.

Copies of the act may be obtained from the Equal Employment Opportunity Commission (EEOC) in Washington, D.C.

Companies employing fifteen full-time persons or more are required to file an annual report with the EEOC detailing their employment figures by race and sex in nine job categories, as well as other recruiting and hiring information as indicated on the form.

The purpose of the act and its revisions is to provide equal opportunity for all the protected classes in the act.

Affirmative Action

Companies which provide goods or services to any branch of the federal government in the amount of fifty thousand dollars a year or more are required to file an affirmative action program.

Information may be obtained from the Department of Labor, Washington, D.C. These requirements ensue basically from Revised Order 4 of Executive Orders 11246 and 11375, which outline in detail the Affirmative Action Compliance Programs required of government contractors.

The orders read, in part, "Relief for members of an 'affected class,' who, by virtue of past discrimination, continue to suffer the present effects of that discrimination must either be included in the contractor's affirmative action program or be embodied in a separate written 'corrective action' program.

"An affirmative action program is a set of specific and result-oriented procedures to which a contractor commits himself to apply every good faith effort. The objective of those procedures plus such efforts is equal employment opportunity. Procedures without effort to make them work are meaningless; and effort, undirected by specific and meaningful procedures, is inadequate."

Company Statement on Sexism/Sexual Harassment

On April 11, 1980, the Equal Employment Opportunity Commission published regulations explicitly forbidding sexual harassment of employees. The company has never condoned actions of this nature; however, the fact that these governmental rules have been issued makes it appropriate for this information to be issued.

The new EEOC rules set forth three criteria for determining whether an action constitutes unlawful harassment. Unwelcome sexual advances, requests for sexual favors, and other verbal or physical conduct of a sexual nature become illegal if:

1. The employee's submission is an explicit or implicit condition of employment
2. The employee's response becomes a basis for employment decision such as promotions, compensation, and benefits
3. The conduct interferes with the employee's performance, creating a hostile, intimidating, or offensive environment.

Any employee determined to have engaged in conduct such as that cited will be dealt with firmly and appropriate sanctions, including termination of employment, will be considered. Since the company will be held

275

responsible for the acts of its supervisory employees, you must ensure that all supervisors in your department receive a copy of this policy.

Moreover, you should review the manner and style in which your department handles business situations to prevent any unintentional actions which might be misinterpreted as violating these guidelines.

Company Statement on Drug Use

Neither the buying, selling, nor use of illegal drugs will be tolerated on any company premises. Please be advised that the use of illegal drugs on any company premises will be cause for instant dismissal.

Be further advised that the buying or selling of illegal drugs on any company premises will be cause for instant dismissal as well as the reporting of the transaction to the proper law enforcement authorities.

Since the company will be held responsible for the acts of its supervisory employees, you must ensure that all employees in your department are aware of this policy.

Company Statement on Equal Opportunity

The company is committed to equal employment opportunity and will provide equal employment and advancement opportunity for all qualified individuals without regard to race, color, sex, religion, age, national origin, or handicap. The company will seek to affirmatively encourage the full participation of women and minorities in all areas and at all levels of the company.

This policy extends to all employees and applicants for employment as well as to all aspects of the employment relationship, including recruitment, placement, promotion, compensation, and benefits.

It is the responsibility of all managers and supervisors to ensure that all personnel actions comply with the principle of equal opportunity.

Company Statement on Solicitation/Selling on the Premises

Employees will be solicited for contributions on the premises only by recognized charities approved by the company.

Employees may suggest charities for solicitation to _____
_____, which will be submitted for approval.

Canvassing or solicitation by an outsider is not permitted on the premises. Should you be approached on the premises by an outside solicitor, report it immediately to Security.

There will be no selling of any merchandise by any employee or outsider permitted on any company premises at any time. Employees selling anything on the premises may be dismissed immediately.

Company Statement on Company Behavior

The company values, and deems it most important to preserve, its reputation for honesty and integrity.

The use of any funds or other assets of the company, or the providing of any services for any purpose which is unlawful or which does not conform to ethical and acceptable business practices is prohibited.

Detailed codes of conduct are available from the company regarding the following:

1. Employee safety and health
2. Nepotism
3. Conflicts of interest
4. Political contributions
5. Payments to labor organizations
6. Dealings with customers, including payment to customers, receiving payment from customers, placing orders with customers as a consideration for receiving business, paying excessive fees or bonuses, or fraudulent or improper billing to the company's customers
7. Dealings with suppliers, including making no payments other than for legitimate goods or services; accepting fees, bribes, or kickbacks from suppliers; use of the company's services in return for placing orders with suppliers, or purchase of advertising for other than general company use.
8. Compliance with the Securities Exchange Act of 1934, as amended by the Foreign Corrupt Practices Act of 1977, applicable both domestically and abroad

All levels of management are responsible for ensuring compliance with these codes by employees under their supervision.

Any company employee who violates any provision of this code may be subject to severe sanctions, including dismissal and personal liability for any damages sustained by the company as a result of such improper conduct.

Do's And Dont's Of Interviewing

In an attempt to find a suitable employee for a position within the company, the interviewing manager or supervisor might pose questions or make statements to the candidate(s) that violate certain fair employment laws. As a result of these unlawful questions or statements, the applicant(s) may file a charge of discrimination against the company with any of the local, state, or federal agencies.

Following are examples of common questions or statements, some of which are quite innocent but can be the basis for a racial discrimination charge. Therefore, they must be avoided when interviewing any applicant for employment. It is good to keep in mind that all questions or statements directed to the applicant for employment be entirely *job-related*.

1. Age
"I am looking for (or I prefer) a young person for this job."

Any attempt on the part of the interviewer to limit, segregate, or classify prospective employees from an employment opportunity because of age is violating the Age Discrimination Act of 1967. Likewise, using printed or published ads which indicate a preference or specification for age is prohibited. However, to set a minimum age such as "person over 21" is acceptable because it includes a vast hiring range and does not exclude the group between 40 and 62.

2. Sex
All questions pertaining to the applicant's children, children's ages, marital status, intention to marry, plans to have children, birth control practices, spouse's occupation, income, or likelihood of transfer are prohibited, as well as any statement that would imply that a woman would not be considered for a particular type of job.
Also, statements that reflect stereotyped myths about women:

"They are too emotional."
"They never stick to a job."
"The work is too heavy for a woman."
"They have a high turnover rate."

According to the 1972 Civil Rights Act, sex is rarely a bona fide occupational qualification (BFOQ). (A BFOQ is any qualification which is reasonably necessary to carry on normal business operations.) Individuals must be considered for employment on the basis of their individual capacities alone and not on the basis of certain characteristics attributable to their group. It is difficult for the employer to prove that race, creed, color, national origin, ancestry, age, marital status, or sex is a bona fide occupational qualification.

An employer cannot refuse to hire women because of assumptions or stereotyped myths about women. Some women may be able to do the job, and each case must be considered individually. Men are protected under the law, too.

Many states have protective laws for women, so called because they prohibit the lifting of weights, provide for taking mandatory breaks, and so forth. These laws, though still in effect, are superseded by the Civil Rights Act of 1972.

3. Character
(1) "Have you ever been arrested or convicted of any crime?"

Under most state fair employment laws, the portion regarding "arrest" is illegal regardless of the purpose for which such information is sought. While inquiries (written and oral) as to arrests are strictly forbidden, asking the applicant if he or she has ever been convicted is not.

Watch how you use the conviction information! Was the conviction for an offense which has relationship to the job being recruited for?

(2) Inquiry or investigation into credit ratings.

Inquiry into an individual's credit rating is totally unrelated to employment and may be deemed discriminatory.

4. National Origin
Inquiry into the language commonly used by the applicant is illegal. Inquiry into lineage, ancestry, national origin, descent, parentage, or nationality is prohibited.

5. Race
Inquiry into complexion or color of skin is prohibited.

6. Religion Or Creed
Inquiry into an applicant's religious denomination, religious affiliations, church, parish, or religious holidays observed is prohibited.

7. Residence
Inquiry into last number of places of residence is not job-related and can be construed as being discriminatory.

8. Tests, Oral Or Written
Tests, oral or written, which are not validated, are illegal. The criterion for administering tests is that they must be related to the position the applicant is applying for, and the tests used are validated ones—that is, they are free of racial and cultural bias.

9. Racial, Ethnic, Or Sex Jokes Or Stories

Do not tell racial or ethnic stories to potential candidates. Usually, the joke or story has a double meaning, one of which probably is most offensive in the view of the female or minority applying for the job.

If the applicant is turned down for the position, your story or joke might be used to indicate your alleged sexism or racism, or your insensitivity when a complaint is filed with a compliance agency.

Stick to questions and statements during the interview which will solicit from the applicant job-related knowledge or aptitude.

10. Writing Specifications For Applicants

Be careful. Watch the job specifications written by you for use by the employment section in seeking applicants for the opening in your department. Have you requested a female? Or a male? Or a high school graduate (when such education is not required in order to do the job)? Before you write your specification, check with the employment section regarding the types of qualifications which you can realistically require in an applicant. If your expectations are too high, then you might be charged—albeit unintentionally—with a racial or a sex discrimination charge.

What Employees Can Do About Sex/Race Discrimination

If you believe that...

1. An employee of the company does not take your career and career goals seriously by action as if those goals are inappropriate for members of your sex or race.
2. You are denied resources, opportunities, or promotions for sexist or racist reasons.
3. Supervisors or managers ignore or make fun of you because of your sex or race.
4. You are pressured by a supervisor or manager to participate with him or her in social and/or sexual activities.

Employees often feel powerless in such situations, but there are people in the company who are available and willing to talk to employees about these problems. Such situations as those described above are not approved by the company. In most instances they occur out of lack of sensitivity or misunderstanding and need only to be brought to the attention of the person involved to be eliminated. Sex discrimination, sexism, and sexual harassment are considered unethical and illegal and are subject to official company disciplinary action, as are actions of race discrimination.

Actions you can take...

1. Talk to the company member who has offended you. Carefully explain why you view the particular comment, joke, or action taken as sexist or racist. Frequently people are not aware of how their remarks or actions affect someone else, and communicating your feelings to the employee might be most helpful to him or her in avoiding such situations in the future. Regard the meeting as a consciousness-raising session in which you help the person to understand how you feel.

2. If you feel uncomfortable meeting the employee alone, it may be appropriate to take an observer with you, perhaps another member of your department or a member of the personnel department.

3. Another alternative is to ask for a joint meeting with the employee and his or her supervisor.

4. Or you may write to the employee. State the facts about the incident(s), how it made you feel, and how the situation can be remedied. Keep a copy of the letter to show his or her department head if the situation is not remedied.

5. If these remedies are not satisfactory, please speak to the affirmative action/EEO officer, the division president, or the president of the company, and keep a copy of your letter requesting such an appointment.

Index

INDEX